D O U B L E
S T I T C H

BLACK WOMEN WRITE ABOUT
MOTHERS & DAUGHTERS

EDITED BY

Patricia Bell-Scott
Beverly Guy-Sheftall
Jacqueline Jones Royster
Janet Sims-Wood
Miriam DeCosta-Willis
and Lucille P. Fultz

HarperPerennial
A Division of HarperCollinsPublishers

DOUBLE STITCH. Copyright © 1991 by Patricia Bell-Scott, Beverly Guy-Sheftall, and The SAGE Women's Educational Press, Inc. Afterword copyright © 1991 by Paula Giddings. All rights reserved. Printed in the United States of America. No part of this book may be used or reproduced in any manner whatsoever without written permission except in the case of brief quotations embodied in critical articles and reviews. For information address HarperCollins Publishers, Inc., 10 East 53rd Street, New York, NY 10022.

HarperCollins books may be purchased for educational, business, or sales promotional use. For information please write: Special Markets Department, HarperCollins Publishers, Inc., 10 East 53rd Street, New York, NY 10022.

First HarperPerennial edition published 1993.

Designed by Christine Leonard Raquepaw

Library of Congress Cataloging-in-Publication Data

Double Stitch : black women write about mothers & daughters / edited by Patricia Bell-Scott . . . [et al.].
    p.   cm.
  Originally published: Boston: Beacon Press, c1991.
  Includes bibliographical references and index.
  ISBN 0-06-097503-2 (pbk.)
  1. Mothers and daughters—United States—Literary collections.
2. Mothers and daughters—United States—History. 3. American literature—Afro-American authors. 4. Afro-American women—Literary collections.
5. Mothers and daughters in literature. 6. American literature—Women authors.
7. Afro-American women in literature. 8. American literature—20th century.
I. Bell-Scott, Patricia.
[PS509.M6D6 1993]
810.8' 0352042—dc20   92-53416

    95 96 97 RRD 10 9 8 7 6

DOUBLE STITCH IS DEDICATED TO
THE WOMEN WHO MOTHERED US:

Dorothy Wilbanks
Ernestine Varnado Guy
& Lillian Varnado Watkins
Lilla Ashe Mitchell
Hazel Sims
Beautine DeCosta Lee
Minnie Logan Fultz
& Countess Barnes Walker

CONTENTS

Foreword / *Maya Angelou*   xi
Preface / *Johnnetta B. Cole*   xiii
Introduction / *Patricia Bell-Scott & Beverly Guy-Sheftall*   1

PART ONE / THREADING THE NEEDLE: BEGINNINGS

Introduced by Patricia Bell-Scott   5

Newborn / *Valerie Jean*   7
Birth of the Black Life / *Nubia Kai*   9
A poem for my mother, Nubia Kai Al-Nura Salaam /
   Malia Kai   10
Insomniac / *Esperanza Cintrón*   11
Baby Faith / *Michele Wallace*   12
Closets and Keepsakes / *Willi Coleman*   21
Dear Mama / *Sonia Sanchez*   24
The Thursday Ladies / *Karla F. C. Holloway*   27
Images of Motherhood in Toni Morrison's BELOVED /
   Lucille P. Fultz   32
The Meaning of Motherhood in Black Culture and Black
   Mother-Daughter Relationships / *Patricia Hill Collins*   42

PART TWO / PIECING BLOCKS: IDENTITIES

Introduced by Beverly Guy-Sheftall   61

The Power of Names / *Irma McClaurin*   63
Touching/Not Touching: My Mother / *Toi Derricotte*   64
On the Spirt of Mildred Jordan / *June Jordan*   66
Mom de Plume / *SDiane Bogus*   67
Lessons / *Pearl Cleage*   71
Mothers of Mind / *Elsa Barkley Brown*   74
Black Mothers and Daughters: Traditional and New
   Perspectives / *Gloria I. Joseph*   94

PART THREE / STITCHING MEMORIES: HERSTORIES

Introduced by Lucie Fultz   107

Something Domestic / *Dolores Kendrick*   109
Mother, in Sunlight / *Louise Robinson-Boardley*   112
The Taste of Mother Love / *Gloria T. Hull*   113
Old Photo from a Family Album: 1915 / *Pinkie Gordon
   Lane*   115
Ah, Momma / *June Jordan*   117
Precious Memories / *Belvie Rooks*   119
"Hush. Mama's Gotta Go Bye-Bye" / *Renita Weems*   123
Smoothing the Tucks in Father's Linen: The Women of
   Cedar Hill / *Miriam DeCosta-Willis*   131

PART FOUR / FRAYING EDGES: TENSIONS

Introduced by Janet Sims-Wood   139

Beatrice's Neck / *Ann T. Greene*   141
Successions / *Valerie Jean*   146
Stepmother / *Irma McClaurin*   148
Reflections of a "Good" Daughter / *Bell Hooks*   149
A Daughter Survives Incest: A Retrospective Analysis /
   Linda H. Hollies   152
Turbulence and Tenderness: Mothers, Daughters, and
   "Othermothers" in Paule Marshall's BROWN GIRL,
   BROWNSTONES / *Rosalie Riegle Troester*   163

PART FIVE / BINDING THE QUILT: GENERATIONS

Introduced by Miriam DeCosta Willis   173

Lineage / *Margaret Walker*   175
Family Tree / *Kate Rushin*   176
At Midday / *Naomi Long Madgett*   178
Double Exposure / *Saundra Sharp*   179
Four Women / *Esperanza Cintrón*   181
To My Daughters / *Saundra Murray Nettles*   186
Dyad/Triad / *Annette Jones White*   188
In Search of Our Mothers' Gardens / *Alice Walker*   196

PART SIX / LOOSENING THE THREADS: SEPARATIONS

Introduced by Jacqueline Jones Royster 207

The Lost Daughter / *Marilyn Nelson Waniek*   209
"Mawu" / *Audre Lorde*   211
Prose Poem: Portrait / *Pinkie Gordon Lane*   212
On that Dark and Moon-Less Night / *Judy Scales-Trent*   213
Connected to Mama's Spirit / *Gloria Wade-Gayles*   214
To My Mother's Vision / *SDiane Bogus*   239
Last Christmas Gift from a Mother / *Lois F. Lyles*   241

Afterword / *Paula Giddings*   253
Suggested Readings / *Janet Sims-Wood*   257
Contributors   265

FOREWORD

Maya Angelou

She stood before me, a dolled up pretty yellow woman, seven inches shorter than my six-foot bony frame. Her eyes were soft and her voice was brittle.

"You're determined to leave? Your mind's made up?"

I was seventeen and burning with rebellious passion. I was also her daughter, so whatever independent spirit I had inherited had been increased by living with her and watching her for the past four years.

"You're leaving my house?"

I collected myself inside myself and answered, "Yes. Yes, I've found a room."

"And you're taking the baby?"

"Yes."

She gave me a smile, half proud and half pitying.

"Alright, you're a woman. You don't have a husband, but you've got a three-month-old baby. I just want you to remember one thing. From the moment you leave this house, don't let anybody raise you. Every time you get into a relationship you will have to make concessions, compromises, and there's nothing wrong with that. But keep in mind Grandmother Henderson in Arkansas and I have given you every law you need to live by. Follow what's right. You've been raised."

More than forty years have passed since Vivian Baxter liberated me and handed me over to life. During those years I have loved and lost, I have raised my son, set up a few households and walked away from many. I have taken life as my mother gave it to me on that strange graduation day all those decades ago.

In the intervening time when I have extended myself beyond my reach and come toppling humpty-dumpty-down on my face in full view of a scornful world, I have returned to my mother to be liberated by her one more time. To be reminded by her that although I had to compromise with Life, even Life had no right to beat me to the ground, to batter my teeth into my throat, to make me knuckle down and call it Uncle. My mother raised me, and then freed me.

And now, as I have read this amazing collection of poems, essays, studies, and short stories on Black mothers and daughters, my attention is called to a bedroom adjoining mine where my once feisty mother lies hooked by pale blue wires to an oxygen tank, fighting cancer for her life.

Each account in this book brings me closer to Vivian Baxter, and each mother makes me think of Frederick Douglass's mother, enslaved on a plantation eleven miles from her infant son. Yet, who after toiling a full day, would walk the distance just to look at her child; then return just in time to begin another day of labor. Each poem makes me know again as if for the first time that the most moving song created during my people's turmoil of slavery was and remains, "Sometimes I feel like a motherless child."

As a mother and a daughter myself, I shall cherish *Double Stitch*. I will read it to myself, buy it for others, and have already begun to quote from it to friends. I have chosen certain poems and essays, for I shall take them to my mother's room and there we will laugh and cry together.

Sisters, Daughters, Mothers, thank you for the quilt. I'm so glad all our faces and graces and warts and neuroses are preserved in its rich design, and being now reminded of past gifts, I pray I shall have the courage to liberate my mother when the time comes. She would expect that from me.

PREFACE

Johnnetta B. Cole

I am, of course, a daughter, as every girl child and woman is, regardless of where she was born, the color of her skin, the sound of her speech or the number of her possessions. The woman who bore me is no longer alive, but I seem to be her daughter in increasingly profound ways. I have no daughters. That is to say, I have not borne any female children. And yet, I am a surrogate mother to many daughters, 1700 of whom are students of Spelman College.

Double Stitch is about all Black women, for each of us is a mother or daughter or both. In this powerful collection of essays, poems, fiction, and personal narratives, each writer speaks out of her own daughterhood, motherhood, or an analysis of another's particular encounters with this universal experience of femaleness.

What is it about this relationship that sets it apart from all others? Because so little has been written about Black mother-daughter relationships, we go to this anthology with great anticipation that insights will be there, boldly presented by some, perhaps only hinted at by others. There is no disappointment here. In the complexities of the many lives that are woven among these pages, several themes emerge about the nature of Black mother-daughter relationships.

The first is that these relationships are quite simply like Black female folks in general—amazingly diverse, despite similarities that bind us together. There are profound differences based on class, sexual preference, age, to name only a few variables. Of course, these relationships are shaped by the commonality of Blackness in a White world. Regardless of how she responds—including with silence—every African-American mother has wondered, in the words of Margaret Burrough's poem: What shall I tell my children who are Black?

There is a sense in which Black mothers and daughters share a collective history. Even though today's Black mothers and daughters were not there, their racial memory includes African men, women, and children being torn from their land and shipped like cargo into slavery in the interest of White men's greed. In the New World, children were literally taken from their mothers' arms in one of the most cruel systems devised in the West.

African-American women also share memories about mothers, aunts, or daughters who worked in Miss Ann's kitchen; mothers and daughters who have waited their turn to have a beautician's hot comb straighten out the kink in their hair; countless mothers who have held their newborn daughters and prayed that they would know as many of their joys and as few of their pains as possible as they grew into both their Blackness and their womanness.

Because of the countless ways in which individual mothers and daughters are different, is it any wonder that Black mother-daughter relationships are presented in all their various forms and stages of development? Mothers and daughters can be competitors or conspirators. Their relationship can be synergistic or parasitic; they can be adversaries or the closest of friends and allies.

A second theme which emerges from this collective portrait is that sexism is a relevant reality if one wishes to understand Black mother-daughter relationships. We are reminded that Black mother-daughter relationships, compared with mother-son relationships, have received very little attention in literary or social science analyses. It is hard to find a satisfactory explanation for this difference other than to say that this is one of the many expressions of sexism in the culture. There are other ways in which Black mother-daughter relationships are influenced by gender discrimination. Though patriarchy is perhaps not expressed in exactly the same ways in African, African-Caribbean, or African-American communities as it is among Euro-Americans, sexism clearly exists in Black communities all over the globe. Black females receive unequal pay for equal work; are the victims of physical and sexual abuse; and, from their early days on earth, are relegated to a role that is at best secondary—whether it is in church, on the hospital staff, in the public school hierarchy, or among elected officials.

In other words, relationships between Black mothers and daughters are profoundly affected by the subtleties as well as the brutalities of sexism within and without African-American communities. Among the rules of patriarchy are that all women are to be mothers, a rule applied to Black women no less than to White women. This ideal persists despite the fact that not all women are biological mothers and many women do not wish to be. What is of particular interest with respect to Black women in America is that racism and poverty frequently bring about situations in which many Black children will have surrogate mothers. These are the women who care for our young and fill in for mothers who cannot be there. This means that many young African-American girls have multiple models of "mother."

There is a third theme that is clearly drawn in *Double Stitch*. Mother-daughter relationships must be worked on if each person in the dyad is to grow in positive ways. We know this, in part, because of the turmoil we see in the lives of those Black women who never consciously come to grips with this powerful relationship.

What is it about this relationship among Black women over time that is potentially problematic? Perhaps it is quite simply that which haunts any mother and her daughter. Daughters ask, how can I be of this woman and yet resist being dominated by her? Blessed are those mothers who are courageous enough to help their daughters find answers.

This pioneering anthology tells us much about the "turbulence and tenderness" which characterizes Black mother-daughter relationships at various points in the life cycle. And, in a challenging way, it leaves unexplored territory. At Spelman College, the home of *SAGE: A Scholarly Journal on Black Women*, and therefore the birthplace of this volume, we are proud surrogate mothers of *Double Stitch*.

INTRODUCTION

Patricia Bell-Scott & Beverly Guy-Sheftall

What my mother teaches me are the essential lessons of the quilt: that people and actions do move in multiple directions at once.

ELSA BARKLEY BROWN

It is appropriate that the quilt is the central metaphor for this collection of readings on Black mothers and daughters. Fashioned from the materials of everyday life and associated with love and family, quilts in all their various textures and splendid beauty have been a central part of African-American material culture for generations, especially for the womenfolk. As an essential element of women's culture, quilts offer a framework for conceptualizing mother-daughter relations.[1]

It is also appropriate that this collection carry the title *Double Stitch*. This term describes a strengthening and decorative technique symbolic of the bonding between mothers and daughters. Just as the double stitch stabilizes and embellishes a fragile design, the mother-daughter tie lays the groundwork upon which subsequent relationships are built and elaborated.

In Colonial America, women took scraps of cloth that had been worn and suffused with memories of the family's daily life, and they made quilts which were both functional and creative. Diverse bits of discarded cloth, stitched together in various patterns, provided warmth for the body and beauty for the eye. In a preindustrial, agricultural society, young girls learned in homes and schools the sewing and quilting skills which prepared them for their traditional roles as wives and mothers.

In the Southern plantation system, dependent largely on slavery for its existence, the cotton which fueled the economy of the United States also fashioned folk culture for Blacks and Whites alike. Slave women who did the economic bidding of their masters or mistresses by picking cotton from sunup to sundown returned to slave quarters to labor late into the night producing home textile goods for White families, using scraps from garments and linen for the welfare of their own families.

Black slave women quilted resourcefully and imaginatively, making tops of worn-out clothes and scraps which belonged to the master's family or their own. Rags and sometimes worn-out quilts, which were cut into strips and squares, were also used. These quilts adorned ugly slave cabins and provided warmth from the cold for kinfolks. They were, in addition, a source of pride and self-esteem.

Quilting sessions, whether large or small, provided a needed social outlet and a respite from backbreaking work. Going from cabin to cabin helping friends make bedcovers also promoted a sense of community and group identity.[2] Whether strip quilting, the most common example of African-American material culture, or patchwork, the most important part of this tradition was the transmission of skills and of a value system handed down from grandmother, to mother, to granddaughter. Bonds were strengthened when a mother taught her daughter to quilt; as the mother imparted skills, techniques, and aesthetic design principles, she, perhaps most significantly, forged a bond essential to the survival of the family, and by extension, the community.

This African-American cultural tradition was rooted in America, but also separate and apart from developments in the young nation. Though African-American quilting goes back as far as the Colonial era, it would be a mistake to assume, as many scholars have in the past, that this tradition is entirely European. More recent scholars have pointed out that though slaves brought from West and Central Africa were unfamiliar with the three-layered bed quilt (top, batting, backing) associated with Euro-Americans, African slave women and men brought with them textile skills (piecing, appliqué, and embroidery) needed in the construction of quilts.[3] Africans also brought with them family and kinship traditions; and these, too, were adapted on American soil.

The primary goal of *Double Stitch* is to demonstrate the development of the Black mother-daughter bond and the range of experiences and traditions which have shaped it. Like quilting, it has been advantaged or disadvantaged by the innate ability, resourcefulness, and environment of the women and girls who have created the patterns, rhythms, order, and dissonance of the basic design.

The second objective of *Double Stitch* is to introduce *SAGE: A Scholarly Journal on Black Women* and its writers and editorial group to a broad audience. Many of the selections in this collection first appeared in two special issues, "Mothers and Daughters" I and II. This journal, now in its eighth year, is the only interdisciplinary periodical devoted exclusively to the new scholarship on Black women.

Finally, this book represents the culmination of a dream to place a neglected relationship in the spotlight. Despite heightened interest in the problems of Black families and the emergence of feminist social science, the mother-daughter dyad has received scant attention from scholars of any persuasion. *Double Stitch* also reflects our womanist orientation and privileges the diverse voices among us.

This anthology would have been impossible without our mothers—biological and symbolic—and our sister editors. Without their support and work, its design would have surely suffered. We thank the women who offered their fiction, essays, poetry, and narratives as the foundation for our "quilt." We are also indebted to Maya Angelou, Johnnetta B. Cole, Paula Giddings, and Bets Ramsey and the Senior Neighbors of Chattanooga, whose material provided an elegant and sturdy border.

We are eternally grateful for the love and criticism given by all our womenkin. They have taught us that people—including mothers and daughters—do indeed move in many directions at once. We offer *Double Stitch* as a token of our love. It is for the women in our past and present; it is also for us.

NOTES

1. See Elsa Barkley Brown, "African-American Women's Quilting: A Framework for Conceptualizing and Teaching African-American Women's History," *SIGNS: Journal of Women in Culture and Society* 14 (Summer 1989):921–29, for a discussion of this framework.

2. See Gladys-Marie Fry, *Stitched from the Soul: Slave Quilts from the Antebellum South* (New York: Dutton Studio Books, 1990) and Pat Ferrero, Elaine Hedges, and Julie Silber, *Hearts and Hands: The Influence of Women and Quilts on American Society* (San Francisco: The Quilt Press, 1987), p. 16.

3. Eva Ungar Grudin, *Stitching Memories: African-American Story Quilts* (Amherst: Williams College Museum of Art, 1990), pp. 7–9, and M. Akua McDaniel, "Black Women Making Quilts of Their Own," *Art Papers* 2 (September/October 1987):20.

PART 1

1

THREADING THE NEEDLE: BEGINNINGS

Quilting was a practical skill taught to women by their mothers as a means of supplying warm bedding. But quilt tops and backs also reveal and reflect the cultural roots and the aesthetic choices of the women who made them.

MAUDE SOUTHWELL WAHLMAN
and JOHN SCULLY

This section—"Threading the Needle"—mirrors the formation of the mother-daughter bond. Like the quilt, the strength and character of this relationship depends in part upon the richness and stability of the tools used in its making. Just as the sharpness of the needle or the elasticity of the thread can impair or enable the quilter's design, the mother's psyche or the circumstances of a daughter's birth can impair or enable mother-daughter relations.

In "Newborn," Valerie Jean evokes the "rhythm pull" between an infant daughter and her mother. Like the novice quilter who learns to set a tempo with her stitching, the new mother comes to appreciate the rhythm of her suckling babe. This dynamic, representative of the interplay between the individual and collective needs of mothers and daughters, is a lifelong source of tension and renewal.

Nubia Kai and daughter Malia celebrate biological birth and psychological affirmation in "Birth of the Black Life" and "A poem for my mother." Esperanza Cintrón's "Insomniac" depicts a mother's intuition of a toddler daughter's need for protection from dangers real and imagined. How grandmothers, mothers, sisters, and other women teach "daughters" through stories, with discipline, and by example is dramatically demonstrated in Michele Wallace's "Baby Faith," Willi Coleman's "Closets and Keepsakes," and Karla F. C. Holloway's "The Thursday Ladies." And the pain of bonds severed by death and the evil of slavery are depicted in Sonia Sanchez's "Dear Mama" and Lucie Fultz's "Images of Motherhood in Toni Morrison's *Beloved*.

This section concludes with Patricia Hill Collins's essay, "The Meaning of Motherhood in Black Culture and Mother-Daughter Relationships." By detailing the competing Eurocentric and Afrocentric perspectives of Black motherhood and the uniqueness of motherhood in African-American communities, Collins illuminates the complexity of contemporary mother-daughter relations.

As a composite, these selections give testimony to the survival and transformation of the mother-daughter tradition on American soil. Reminiscent of the quilt and double stitch, these traditions have given us comfort, support, and beauty.

Patricia Bell-Scott

NEWBORN

Valerie Jean

Like the layered heat of
a summer sun, you awaken early.
Soft, your cries reach in-

to my dreams and motion me awake
to rock you. Your skin
bunches warm, elastic. Quick,

your small mouth stretches
wide around my tender breast. I tense,
a burn like flash-fires.

Slowly, I melt into the rhythm pull,
giving. This makes the pain
bearable as you tug me towards some

semblance of where we both
began. I think I am awake and watching
your eyes flicker sparks

that stare, unfocused. I imagine
you still see the cloudy,
enclosed waters from the place you were

before you passed through me,
to air. Unseen, like wind shifts, you
are sudden breath, a panting

deep that opens fear up in my heart. I
have to hurry, feeling
your lips set and hardening, feeling

your jaws lock and your tongue
sticking, before you get too used to flesh.
Before you learn to bite

down hard, I must teach you how
to eat of the earth
and how to drink the water.

BIRTH OF THE BLACK LIFE
(Malia Kai, born day of the eclipse aquarius 30 72)

Nubia Kai

After the eclipse
came the dawn
the afternoon snow showered
the metallic forests of djinns
then, a dewdrop on the pavement
growing, alive, as strong as
grass lifting skyscrapers

in this horrible tomb
there are wombs
budding even in defiant winters

Malia,
you are not the warrior we conjured
but you are the jewel of the warrior
mother of sons & daughters & nations
scaling eternity

child of my loins
child of your father's left side
you could inspire tenderness
and love of distances
even in the nows raging fire

After the eclipse
when the full moon and sun have parted
a dewdrop forms on the pavement
overshadows death, lining the frozen streets
life is born
born is life
again, the day melts into forever.

A POEM FOR MY MOTHER, NUBIA KAI AL-NURA SALAAM

Malia Kai

When Allah made
The sun,
He had
You in mind.

INSOMNIAC

Esperanza Cintrón

Bare feet padding
down a carpeted hallway
She calls me
Her tiny voice
comes to stand in the doorway
Plump fingers
pull on fat pig tails
rub widening eyes
Round belly pokes out
of cotton nightie
Toes on cold linoleum,
she considers thirst
uncloseted monsters
or watery nightmares
the best excuse
for being up this late
lips pout
she cd always make me smile
so I,
hold out my arms
& she comes tumbling in.

BABY FAITH

Michele Wallace

The rumor was that Harlem Hospital maternity had sent some families home with the wrong babies that year, so babies had to be named before their mothers left delivery. But my grandmother Willi Posey was depressed and uninterested in naming her newborn baby girl. In an effort to rouse my grandmother's spirits, and bestow upon the child the quality she was most likely to need, a nurse suggested helpfully, "Why don't you name her Faith?" It was, after all, 1930, the height of the Great Depression. Although my grandfather had one of the rare good jobs a Black man could have in the period—he drove a truck for the Department of Sanitation—my grandmother, who was always ambitious, faced her future as Harlem housewife and mother of three through the grief of having lost a two-year-old son to pneumonia only six months before. Yet she stirred herself sufficiently to give to my mother her own first name Willi as a middle name.

There's always been a gift among the women in my family for making things. We trace it back to my great-great-great grandmother Susie Shannon and her daughter Betsy Bingham, both house slaves and quilt makers in antebellum Florida. Skipping the generation of my great-grandparents, who were preachers and teachers, it survived in my grandmother Willi Posey, whom I called Momma Jones, as part of the generation that came North. Once her children were grown, she worked sewing in the factories in the garment district, while launching herself as a prominent Harlem club-woman and fashion designer. When I was little, she was always quitting her job downtown because of some white male boss whose authority she could not abide, always sewing or cutting a pattern or fitting a dress or a suit on a model or a customer. All of us—my mother, my aunt, my sister, and I—modelled in her fashion shows. These lavish, musical extravaganzas—more social than financial successes—showcased my grandmother's penchant for the theatrical.

The work of my mother Faith Ringgold, as feminist performance artist, painter, soft sculptor, and quilt maker seems the culmination of this tradition. At various times, all of us have been her collaborators. Momma Jones, in particular, made Faith's tankas (cloth frames) for paintings, clothing for her soft sculpture, costumes for her performances, and taught her the rudimentary skills of quilt making. My childhood evenings were often spent in a circle of women, drawing, cutting, sewing—making things.

But along with my mother's and my commitment to Black feminist goals, there has emerged in my family an increasing fascination with naming, storytelling, and language. Perhaps the ultimate manifestation, thus far, has been Faith's own increasing reliance on storytelling in her art, from the picaresque Black feminist tale of "The Who's Afraid of Aunt Jemima Quilt" to the autobiographical photo-essay of "Change: Faith Ringgold's Over 100 Pounds Weight Loss Story Quilt" and performance. Both performance and quilt feature photographs and text illustrating the "changes" wrought upon her body and spirit, as sister, wife and mother, from childhood to the present.

Like Milkman's search for Pilate's "gold" in Toni Morrison's *Song of Solomon*, which leads him to uncover the conundrum of names in his family, we knew that the feminist notion of history, continuity, and tradition was a way to remember what we could no longer afford to forget about the patterns of being a Black woman. It wasn't only that naming ourselves had been a heady privilege for Blacks ever since the collective "misnaming" of slavery. It was also that we would no longer be Alice Walker's "Saints" in search of our mother's gardens. We weren't rural, but urban, nor bound to the land or religion or anything but each other. Momma Jones never kept a garden, but she wrote all the time—letters to her family, notes to herself, plans and sketches for future fashions—in a large, imperial hand. Yet it never occurred to her to organize these materials because somebody might want to read them.

Quite early, my sister and I were persuaded that the world was most profoundly known through the accretion of language, the nuances of interpretation, anecdotal accumulation and overlay. Although Faith grew up hearing the story of how the nurse had named her, Momma Jones didn't tell her that her middle name was Willi. Faith thought her middle name was Elizabeth until her marriage in 1950 required that she obtain a copy of her birth certificate. I grew up hearing my mother tell this story about Momma Jones, who never explained. It was part of an endless performance of stories about life on Harlem's Edge-combe Avenue and beyond, that were told and retold by Momma Jones, Faith, my Aunt Barbara and my stepfather Burdette Ring-gold. Not only did visitors bring newer, less familiar stories, thanks to the intellectual curiosity of my then protofeminist mother, I had access to a vast store of Afro-American music as well as books.

As infants, my sister and I often accompanied my mother to the 42nd Street Library, our own copies of "The Cat in The Hat" or "Eloise" in tow. (Kenneth Clarke's research had resulted in Black dolls, but not yet Black books for children.) Momma Jones began teaching me how to read when I was three. Later, I remember visits to the bookstore offered up, along with the movies, as the ultimate weekend entertainment. "Why" questions were chased down and settled with books and music, as well as stories. From their first appearance, James Baldwin's books—which would subsequently inspire Faith's first series of political paintings on the Civil Rights Movement—were primary texts in our house, along with the records of Dinah Washington, Billie Holiday, and Nina Simone.

Again in Harlem Hospital, fifty years later, another Faith Willi was born in our family to my sister Barbara Faith Wallace, Ph.D. student in theoretical linguistics at CUNY's Graduate Center. The cold, grey dawn of March 1, 1982, Faith woke up abruptly to announce that Baby Faith had arrived within minutes of her birth, which a call to the hospital soon confirmed. Barbara shared a hospital room with five other women, all Black and Latina. Each woman held a baby, gingerly, in her arms. But the room was absolutely silent except for Barbara chattering away full speed to the new Faith Willi as though it were not a new conversation but an old conversation interrupted.

At the time, Barbara and I were living together in what had been Momma Jones's apartment in the Lennox Terrace across the street from Harlem Hospital. Momma Jones had died in her sleep at seventy-nine in October of the year before. My sister Barbara and Faith had found the body, as well as the blue wool panels of a winter maternity coat she'd been making for Barbara spread out on a cutting table in the living room.

It had not been a good year for any of us. My sister had suffered a difficult divorce. Pregnancy would indefinitely delay her Ph.D., although she had been awarded an M.A. and an M.Phil. that June in a ceremony that Momma Jones had attended. The first draft of my novel was rejected by my publisher, and I suddenly realized that, for financial reasons, I would be unable to continue graduate school in American Studies at Yale.

Having recently finished her first quilt, "Echoes of Harlem," as a collaboration with Momma Jones, Faith eagerly pursued her interest in this medium. Although she was well known across the country as a feminist artist, with no dealer and no gallery she was making very little money from the sale of her art. My Aunt Barbara, an elementary schoolteacher, who had once dreamed of a Ph.D. in education at Columbia University and who encouraged my interest in writing by introducing me to Langston Hughes's "The Sweet Flypaper of Life" and Ann Petry's *The Street*, would die of a heart attack brought on by acute alcoholism only six months after Baby Faith's birth. She had never reconciled herself to Momma Jones's death.

Prompted by recent speculation that fetuses are receptive to conversation, my sister and I had talked to Baby Faith in the womb throughout Barbara's pregnancy. As writer and linguist, we were eager that Baby Faith would share with us the mystery of words as soon as possible. Thus we continued a family tradition at least one generation old. When Barbara and I were born in 1952, both Faith and her sister Barbara were college students majoring in education at the City College of New York and Hunter College, respectively. As a result, Barbara and I were endlessly probed and tested.

Now we anticipated observing and studying Baby Faith. And she did not disappoint us. Every day was a small adventure. The first time she smiled, I initially mistook it for a burp. During our weekend candlelight dinners, we propped up the five-month-old Baby Faith in her carriage, a steak bone in her hand, so that she might enjoy the conversation. An endlessly expressive "Dah" was her only word. In tribute, Faith did the "Dah Series," six large abstract paintings that channeled the emotions of losing her mother and gaining a first grandchild in a single year. Faith and I collaborated on the Dah Performance #1 in surrealistic masks and costume. The six-month-old Baby Faith watched from the front row and was unafraid.

Everyday, I grow less certain of feminism's definition, of the usefulness of confining it to narrow, monological explanation. Surely it is process, ethos, movement, archive, and article of faith all at once. Its range is simultaneously psychological and international. Black feminism, then, is perhaps her-story, whatever it calls itself, in order to make the world inhabitable for the Faiths, Willis, and Micheles, who would make things with their hands, and with language, and with all of their being; a unique caliber of self-expression and fulfillment; to each her own niche.

Four years later, Faith now has a dealer, the Bernice Steinbaum Gallery in SoHo. In a recent one-person exhibition, she displayed quilts of an unprecedented range, incorporating autobiography, fictional narrative, performance, photo-essay, painting and sewing. She has lost 100 pounds, a pivotal feat of self-love in itself. From January to June, she is a tenured professor of Visual Arts at The University of California in San Diego. The rest of the year, she spends making art, which now sells quite well, in her beloved Harlem. She has been awarded two honorary doctorates of fine arts from The Moore College of Art ('86) and the College of Wooster ('87).

I teach Afro-American Literature, Women's Studies, and Creative Writing at the University of Oklahoma. I write fiction about Black girls with strong mothers, fiction which has not yet found its place. Continuing the work I began in *Black Macho and the Myth of the Superwoman,* I also write about Afro-American culture and literature, and its particular ambivalence about what Toril Moi has called "Sexual/Textual Politics."

My sister Barbara now teaches third grade at P.S. 200 in Harlem. She has switched her dissertation topic from theoretical linguistics to sociolinguistics. Although she says that feminism conflicts with her religious beliefs, she says her research will focus on Black English as spoken by Black women who were raised in Harlem. Barbara says that most Black people speak some degree of Black English. Recent studies identify three levels—basolect, mesolect, and the acrolect, which includes, Barbara tells me, "most professional, middle class, occasional Black English speakers like you and me and our mother Faith Ringgold."

Which causes me to recollect the curious half-Southern, half formal speech Momma Jones sometimes used when talking to strangers, and the way people were always unable to tell the voices of my Aunt Barbara, Faith, myself, and my sister apart. Barbara points out that studies of Black English are rarely done on women: "Linguists have concentrated on men's language because men were the linguists. But women teach children how to speak. In the first five years we are the dominant figures in children's lives."

In July of 1985, Baby Faith was joined by a baby sister Theodora Michele, named after a great-grandmother who is still living and me. On March 1, Baby Faith's fifth birthday, I called their family long distance. After several resounding "Hi's" from the 1½-year-old Teddy, I spoke to Baby Faith. I asked her how she felt on her birthday.

"I'm proud of myself, happy," she said. "I know how to tie my shoes. I know how to read easy books. I'm teaching myself how to read. Sometimes I draw a picture of my family. I help my mother with Teddy. I pass her the diapers. I make milk for Teddy."

"What do you want to be when you grow up?" I ask her. Perhaps to Barbara's credit, this question is not a familiar one. But finally, she says, "I want to be a nurse, and I want to be a lawyer when I grow up. Also I want to be an artist like grandma and a writer, too."

The last time I'd seen Baby Faith had been a year ago, when I visited her in Harlem. She gave me several pieces from a large stack of her drawings, and dashed off a pencil sketch—a "portrait" of me, I think, while I sat there, which she then promptly signed Faith Willi Wallace-Gadsden.

"How will you be all those things at once," I asked.

"If I lose one job I can go on the other," she explained reasonably.

"Are you a feminist?" I asked her.

"What's a feminist?"

"Well, a feminist is somebody who believes in the equality of women to men."

"What's equality?" she asked me.

At the time, I was unable to come up with an answer, perhaps because of the alienation of the telephone, the long distance call, which has linked me to my family these past years. But what I should have done was what Momma Jones or Aunt Barbara or Faith might have done—tell her a story, or perhaps there's an easy book . . .

San Diego, California
April 1987

Postscript

In 1988 Faith won the Guggenheim and has been engaged in many exciting projects and commissions, perhaps chief among them her participation in a benefit for Bishop Tutu, sponsored by Michael Jackson. Her contribution to this effort was a special painting/quilt devoted to Jackson's "Bad." In it she deals with her notion that when you're Black, good is never good enough. Thus "bad" is what you need to be in order to overcome the dangerous forces that compromise your effectiveness. In the corners of the painting, she writes the names of notorious "bad guys" like Rosa Parks, Fannie Lou Hamer, Zora Neale Hurston, Bishop Tutu, Martin Luther King, Michael Jackson, and myself.

Also, Faith has done "Church Picnic," a painted story quilt, and a new acquisition of the permanent collection at the High Museum in Atlanta. The image shows a vast array of Black people attending a church picnic in Atlanta around the turn of the century. The story focuses on the Black community's problem in dealing with a couple who fall in love and choose to marry, despite their class differences and despite the objections of their respective families. Faith suggests that the underlying struggle here is really about how the Black community will define its relationship to freedom and emancipation.

So far, we've engaged in one collaboration called "Dream 2:MLK and The Sisterhood," a story quilt which shows Martin Luther King with Coretta King, Fannie Lou Hamer, Rosa Parks, and Ella Baker, and which includes a text by me, first delivered as a speech commemorating his birthday as an official holiday in Flint, Michigan. The quilt will appear in a special issue of *The Sunday Washington Post Magazine* devoted to the anniversary of Martin Luther King's death on April 4th.

I am no longer teaching at the University of Oklahoma. I am now teaching Women's Studies and American Studies at the University of Buffalo-SUNY. Although I've written very little fiction this year, I have been writing essays on Zora Neale Hurston, Michael Jackson, Spike Lee, and what I call "Variations on Negation: The Heresy of Black Feminist Creativity," which will appear in the Winter '89 issue of *Heresies*. I am also very close to completing my Master's in English at CCNY.

My sister Barbara has just had another baby named Martha. She took a leave of absence from the doctoral program at the City University of New York Graduate Center in order to do so. Although she advanced to candidacy in 1977, and they customarily permit candidates only eight years in which to finish up, they had recently granted her another two years. In the fall, then, she'll have another year in which to complete her dissertation, but she also has the responsibility of three children, and she will soon return to teaching a seventh grade class at P.S. 175 in Manhattan.

Needless to say, I think my sister's ambivalence about getting a Ph.D. runs deep. In fact, I think she has babies *instead* of Ph.D.'s. But I have no children and I have suffered from the same problem, having attempted to pursue graduate degrees on four separate occasions—first in creative writing at CCNY, then in English at NYU, then in Afro-American Studies and American Studies at Yale, and now in English at CCNY.

Perhaps our ambivalence has to do with the pressures incumbent upon Black female speech (and writing) described by Bell Hooks in an essay called "Talking Back."[1] In this essay, Hooks illustrates in poignant detail, drawn from autobiographical reflection, the three levels of speech that occur among Black women: (1) speechlessness, the plight of female children (who should be seen and not heard), the mad and the dead; (2) self-reflexive speech, that speech which is only listened to by other Black women, but ignored by almost everybody else, including Black men; (3) and "talking back," that speech, which usually must be written (in order to become history), that transcends and transforms the barriers of race, class, and sex to address the world.

This third category of speech is the kind that generally gets you in trouble precisely because it problematizes the invariability of classifications of difference. It is also unavoidable in any process of Black female intellectual self-formulation. Although such self-formulation is not *required* as part of the graduate education we usually receive, the ritual of education inevitably raises the spectre of such a process. The problem then becomes how to pursue a degree as part of a graduate education (in history or literature, philosophy or linguistics) which inevitably denies the significance/presence of the Black intellect, in a demonstration of precisely that intellect (female no less!) which the structure of that education denies. These obstacles appear not only in the form of the antipathy of our frequently white male professors but also in the form of financial and child care restrictions and limitations. I also think that the Black community—from family to church to boys on the corner to the men in our lives—exacts a high price for "talking back." And most of us are unwilling, or unable (after a while, it becomes difficult to tell the two apart) to pay it.

Buffalo, New York
March 21, 1988

NOTE

1. See Bell Hooks's most recent book, *Talking Back, Thinking Feminist, Thinking Black* (Boston: South End Press, 1988), which is a collection of her personal essays.

CLOSETS AND KEEPSAKES

Willi Coleman

Closets are the city dweller's storeroom, attic, and basement. Although I've been known to keep boxes under my bed or stuffed behind the sofa, it is the shelves and back recesses of a closet which seem to hold a rare assortment of items. There are some very special memories contained in cardboard boxes and brown paper bags of varying sizes. Such things I make no pretense of wanting to throw away or share with others during sophisticated wine and cheese romps down memory lane. Some things are too precious for either category. Occasionally it is up to scraps of paper and old photographs to link you with yourself through the passing of time and shifts in lifestyles. And so, we move battered boxes and newspaper-protected, oddly shaped bundles into cramped studio or tenth-floor "garden" apartments. Inside these packages are parts of ourselves that we sometimes refuse to share with curious lovers and newfound friends. Decor and lifestyles change, but the stuff in the back of the closet remains a constant beacon calling us back.

Sitting on the floor with the contents of two boxes spread out before me, I feel the weight of a wrinkled brown paper bag. It is heavy and crumpled to fit the shape of its contents. The straightening comb inside has slightly bent teeth, contoured by years of being dropped from less than skillful hands and blackened by just as much use. A few remaining glints of bright metal transport me instantly to a time when I was very small, very southern . . . and quite happy. There was a time . . . there really was a time when hot combs were for holidays and permanents did not exist. Political correctness be damned, we loved the ritual as well as the end results. Both were powerful lines of love held in the hands of women and shaping the lives of girls. The route taken was as old as fire and remains equally as irreplaceable.

I remember being eight years old and sitting on the floor, my head even with my mother's knees. She above me, seated on a chair, shifted her weight from side to side organizing wide tooth comb, brush, pins, straightening comb and serious hair grease.

Her hands pulled, darted, twisted and patted as if she were directing the Sunday morning choir for "Light of the World" Baptist Church. Two smart taps on the left side of my head was the signal for me to turn my head to the right and vice versa. When I allowed my head to wander out of her reach or without her direction my reward was three sharp raps on the top of my head. It never hurt, and the ritual never gave way to verbal directions. It was always three slaps on the head with a wide tooth comb . . . never two or four.

Mama was a creature of habit and our sessions together could halt time, still waters, and predict the future. Any soul-wrenching childhood catastrophe could be borne until it was again my turn on the floor between my mother's knees. On some occasions the first flap of the comb brought not my usual obedient response but a sniffle. On the second flap I escalated to a whimper and the third was almost anticipated by a full-scale yell. Always an overly dramatic child, I played the sniffle, whimper, yell routine for a full three minutes to my one-woman audience. In due time I would quiet down just enough to hear the head tapper inquire in words that never changed . . . "Lil old negro . . . what in the world is wrong with you?" The sentence had a rhythm all its own. Negro came out "knee-grow" and world was drawn out as if to give the sound a chance to circle the entire universe. Mama had her way of pampering each of her children. She did not like "nobody's rotten kids" and had no intentions of raising any in her house. Behavior which would not have been tolerated otherwise received lesser penalties on hair day. The invitation of her words immediately prompted me to unburden myself. It never crossed my mind to hold back the hurt, fear, or anger. Long before I was four I knew that with me on the floor and Mama waving her comb I could get more mileage out of a mere whimper than a loud wail at any other time.

Except for special occasions Mama came home from work early on Saturdays. She spent six days a week mopping, waxing, and dusting other women's houses and keeping out of reach of other women's husbands. Saturday nights were reserved for "taking care of them girls' hair" and the telling of stories. Some of which included a recitation of what she had endured and how she had triumphed over "folks that were lower than dirt" and "no-good snakes in the grass." She combed, patted, twisted, and talked, saying things which would have embarrassed or shamed her at other times. There were days when I was sure that she had ceased to be the mother we all knew. The smell of warm oils, clean hair, and a Black working woman's anger had transformed her into somebody else. She talked with ease and listened with undivided attention. Sometimes the magic lasted for hours. By the time my sister had taken her place on the floor I had covered the two blocks to the store. With whatever change could be squeezed out of Mama's "four dollars a day plus carfare," I would carefully choose day-old pastry and get back home before my sister's last plait was in place. There never was a time when I did not wonder just what tales and secrets I had missed. The eleven months which separated my sister and me were, I suspected, most evident in what was said during my absence.

But even this small slight has carved out a warm place to hide in my memories. For, at my mother's signal, I had moved away from those Saturday hair sessions, as if from a safe harbor, carrying with me: "Child, go look at yourself in the mirror." It was always said as if whatever I saw surpassed good and bordered on the truly wonderful. And I, searching for my own reflection, walked away oblivious to the love and life-sustaining messages which had seeped into my pores as I sat on the floor of my mother's kitchen.

DEAR MAMA

Sonia Sanchez

It is Christmas eve and the year is passing away with calloused feet. My father, your son, and I decorate the night with words. Sit ceremoniously in human song. Watch our blue sapphire words eclipse the night. We have come to this simplicity from afar.

He stirs, pulls from his pocket a faded picture of you. Blackwoman. Sitting in frigid peace. All of your biography preserved in your face. And my eyes draw up short as he says, "her name was Elizabeth but we used to call her Lizzie." And I hold your picture in my hands. But I know your name by heart. It's Mama. I hold you in my hands and let time pass over my face: "Let my baby be. She ain't like the others. She rough. She'll stumble on gentleness later on."

Ah Mama. Gentleness ain't never been no stranger to my genes. But I did like the roughness of running and swallowing the wind, diving in rivers I could barely swim, jumping from second story windows into a saving backyard bush. I did love you for loving me so hard until I slid inside your veins and sailed your blood to an uncrucified shore.

And I remember Saturday afternoons at our house. The old sister deaconesses sitting in sacred pain. Black cadavers burning with lost aromas. And I crawled behind the couch and listened to breaths I had never breathed. Tasted their enormous martyrdom. Lives spent on so many things. Heard their laughter at Sister Smith's latest performance in church—her purse sailing toward Brother Thomas's head again. And I hugged the laughter round my knees. Draped it round my shoulder like a Spanish shawl.

And history began once again. I received it and let it circulate in my blood. I learned on those Saturday afternoons about women rooted in themselves, raising themselves in dark America, discharging their pain without ever stopping. I learned about women fighting men back when they hit them: "Don't never let no mens hit you mo than once girl." I learned about "womens waking up

From *Under a Soprano Sky*, by Sonia Sanchez (Trenton, NJ: Africa World Press, 1989).

they mens" in the night with pans of hot grease and the compromises reached after the smell of hot grease had penetrated their sleepy brains. I learned about loose women walking their abandoned walk down front in church, crossing their legs instead of their hands to God. And I crept into my eyes. Alone with my daydreams of being woman. Adult. Powerful. Loving. Like them. Allowing nobody to rule me if I didn't want to be.

And when they left. When those old bodies had gathered up their sovereign smells. After they had kissed and packed up beans snapped and cakes cooked and laughter bagged. After they had called out their last goodbyes, I crawled out of my place. Surveyed the room. Then walked over to the couch where some had sat for hours and bent my head and smelled their evening smells. I screamed out loud, "oooweeee! Ain't that stinky!" and I laughed laughter from a thousand corridors. And you turned Mama, closed the door, chased me round the room until I crawled into a corner where your large body could not reach me. But your laughter pierced the little alcove where I sat laughing at the night. And your humming sprinkled my small space. Your humming about your Jesus and how one day he was gonna take you home . . .

Because you died when I was six Mama, I never laughed like that again. Because you died without warning Mama, my sister and I moved from family to stepmother to friend of the family. I never felt your warmth again.

But I knew corners and alcoves and closets where I was pushed when some mad woman went out of control. Where I sat for days while some woman raved in rhymes about unwanted children. And work. And not enough money. Or love. And I sat out my childhood with stutters and poems gathered in my head like some winter storm. And the poems erased the stutters and pain. And the words loved me and I loved them in return.

My first real poem was about you Mama and death. My first real poem recited an alphabet of spit splattering a white bus driver's face after he tried to push cousin Lucille off a bus and she left Birmingham under the cover of darkness. Forever. My first real poem was about your Charleswhite arms holding me up against death.

My life flows from you Mama. My style comes from a long line of Louises who picked me up in the night to keep me from wetting the bed. A long line of Sarahs who fed me and my sister and fourteen other children from watery soups and beans and a

lot of imagination. A long line of Lizzies who made me understand love. Sharing. Holding a child up to the stars. Holding
your tribe in a grip of love. A long line of Black people holding
each other up against silence.

I still hear your humming Mama. The color of your song calls
me home. The color of your words saying, "Let her be. She got
a right to be different. She gonna stumble on herself one of
these days. Just let the child be."

And I be, Mama.

THE THURSDAY LADIES

Karla F. C. Holloway

for Gloria and her memory

I wasn't coaxed awake that morning. My sister didn't nudge me off her side of the bed. Mama didn't call, quietly expecting no answer, or louder, getting irritated. No summer morning breeze blew through our window, rattling the shell chimes I'd made on the back porch. Nothing Sunday woke me up—no vaseline-shined shoes waiting to be worn or church waiting to be filled. Nothing but the intermittent squeak of the back screen door, followed by muffled good mornings ". . . them sweeties still sleep?" constantly echoing through the house woke me. I knew it was Thursday after the fourth or fifth squeak . . . and so I punched Shirley in the back and told her "Get up—those ladies are back."

We called them the Thursday ladies. But they could have been the summer ladies or weekday ladies or servant ladies. They were all of those things. In our small Michigan town ours was one of the few Black families. We lived apart from the town's center. I never knew the reason we lived past the main highway, almost to the church we shared with the next town's Black Baptist congregation. I wasn't sure whether it was to be close to the church where we spent so much of our family time or to be distant from the town that had only grudgingly admitted us into the outskirts of its community. It was the town where my Papa brought Mama after they'd married and left Sedalia, and he'd made a living for all of us there. Mama, me, my sister Shirley, and my three brothers. My brothers were gone now, army, college, dead (hit by a car in the town my mama avoided) and only me and Shirley were home. Mama was obviously proud that her family had made it—even into the fringes of that community where we lived. So she accepted the town because it grounded our family. But Shirl and me thought she must have hated it some too by the way she never went to town unless it was to shop (on Wednesday) or to school to see about us.

Those ladies were the most constant event in our lives. They connected the time before our brother Junior (we called him

June Bug) died and the time after. They'd always been coming on Thursday, and they were always the same.

I don't mean that they were all softly warm brown. Some were night-dark, deep black women with loving, caring eyes. Some were high-yellow. Like Mama. Some were so slender that I wondered how they took care of all those children they always talked about. They were too fragile, I thought. Some were large and big-boned, and their gentleness was marked in their smiles and the weariness in their eyes. They carried pocketbooks when they came to see us; they all wore the same shoes—"nurse's shoes" Shirl and I called them—and they never acknowledged that they knew. Shirl and I would sneak down the hall when we heard them coming, hide behind the stove closet (where Mama kept cooking stuff), and spend most of Thursday listening to the strange community that entered our kitchen.

They didn't talk like us—me, or Shirl or Mama. They sounded like M'dear, our grandmama back in Sedalia. They kissed (when we came out to grab a biscuit or bacon) like those ladies in M'dear's church. Their voices were soft and their feelings were loud. And Mama smiled more on those summer Thursdays than on any other day.

Their community was well-established. They had ritualized those mornings spent in Mama's kitchen, the evenings on our porch. All of the ladies worked for white families who had come to Michigan to escape the summer heat of places like Charleston or Natchez or New Orleans. They brought their "girls" with them to take care of the children (and them) while they vacationed in our Lake Michigan town. These ladies weren't on vacation—except on Thursday. That was their day off and the day when they gathered in the home of one of the only Black families in town and relieved themselves of the burdens of working for white folks. So Shirl and I knew to come to the kitchen without coaxing that morning, and to be there while they were coming, slowly filling in the spaces around our kitchen table, leaning up against the cupboard, standing duty near the ice box in case someone wanted something, or helping Mama roll biscuits. Shirl and I knew they'd talk first about their "people" and we didn't want to miss any of the ritual. "Girl, you should'a seen . . ." or "She didn't have no better sense than to . . ." or "Well, what chu do when they . . . ?" We'd listen in on the fascinating world of Southern white women who didn't seem to want to see their children all day (except after their naps, or after they'd been fed, or after they were dressed for bed). That would intrigue us, but even more compelling was the aura of the community of these Black women who talked like M'dear and who were absolutely out of place in our sophisticated preadolescent vision of the world. I think now that we kind of resented the woman our mother became on Thursdays because on those days she was happy in ways that we never could make her and she laughed at things we didn't think were funny, and she seemed a part of them instead of us.

So most Thursdays, we'd pick on these ladies like they picked at the white folks they worked for. "Girl, did you see those ankles on that lady by the window?" We'd exaggerate their dialect and ridicule the country manners that caused the younger ladies to call our Mama "Ma'am." "Yes, chile!" I'd pitch my voice real high to sound thin and reed-like like the cocoa-brown lady who'd just joined the group this summer. "Lawd knows my feet cain't take much more of runnin after these chillun." I rubbed my feet like I had seen her do. "Mah Jesus—mah ankles so swole I speck they'll bust!"

"Do Jesus!" Shirl would roll her eyes up and then we'd hit the floor, laughing at our laughing at them. But we'd make sure to get down the hall before the talk about their people was done and shifted to the talk about what they were going to do on their day off.

Our house was the base for Thursday breakfast, supper, late night talk and a kind of gathering of spirit that I didn't understand then, but respected (or feared, or envied) for the strength that was obviously a part of these women's meetings.

On that Thursday Mamie, the new lady, announced she was going to the movie house in town. The other ladies just glanced at her, a smiling acknowledgement of her intent and went on back to their conversations. They were talking about men . . . and that was the ritual talk (after breakfast and before the late afternoon lethargy when a lot of them napped on the porch swing or on the davenport in the living room) that Shirl and I had to be really quiet and careful listeners for, because we reviewed it in our beds Thursday nights. So we didn't pay much attention when Mamie put her bag on her left arm, pulled on her gloves (like she was going to church, Shirl said later) and straightened that black triangle hat she always wore. She went out the front door. We heard it bang shut, but our attention quickly went back to their conversation—certain we'd hear something new about men, something that demanded review, or experimentation or a conference with some of our older girl friends from church. So we sat, our backs firmly pressed against the hall wall, munching peaches and collecting the seeds for planting in our backyard spot that we always forgot the location of.

We did hear Mamie come back. The door's slam punctuated a point that one of the older ladies made: ". . . ain't that just like them mens." And the noise broke our concentration, because it was too early. By the time the movie let out, we should have been back in the kitchen, cutting up tomatoes for supper or heating the frying pan in the oven for the corn bread being stirred on the table. But she was too early for that evening kitchen time. And so Shirl and I looked at each other, then at her, sure we would see some indication of why Mamie had returned too early from the movie house.

But she just smiled—and said, "Scuse me, y'all," in that high squeaky voice of hers and shyly (we agreed later her moves weren't sneaky, just shy) made her way through the living room, past us in the hall and down the passage to the bathroom. She closed the door and turned the water on. We could hear her tinkling into the toilet and the flush even though the water was running. Then she came back out, smiled that "scuse me, y'all" smile and the front door slammed behind her. We jumped up and ran back to the kitchen window where we could see her making her way back down the road to town—back to the movie house.

We looked at each other for just a moment until the truth hit us and then we burst into hysterical, derisive laughter. "She came back just to use the bathroom!" Shirl shouted.

"Countre-e-e-e-e!" I giggled. "Maybe she thought the toilet was outside the movie house and she just kept on walking till she got back here!"

"Maybe the girl on the 'Ladies' sign didn't look enough like her so she didn't think she could go in!" Shirl's voice was broken by the hilarity that had descended on us both.

I yelled back, "Maybe she couldn't read!"

We were both just about overcome with her obvious ignorance and our own delightful sophistication when Mama appeared in the kitchen doorway. She spoke to us in a voice that controlled her rage but could not suppress her unhappiness. Later we both said that we thought she was going to cry instead of talk, but she did talk and it seemed to come out of a memory. Shirl said later that it felt like she hadn't even been in the kitchen with us.

"Maybe," Mama said quietly "maybe in that little country town in Mississippi that's so funny and so foreign to you two, where Mamie works her life away in a home that will never be hers and for a family that will never love her back . . . maybe the bathrooms in movie houses there say something that hurts her so bad she wishes she couldn't read."

And she looked at us like she knew we didn't know what she meant and went back to the room and to her community of Thursday ladies who lived the memory Mama had left in Sedalia.

IMAGES OF MOTHERHOOD IN TONI MORRISON'S *BELOVED*

Lucille P. Fultz

> the fact that another man had the power to
> tear from our cradle the new-born babe
> and sell it in the shambles [marketplace]
> like a brute, and then scourge us if we dare
> to lift a finger to save it from such a fate,
> haunted us for years.
>
> WILLIAM CRAFT,
> *Running a Thousand Miles for Freedom*

> It seems less degrading to give one's self,
> than to submit to compulsion. There is
> something akin to freedom in having a
> lover who has no control over you, except
> that which he gains by kindness and
> attachment.... There may be sophistry in
> all this; but the condition of a slave
> confuses all principles of morality, and, in
> fact, renders the practice impossible.
>
> HARRIET JACOBS,
> *Incidents in the Life of a Slave Girl*

The relationship between slave mothers and their children is one of the overarching issues in Toni Morrison's *Beloved*.[1] Marianne Hirsch rightly argues that in *Beloved* Morrison "has opened the space for maternal narrative in feminist fiction."[2] Morrison's text begins with a historical fact, which it transforms into a fictional artifact. Morrison takes the case of Margaret Garner and "invents" Sethe Suggs. "I had a few important things," Morrison says, but "the rest was novel writing."[3]

In January 1856 a pregnant Margaret Garner, her husband, their four children, and her husband's parents crossed the frozen Ohio River in a daring attempt to gain their freedom. They had joined nine other fugitives from Kentucky. The Garners made their way to the home of a relative, an exslave. Because this refuge was considered unsafe, plans were made to move them to a safer station. But before these plans could be effected, their hiding place was discovered and surrounded by their slave-

holders, U.S. marshals, and a large posse. The Garners, vowing
never to return to slavery, boarded the doors and windows in
hopes of forestalling their capture. When it was clear that the
family would be taken, Margaret took a butcher's knife and slit
the throat of her baby girl. She struck the two boys with a shovel,
but was restrained before she could do further harm to her
children and herself.

Margaret is reported to have said: "if they had given [me]
time, [I] would have killed them all." Reverend Bassett, who
spoke with Margaret, Sethe's historical counterpoint, no doubt
summarized the feelings of most slaves: "She . . . told the story
of her wrongs. She spoke of her days of sufferings, of her nights
of unmitigated toil."[4]

Much of the literature of slavery has focused on the external
conditions of the slaves and patriarchal themes of the Southern
plantation.[5] For example, in discussing their escapes, many fugitives from slavery were constrained by an abolitionist agenda;
they were to emphasize especially the effects of the dehuman-
izing conditions of the system upon the African-American family. These early slave narratives foregrounded the beatings,
abortive escapes, and the long days and short nights on the
plantations.

Beloved evinces the ways in which personal interchange did
more to heal and bind former slaves than did public, formulaic
self-representations. Clearly, the desire for intimacy emerges
from the eponymous character's question about Sethe's relations
with her mother. "Your woman she never fix up your hair?" is
a personal question about an everyday aspect of mother-daughter
bonding. Sethe speaks directly to Beloved in a manner that is
corrective and informative:

> My woman? You mean my mother? If she did, I don't
> remember. I didn't see her but a few times out in the
> fields, and once when she was working indigo. By the
> time I woke up in the morning, she was in line. If the
> moon was bright they worked by its light. Sunday she
> slept like a stick. She must of nursed me two or three
> weeks—that's the way the others did. Then she went
> back in rice and I sucked from the other woman whose
> job it was. So to answer you, no. I reckon not. She
> never fixed my hair nor nothing. (60)

Beloved's question about Sethe's relationship with her mother
addresses the central strategy of the novel, namely the multi-

valent delineation of ancestral relations. By calling into question
the nature of relations between mothers and daughters, the novel
questions other subjective relations as well. Thus Beloved's
question is at once contemporaneous and contemporary. Sethe's
answer to Beloved's question is also an answer to the African-
American female reader.

Bensman and Lilienfeld[6] have concluded from their studies
that information sharing is a "necessity" and the "*desideratum*
of friendship," since friends use their relationship to "unburden
themselves, a burden that ordinarily causes isolation from the
public and official culture," which frequently condemns or es-
chews information which it perceives to be of a private nature"
(149). Bensman and Lilienfeld argue that by valorizing the "private, the unique, the individual, we usually do so by devaluing
the public, the social, the collective" (ix). In a recent interview,
Morrison corroborated this view: "I was trying to make it a
personal experience. The book was not about the institution—
Slavery with a capital S. It was about these anonymous people
called slaves. What they do to keep on, how they make a life,
what they're willing to risk, however long it lasts, in order to
relate to one another."[7]

The plethora of narratives by and about slaves corroborates
the notion that it was much easier for slaves to discuss their
physical experiences in bondage. But few exposed their interior lives: their private thoughts and psychological bruises. To
the extent that *Beloved* foregrounds the mental lives of a few
slave women, it is a revision of the nineteenth-century slave
narratives.

The novel foregrounds the opposition between the slave mother's natural rights and the slaveholder's legal/economic claims.
In *Beloved* Morrison, like many other African-American women
writers, is "less concerned with external historical events than
with how these events are filtered through the psychological
process."[8] The text configures the agonizing memories of slave
women's experiences as mothers. Several women in the novel
bear deep scars connected with their roles as slave mothers:
some have taken drastic measures to thwart the master's will;
others have quietly endured their pain.

Ella, the first Black woman Sethe meets when she crosses the
Ohio River, has limited her reactions to verbal violence against
her slaveholders—a father and son—who "kept her locked in
a room for themselves for more than a year." As she puts it:
"You couldn't think up what them two done to me" (119). She

terms them the "lowest yet." Thus when Ella meets Sethe and her day-old child with its "tiny, dirty face poking out of the wool blanket," she admonishes Sethe, "Don't love nothing" (91). This admonition results from Ella's having spent puberty "in a house where she was shared by father and son" from whom she acquired a "disgust for sex and against whom she measured all atrocities. A killing, a kidnap, a rape . . . Nothing compared to 'the lowest yet.' " During this period of victimization Ella urged restraint on her husband, knowing any protestation or intervention by him would result in his death. Moreover, she was confident that she would eventually escape and join him.

Baby Suggs, Sethe's mother-in-law, epitomizes the slave woman who bore numerous children and watched as they were snatched from her one by one. As she tells Sethe, "I had eight. Every one of them gone away from me. Four taken, four chased, and all, I expect, worrying somebody's house into evil," by which she means they have probably died and are wreaking revenge as ghosts. "My first-born," Ella muses. "All I can remember of her is how she loved the burned bottom of bread. Can you beat that? Eight children and that's all I remember" (5). Her statement suggests that bereaved slave mothers in bondage stashed away bits and pieces of their offspring in their psyches.

Repeatedly, in both factual and fictional narratives, we hear of slaves trying to track down lost relatives by rehearsing some physical characteristic or some peculiar gesture. George Rawick, among others, notes that in interviews many of the slaves retained memories of their "family histories," including details about African ancestors. Many "knew their precise relationship with brothers and sisters and half-brothers and half-sisters and obviously valued these relationships."[9]

Both Sethe and Baby Suggs epitomize the slave mother's position in relation to her children:

> All of Baby's life, as well as Sethe's own, men and
> women had been moved around like checkers. Anybody
> Baby Suggs knew, let alone loved, who hadn't run off
> or been hanged, got rented out, loaned out, bought up,
> brought back, stored up, mortgaged, won, stolen, or
> seized. So Baby's eight children had six fathers. What
> she called the nastiness of life was the shock she re-
> ceived upon learning that nobody stopped playing check-
> ers just because the pieces included her children. (23)

As a palliative for the loss of her two daughters who were sold before they had cut their "adult teeth," Baby Suggs was allowed to keep her son Halle. She was also told that in return for sleeping with a "straw boss" she could keep her third son, but the child was sold nonetheless. Baby felt that she was unable to love the offspring of her union with the straw boss, "and the rest she would not [love]" (23) because she knew she would lose them. Though she contends "it was not worth the trouble to try to learn features you would never see change into adulthood," she does recall some characteristic gesture of the eight, and the pain of not seeing them develop into mature human beings haunts her until her death:

> Seven times she had . . . held a little foot; examined the fat fingertips with her own—fingers she never saw become the male or female hands a mother would recognize anywhere. She didn't know to this day what their permanent teeth looked like; or how they held their head when they walked. Did Patty lose her lisp? What color did Famous' skin finally take? Was that a cleft in Johnny's chin or just a dimple that would disappear soon's his jawbone changed? Four girls, and the last time she saw them there was no hair under their arms. Does Ardelia still love the burned bottom of bread? All seven were gone or dead. What would be the point of looking too hard at that youngest one? (139)

Through Baby Suggs and the other slave women, Morrison delineates the dilemma of slave mothers caught in the web of a cultural and economic system that sought to denature human feelings and sever family ties. Baby Suggs's interior monologue undermines that system by arguing for the deep, abiding love of all mothers for their offspring. Her gesture at hardening herself for the inevitable, yet somehow clinging to tiny memories of her children, challenges the argument that slave women lost interest in their children as easily as they were stripped of physical contact with them. In articulating Baby Suggs's feelings, Morrison challenges not only the slave system but those detractors who accused slave mothers of callous disregard for their offspring.

The slave mother, living in a society in which the demands of the slaveholder nearly always infringed upon her loyalty to her own, had to sequester her love for her children in the crowded slave quarters and in the quiet regions of her heart. Morrison's refiguration of slavery evinces the effects of the displacement of the slave family in the limited access slave children had to their parents. Witness, for example, Sethe's contacts with her mother, "who was pointed out to her by an eight-year old child who watched over the young ones—pointed out as the one among many backs turned away from her, stooping in a watery field. . . . What she saw was a cloth hat as opposed to a straw one" (31).

This episode exposes the system which breaks the fundamental relation between child and parent, the one human the child recognizes above all others. Sethe knows her mother primarily by her headgear and by "a circle and a cross burnt right in the skin." The mother, moreover, makes herself known to Sethe by the cruel hieroglyphics on her body: "This is your ma'am . . . I am the only one got this mark now. The rest dead. If something happens to me and you can't tell me by my face, you can know me by this mark" (61).

Because Sethe does not understand the cruel significance of the scar, she pleads for some mark by which her mother will recognize her as well. Sethe's plea is for some recognizable bond between herself and her mother. "But how will you know me? [Sethe asks]. Mark me, too. . . . Make the mark on me too." Her mother's response is a slap across the face, which Sethe does not understand until some years later when her own back—scored by a White man's whip—becomes a grotesque image of the "family tree."

Socialization begins with the nuclear family and is passed from one generation to another through cultural and historical consciousness. Sethe, however, is denied this socialization. More importantly she has had no role model for motherhood. All that remains of her mother is the memory of a cloth headdress and a mark scored in the flesh. When her mother is hanged and burned, Sethe looks for the stigma. Only then does she learn that her mother had borne several children by White men but threw those children away. Sethe alone she kept because she was conceived by a Black man. All this Sethe learns, not from her mother, but from Nan, a slave and a close friend of her mother's.

Sethe's relation with her children differs markedly from that of the other slave women in the novel. First of all, as her mother-in-law reminds her, Sethe has had "the amazing luck of six whole years of marriage" to one man who "fathered every one of her children" (23). Second, she has found ways to maintain a close physical relationship with her children for two important reasons: because of her fierce attachment to them and because of the level of respect Garner has accorded the slaves on his

farm. Sethe is determined that her children will not suffer the
fate of other slave children left in the care of nannies who had
to nurse White babies first, leaving little milk, if any, for the
slave children. ("Nan had to nurse white babies and me too
because Ma'am was in rice. The little white babies got it first
and I got what was left or none.") Equating milk with motherhood
and the natural link between mother and child, Sethe is horrified
by the notion that someone else could preempt her children's
claim to their birthright. "Nobody will ever get my milk no more
except my own children" (200).

Having been denied the nurturing of a mother and lacking an
appropriate model for motherhood, Sethe is determined that her
daughter will not suffer parental neglect. Yet, in order to protect
her child from the consequences of life in slavery, she must first
free her at whatever sacrifice.

Through desire and knowledge Sethe achieves subjectivity for
herself and her children. She refuses to subscribe to the system
that treats her and her family as objects. Her description of her
children's running free around the farm and of her infant daughter lying in a basket defies the notion that the slave mother was
careless of her children's well-being and indifferent to their
childish whims. During her period of insanity and isolation,
when she has been driven mad by what she terms her "remem-
ories," Sethe recalls the period in slavery when she sought to
protect her children from harm and bondage. She paints a picture
of her children in a kind of Eden before Mrs. Garner's brother
came to manage the farm: "The ground raised up from the second
patch [where potatoes and pumpkins were planted]. Not a hill
exactly but kind of. Enough for Buglar and Howard to run up
and roll down, run up and roll down. That's the way I used to
see them in my dreams, laughing, their short fat legs running
up the hill."

This is an apostrophe to Beloved, who she presumes is the
reincarnation of the murdered infant: "I put my hoe down and
cut across the side yard to get to you. . . . Still asleep. I wanted
to pick you up in my arms and I wanted to look at you sleeping
too. Didn't know which; you had the sweetest face" (192). Sethe
recalls removing the child in her basket to a shady spot in the
grape arbor to protect her from the blazing sunlight. "Cool in
there and shady. I set you down on a little table and figured if
I got a piece of muslin the bugs and things wouldn't get to you."
(192).

This tenderness converts to terror when Sethe realizes that schoolteacher's motives are both economic and pseudoscientific. Sethe recalls that once she understood "why schoolteacher measured [her]" she "had trouble sleeping" (186). In her revulsion at this use of her body, Sethe is acting out a rebellion against the theory and practice of racism. Her anxiety is more than justified since, according to her account, his nephews held her down and sucked her milk. "They handled me like I was a cow" (200). She vows to protect her daughter from similar atrocities, "no one, nobody on this earth, would list her daughter's characteristics on the animal side of the paper" (251). Thus, when schoolteacher comes to Cincinnati to reclaim them, Sethe, in a desperate act of defiance, tries to forestall him by murdering her child. With a terrifying gesture of murderous love she asserts her maternal autonomy to save her daughter from what she believes is a condition worse than death. Sethe is, nevertheless, frightened by her passionate claims because she knows that "Unless carefree, motherlove was a killer" (132). Moreover Sethe avers: "When I explain it she'll understand" (200).

Paul D, like Ella, worries that Sethe has loved her children too much. He terms it "dangerous" for a former slave "to love anything that much . . . especially if it was her children she had settled on to love. The best thing, he knew, was to love just a little bit, so when they broke its back or shoved it in a croaker sack, well maybe you'd have a little left over for the next one" (45). Stamp Paid alone seems to understand the infanticide. He tells Paul D, "She ain't crazy. She love those children. She was trying to outhurt the hurter" (234).

Attempting to understand Sethe's toughness, Paul D searches her eyes. He describes her face as a "mask with mercifully punched out eyes. . . . [which] did not pick up a flicker of light." He concludes that schoolteacher's treatment of the slaves at Sweet Home "punched the glittering iron out of Sethe's eyes, leaving two open wells that did not reflect light" (9). Paul D suggests that there is a connection between Sethe's iron eyes and her fierce attachment to her children.

In her gesture of drawing her children to her and her efforts to deflate schoolteacher's power by reclaiming them as hers alone, Sethe creates around herself something analogous to an "event horizon."[10] She tells Paul D that she cannot permit him to criticize Denver. "I can't hear a word against her. I'll chastise her. You leave her alone," Sethe warns him. And when Paul D reminds her that Denver is grown, Sethe counters: "I don't care what she is. Grown don't mean nothing to a mother. A child is a child. They get bigger, older, but grown? . . . In my heart it don't mean a thing" (45).

Commenting on Sethe's love for her children, Morrison notes that "Under the theatrical conditions of slavery, if you made that claim . . . that you are the mother of these children you were claiming the right to say something about what happens to them." Morrison terms Sethe's commitment to her children "an excess of maternal feeling, a total surrender."[11] This surrender is configured in Sethe's desire to protect her daughter from the ills she suffered as a female slave. Morrison demonstrates the destructive potential of this kind of love. For example, when Sethe is confronted with the ultimate reality of the slaveholder's power over her and her daughter, she resorts to murder in order to protect her daughter from the indignities she herself had suffered. Convinced that her gesture was the right one, she vows to explain to the Beloved, the murdered daughter "reincarnated," that "if I hadn't killed her she would have died and that is something I could not bear to happen to her."

Beloved reconfigures the dynamics of motherhood under slavery, but it does not judge the morality of Sethe's radical act of reclamation. Independent of how Sethe's deed is judged, Morrison insists that North American slavery produced more than cotton and rice. That so-called "peculiar institution" produced monsters among slaveholders and slaves as well. Yet Morrison does not represent Sethe as a simple victim of her oppressors. She presents a complex character who refuses to succumb to a system designed to undermine all human feelings and negate the very notion of motherhood.

NOTES

1. Toni Morrison, *Beloved* (New York: Knopf, 1987). All further parenthetical references are to this edition.

2. Marianne Hirsch, *The Mother/Daughter Plot: Narrative, Psychoanalysis, Feminism* (Bloomington: Indiana University Press, 1989), p. 198.

3. Mervyn Rothstein, "Toni Morrison, in Her New Novel, Defends Women," *New York Times*, 26 August 1987, p. C17.

4. Middleton Harris and others, eds., *The Black Book* (New York: Random House, 1974), p. 10. See also *The Liberator* (Jan.–Apr. 1856); the *New York Daily Tribune* (Jan.–Apr. 1856); Levi Coffin, *Reminiscences* (Cincinnati: Western Tract Society, 1876); and Julius Yanuck, "The Garner Fugitive Case," *The Mississippi Valley Historical Review* 40 (1953): 47–66.

5. See, for example, Harriet Wilson, *Our Nig, or Sketches from the Life of a Free Black* (New York: Vintage Books, 1973); Harriet Jacobs, *Incidents in the Life of a Slave Girl* (New York: Harcourt Brace Jovanovich, 1973), p. 55; Henry Bibb, *Narrative of the Life and Adventures of Henry Bibb, an American Slave* (1855; New York: Negro Universities Press, 1969); William Craft, *Running a Thousand Miles for Freedom, or The Escape of William and Ellen Craft from Slavery*, in *Great Slave Narratives*, ed. Arna Bontemps (Boston: Beacon, 1969).

6. Joseph Bensman and Robert Lilienfeld, *Between Public and Private: The Lost Boundaries of the Self* (New York: The Free Press, 1979).

7. Bonnie Angelo, "The Pain of Being Black," *Time* 133 (22 May 1989): 120.

8. Jane Campbell, *Mythic Black Fiction: The Transformation of History* (Knoxville: University of Tennessee Press, 1986), p. xiii.

9. George P. Rawick, ed., *The American Slave: A Composite Autobiography*, vol. 6, *Alabama and Indiana Narratives* (Westport, CT: Greenwood Press, 1972), p. 90.

10. Stephen Hawking, *A Brief History of Time: From the Big Bang to Black Holes* (New York: Bantam, 1988), describes an "event horizon" as the region surrounding a black hole "from which it is not possible to escape." This boundary "acts rather like a one-way membrane" through which objects . . . can fall but nothing can ever get through the event horizon" (89).

11. Marsha Darling, "In the Realm of Responsibility: A Conversation with Toni Morrison," *The Women's Review of Books* 6 (March 1966): 9.

THE MEANING OF MOTHERHOOD IN BLACK CULTURE AND BLACK MOTHER-DAUGHTER RELATIONSHIPS

Patricia Hill Collins

"What did your mother teach you about men?" is a question I often ask students in my courses on African-American women. "Go to school first and get a good education—don't get too serious too young," "Make sure you look around and that you can take care of yourself before you settle down," and "Don't trust them, want more for yourself than just a man," are typical responses from Black women. My students share stories of how their mothers encouraged them to cultivate satisfying relationships with Black men while anticipating disappointments, to desire marriage while planning viable alternatives, to become mothers only when fully prepared to do so. But, above all, they stress their mothers' insistence on being self-reliant and resourceful.

These daughters, of various ages and from diverse social class backgrounds, family structures and geographic regions, had somehow received strikingly similar messages about Black womanhood. Even though their mothers employed diverse teaching strategies, these Black daughters had all been exposed to common themes about the meaning of womanhood in Black culture.[1]

This essay explores the relationship between the meaning of motherhood in African-American culture and Black mother-daughter relationships by addressing three primary questions. First, how have competing perspectives about motherhood intersected to produce a distinctly Afrocentric ideology of motherhood? Second, what are the enduring themes that characterize this Afrocentric ideology of motherhood? Finally, what effect might this Afrocentric ideology of motherhood have on Black mother-daughter relationships?

COMPETING PERSPECTIVES ON MOTHERHOOD

The Dominant Perspective:
Eurocentric Views of White Motherhood

The cult of true womanhood, with its emphasis on motherhood as woman's highest calling, has long held a special place in the gender symbolism of White Americans. From this perspective, women's activities should be confined to the care of children, the nurturing of a husband, and the maintenance of the household. By managing this separate domestic sphere, women gain social influence through their roles as mothers, transmitters of culture, and parents for the next generation.[2]

While substantial numbers of White women have benefited from the protections of White patriarchy provided by the dominant ideology, White women themselves have recently challenged its tenets. On one pole lies a cluster of women, the traditionalists, who aim to retain the centrality of motherhood in women's lives. For traditionalists, differentiating between the experience of motherhood, which for them has been quite satisfying, and motherhood as an institution central in reproducing gender inequality, has proved difficult. The other pole is occupied by women who advocate dismantling motherhood as an institution. They suggest that compulsory motherhood be outlawed and that the experience of motherhood can only be satisfying if women can also choose not to be mothers. Arrayed between these dichotomous positions are women who argue for an expanded, but not necessarily different, role for women—women can be mothers as long as they are not *just* mothers.[3]

Three themes implicit in White perspectives on motherhood are particularly problematic for Black women and others outside of this debate. First, the assumption that mothering occurs within the confines of a private, nuclear family household where the mother has almost total responsibility for child-rearing is less applicable to Black families. While the ideal of the cult of true womanhood has been held up to Black women for emulation, racial oppression has denied Black families sufficient resources to support private, nuclear family households. Second, strict sex-role segregation, with separate male and female spheres of influence within the family, has been less commonly found in African-American families than in White middle-class ones. Finally, the assumption that motherhood and economic dependency on men are linked and that to be a "good" mother one must stay at home, making motherhood a full-time "occupation," is similarly uncharacteristic of African-American families.[4]

Even though selected groups of White women are challenging the cult of true womanhood and its accompanying definition of motherhood, the dominant ideology remains powerful. As long as these approaches remain prominent in scholarly and popular discourse. Eurocentric views of White motherhood will continue to affect Black women's lives.

Eurocentric Views of Black Motherhood

Eurocentric perspectives on Black motherhood revolve around two interdependent images that together define Black women's roles in White and in African-American families. The first image is that of the Mammy, the faithful, devoted domestic servant. Like one of the family, Mammy conscientiously "mothers" her White children, caring for them and loving them as if they were her own. Mammy is the ideal Black mother for she recognizes her place. She is paid next to nothing and yet cheerfully accepts her inferior status. But when she enters her own home, this same Mammy is transformed into the second image, the too-strong matriarch who raises weak sons and "unnaturally superior" daughters.[5] When she protests, she is labeled aggressive and unfeminine, yet if she remains silent, she is rendered invisible.

The task of debunking Mammy by analyzing Black women's roles as exploited domestic workers and challenging the matriarchy thesis by demonstrating that Black women do not wield disproportionate power in African-American families has long preoccupied African-American scholars.[6] But an equally telling critique concerns uncovering the functions of these images and their role in explaining Black women's subordination in systems of race, class, and gender oppression. As Mae King points out, White definitions of Black motherhood foster the dominant group's exploitation of Black women by blaming Black women for their characteristic reactions to their own subordination.[7] For example, while the stay-at-home mother has been held up to all women as the ideal, African-American women have been compelled to work outside the home, typically in a very narrow range of occupations. Even though Black women were forced to become domestic servants and be strong figures in Black households, labeling them Mammys and matriarchs denigrates Black women. Without a countervailing Afrocentric ideology of motherhood,

White perspectives on both White and African-American motherhood place Black women in a no-win situation. Adhering to these standards brings the danger of the lowered self-esteem of internalized oppression, one that, if passed on from mother to daughter, provides a powerful mechanism for controlling African-American communities.

African Perspectives on Motherhood

One concept that has been constant throughout the history of African societies is the centrality of motherhood in religions, philosophies, and social institutions. As Barbara Christian points out, "There is no doubt that motherhood is for most African people symbolic of creativity and continuity."[8]

Cross-cultural research on motherhood in African societies appears to support Christian's claim.[9] West African sociologist Christine Oppong suggests that the Western notion of equating household with family be abandoned because it obscures women's family roles in African cultures.[10] While the archetypal White, middle-class nuclear family conceptualizes family life as being divided into two oppositional spheres—the "male" sphere of economic providing and the "female" sphere of affective nurturing—this type of rigid sex role segregation was not part of the West African tradition. Mothering was not a privatized nurturing "occupation" reserved for biological mothers, and the economic support of children was not the exclusive responsibility of men. Instead, for African women, emotional care for children and providing for their physical survival were interwoven as interdependent, complementary dimensions of motherhood.

In spite of variations among societies, a strong case has been made that West African women occupy influential roles in African family networks.[11] First, since they are not dependent on males for economic support and provide much of their own and their children's economic support, women are structurally central to families.[12] Second, the image of the mother is one that is culturally elaborated and valued across diverse West African societies. Continuing the lineage is essential in West African philosophies, and motherhood is similarly valued.[13] Finally, while the biological mother-child bond is valued, child care was a collective responsibility, a situation fostering cooperative, age-stratified, woman-centered "mothering" networks.

Recent research by Africanists suggests that much more of this African heritage was retained among African-Americans

than had previously been thought. The retention of West African
culture as a culture of resistance offered enslaved Africans and
exploited African-Americans alternative ideologies to those advanced by dominant groups. Central to these reinterpretations
of African-American institutions and culture is a reconceptual-
ization of Black family life and the role of women in Black family
networks.[14] West African perspectives may have been combined
with the changing political and economic situations framing
African-American communities to produce certain enduring
themes characterizing an Afrocentric ideology of motherhood.

ENDURING THEMES OF AN AFROCENTRIC
IDEOLOGY OF MOTHERHOOD

An Afrocentric ideology of motherhood must reconcile the competing worldviews of these three conflicting perspectives of motherhood. An ongoing tension exists between efforts to mold the
institution of Black motherhood for the benefit of the dominant
group and efforts by Black women to define and value their own
experiences with motherhood. This tension leads to a continuum
of responses. For those women who either aspire to the cult of
true womanhood without having the resources to support such
a lifestyle, or who believe the stereotypical analyses of themselves as dominating matriarchs, motherhood can be oppressive.
But the experience of motherhood can provide Black women
with a base of self-actualization, status in the Black community,
and a reason for social activism. These alleged contradictions
can exist side by side in African-American communities, families, and even within individual women.

Embedded in these changing relationships are four enduring
themes that I contend characterize an Afrocentric ideology of
motherhood. Just as the issues facing enslaved African mothers
were quite different from those currently facing poor Black
women in inner cities, for any given historical moment the actual
institutional forms that these themes take depend on the severity
of oppression and Black women's resources for resistance.

Bloodmothers, Othermothers, and
Women-Centered Networks

In African-American communities, the boundaries distinguish-
ing biological mothers of children from other women who care

for children are often fluid and changing. Biological mothers or bloodmothers are expected to care for their children. But African and African-American communities have also recognized that vesting one person with full responsibility for mothering a child may not be wise or possible. As a result, "othermothers," women who assist bloodmothers by sharing mothering responsibilities, traditionally have been central to the institution of Black motherhood.[15]

The centrality of women in African-American extended families is well known.[16] Organized, resilient, women-centered networks of bloodmothers and othermothers are key to this centrality. Grandmothers, sisters, aunts, or cousins acted as othermothers by taking on childcare responsibilities for each other's children. When needed, temporary child care arrangements turned into long-term care or informal adoption.[17]

In African-American communities, these women-centered networks of community-based childcare often extend beyond the boundaries of biologically related extended families to support "fictive kin."[18] Civil rights activist Ella Baker describes how informal adoption by othermothers functioned in the Southern, rural community of her childhood:

> My aunt who had thirteen children of her own raised
> three more. She had become a midwife, and a child was
> born who was covered with sores. Nobody was particu-
> larly wanting the child, so she took the child and raised
> him . . . and another mother decided she didn't want to
> be bothered with two children. So my aunt took one and
> raised him . . . they were part of the family.[19]

Even when relationships were not between kin or fictive kin, African-American community norms were such that neighbors cared for each other's children. In the following passage, Sara Brooks, a Southern domestic worker, describes the importance of the community-based childcare that a neighbor offered her daughter. In doing so, she also shows how the African-American cultural value placed on cooperative childcare found institutional support in the adverse conditions under which so many Black women mothered:

> She kept Vivian and she didn't charge me nothin either.
> You see, people used to look after each other, but now
> it's not that way. I reckon it's because we all was poor,
> and I guess they put theirself in the place of the person
> that they was helpin.[20]

Othermothers were key not only in supporting children but also in supporting bloodmothers who, for whatever reason, were ill-prepared or had little desire to care for their children. Given the pressures from the larger political economy, the emphasis placed on community-based childcare and the respect given to othermothers who assume the responsibilities of childcare have served a critical function in African-American communities. Children orphaned by sale or death of their parents under slavery, children conceived through rape, children of young mothers, children born into extreme poverty, or children who for other reasons have been rejected by their bloodmothers have all been supported by othermothers who, like Ella Baker's aunt, took in additional children, even when they had enough of their own.

Providing as Part of Mothering

The work done by African-American women in providing the economic resources essential to Black family well-being affects motherhood in a contradictory fashion. On the one hand, African-American women have long integrated their activities as economic providers into their mothering relationships. In contrast to the cult of true womanhood, in which work is defined as being in opposition to and incompatible with motherhood, work for Black women has been an important and valued dimension of Afrocentric definitions of Black motherhood. On the other hand, African-American women's experiences as mothers under oppression were such that the type and purpose of work Black women were forced to do had a great impact on the type of mothering relationships bloodmothers and othermothers had with Black children.

While slavery both disrupted West African family patterns and exposed enslaved Africans to the gender ideologies and practices of slaveowners, it simultaneously made it impossible, had they wanted to do so, for enslaved Africans to implement slaveowner's ideologies. Thus, the separate spheres of providing as a male domain and affective nurturing as a female domain did not develop within African-American families.[21] Providing for Black children's physical survival and attending to their affective, emotional needs continued as interdependent dimensions of an Afrocentric ideology of motherhood. However, by changing the conditions under which Black women worked and the purpose of the work itself, slavery introduced the problem of how best to continue traditional Afrocentric values under oppressive conditions. Institutions of community-based childcare, informal adoption, greater reliance on othermothers, all emerge as adaptations to the exigencies of combining exploitative work with nurturing children.

In spite of the change in political status brought on by emancipation, the majority of African-American women remained exploited agricultural workers. However, their placement in Southern political economies allowed them to combine childcare with field labor. Sara Brooks describes how strong the links between providing and caring for others were for her:

> When I was about nine I was nursin my sister Sally— I'm about seven or eight years older than Sally. And when I would put her to sleep, instead of me goin somewhere and sit down and play, I'd get my little old hoe and get out there and work right in the field around the house.[22]

Black women's shift from Southern agriculture to domestic work in Southern and Northern towns and cities represented a change in the type of work done, but not in the meaning of work to women and their families. Whether they wanted to or not, the majority of African-American women had to work and could not afford the luxury of motherhood as a noneconomically productive, female "occupation."

Community Othermothers and Social Activism

Black women's experiences as othermothers have provided a foundation for Black women's social activism. Black women's feelings of responsibility for nurturing the children in their own extended family networks have stimulated a more generalized ethic of care where Black women feel accountable to all the Black community's children.

This notion of Black women as community othermothers for all Black children traditionally allowed Black women to treat biologically unrelated children as if they were members of their own families. For example, sociologist Karen Fields describes how her grandmother, Mamie Garvin Fields, draws on her power as a community othermother when dealing with unfamiliar children.

> She will say to a child on the street who looks up to no
> good, picking out a name at random, "Aren't you Miz
> Pinckney's boy?" in that same reproving tone. If the re-
> ply is, "No, *ma'am*, my mother is Miz Gadsden," what-
> ever threat there was dissipates.[23]

The use of family language in referring to members of the
Black community also illustrates this dimension of Black motherhood. For example, Mamie Garvin Fields describes how she
became active in surveying the poor housing conditions of Black
people in Charleston.

> I was one of the volunteers they got to make a survey of
> the places where we were paying extortious rents for in-
> describable property. I said "we," although it wasn't
> Bob and me. We had our own home, and so did many
> of the Federated Women. Yet we still felt like it really
> was "we" living in those terrible places, and it was up
> to us to do something about them.[24]

To take another example, while describing her increasingly successful efforts to teach a boy who had given other teachers
problems, my daughter's kindergarten teacher stated, "You
know how it can be—the majority of children in the learning
disabled classes are *our children*. I know he didn't belong there,
so I volunteered to take him." In these statements, both women
invoke the language of family to describe the ties that bind them
as Black women to their responsibilities to other members of
the Black community as family.

Sociologist Cheryl Gilkes suggests that community othermother relationships are sometimes behind Black women's decisions to become community activists.[25] Gilkes notes that many
of the Black women community activists in her study became
involved in community organizing in response to the needs of
their own children and of those in their communities. The following comment is typical of how many of the Black women in
Gilkes' study relate to Black children: "There were a lot of
summer programs springing up for kids, but they were exclusive . . . and I found that most of *our kids* (emphasis mine) were
excluded."[26] For many women, what began as the daily expression of their obligations as community othermothers, as was the
case for the kindergarten teacher, developed into full-fledged
roles as community leaders.

Motherhood as a Symbol of Power

Motherhood, whether bloodmother, othermother, or community othermother, can be invoked by Black women as a symbol of power. A substantial portion of Black women's status in African-American communities stems not only from their roles as mothers in their own families but from their contributions as community othermothers to Black community development as well.

The specific contributions Black women make in nurturing Black community development form the basis of community-based power. Community othermothers work on behalf of the Black community by trying, in the words of late nineteenth century Black feminists, to "uplift the race," so that vulnerable members of the community would be able to attain the self-reliance and independence so desperately needed for Black community development under oppressive conditions. This is the type of power many African-Americans have in mind when they describe the "strong, Black women" they see around them in traditional African-American communities.

When older Black women invoke this community othermother status, its results can be quite striking. Karen Fields recounts an incident described to her by her grandmother illustrating how women can exert power as community othermothers:

> One night . . . as Grandmother sat crocheting alone at about two in the morning, a young man walked into the living room carrying the portable TV from upstairs. She said, "Who are you looking for *this* time of night?" As Grandmother [described] the incident to me over the phone, I could hear a tone of voice that I know well. It said, "Nice boys don't do that." So I imagine the burglar heard his own mother or grandmother at that moment. He joined in the familial game just created: "Well, he told me that I could borrow it." "*Who* told you?" "John." "Um um, no *John* lives here. You got the wrong house."[27]

After this dialogue, the teenager turned around, went back upstairs and returned the television.

In local Black communities, specific Black women are widely recognized as powerful figures, primarily because of their contributions to the community's well-being through their roles as community othermothers. Sociologist Charles Johnson describes the behavior of an elderly Black woman at a church service in rural Alabama of the 1930s. Even though she was not on the program, the woman stood up to speak. The master of ceremonies rang for her to sit down but she refused to do so claiming, "I am the mother of this church, and I will say what I please." The master of ceremonies later explained to the congregation— "Brothers, I know you all honor Sister Moore. Course our time is short but she has acted as a mother to me . . . Any time old folks get up I give way to them."[28]

IMPLICATIONS FOR BLACK
MOTHER-DAUGHTER RELATIONSHIPS

In her discussion of the sex-role socialization of Black girls, Pamela Reid identifies two complementary approaches in understanding Black mother-daughter relationships.[29] The first, psychoanalytic theory, examines the role of parents in the establishment of personality and social behavior. This theory argues that the development of feminine behavior results from the girls' identification with adult female role models. This approach emphasizes how an Afrocentric ideology of motherhood is actualized through Black mothers' activities as role models.

The second approach, social learning theory, suggests that the rewards and punishments attached to girls' childhood experiences are central in shaping women's sex-role behavior. The kinds of behaviors that Black mothers reward and punish in their daughters are seen as key in the socialization process. This approach examines specific experiences that Black girls have while growing up that encourage them to absorb an Afrocentric ideology of motherhood.

African-American Mothers as Role Models

Feminist psychoanalytic theorists suggest that the sex-role socialization process is different for boys and girls. While boys learn maleness by rejecting femaleness via separating themselves from their mothers, girls establish feminine identities by embracing the femaleness of their mothers. Girls identify with their mothers, a sense of connection that is incorporated into the female personality. However, this mother-identification is problematic because, under patriarchy, men are more highly valued than women. Thus, while daughters identify with their mothers, they also reject them, since in patriarchal families, identifying with adult women as mothers means identifying with persons deemed inferior.[30]

While Black girls learn by identifying with their mothers, the specific female role with which Black girls identify may be quite different than that modeled by middle-class White mothers. The presence of working mothers, extended family othermothers, and powerful community othermothers offers a range of role models that challenge the tenets of the cult of true womanhood.

Moreover, since Black mothers have a distinctive relationship to White patriarchy, they may be less likely to socialize their daughters into their proscribed role as subordinates. Rather, a key part of Black girls' socialization involves incorporating the critical posture that allows Black women to cope with contradictions. For example, Black girls have long had to learn how to do domestic work while rejecting definitions of themselves as Mammies. At the same time they've had to take on strong roles in Black extended families without internalizing images of themselves as matriarchs.

In raising their daughters, Black mothers face a troubling dilemma. To ensure their daughters' physical survival, they must teach their daughters to fit into systems of oppression. For example, as a young girl in Mississippi, Black activist Ann Moody questioned why she was paid so little for the domestic work she began at age nine, why Black women domestics were sexually harassed by their White male employers, and why Whites had so much more than Blacks. But her mother refused to answer her questions and actually became angry whenever Ann Moody stepped out of her "place."[31] Black daughters are raised to expect to work, to strive for an education so that they can support themselves, and to anticipate carrying heavy responsibilities in their families and communities because these skills are essential for their own survival as well as for the survival of those for whom they will eventually be responsible.[32] And yet mothers know that if daughters fit too well into the limited opportunities offered Black women, they become willing participants in their own subordination. Mothers may have ensured their daughters' physical survival at the high cost of their emotional destruction.

On the other hand, Black daughters who offer serious challenges to oppressive situations may not physically survive. When Ann Moody became involved in civil rights activities, her mother first begged her not to participate and then told her not to come home because she feared the Whites in Moody's hometown would kill her. In spite of the dangers, many Black mothers routinely encourage their daughters to develop skills to confront oppressive conditions. Thus, learning that they will work, that education is a vehicle for advancement, can also be seen as ways of preparing Black girls to resist oppression through a variety of mothering roles. The issue is to build emotional strength, but not at the cost of physical survival.

This delicate balance between conformity and resistance is described by historian Elsa Barkley Brown as the "need to socialize me one way and at the same time to give me all the tools I needed to be something else."[33] Black daughters must learn how to survive in interlocking structures of race, class, and gender oppression while rejecting and transcending those very same structures. To develop these skills in their daughters, mothers demonstrate varying combinations of behaviors devoted to ensuring their daughters' survival—such as providing them with basic necessities and ensuring their protection in dangerous environments—to helping their daughters go farther than mothers themselves were allowed to go.

The presence of othermothers in Black extended families and the modeling symbolized by community othermothers offer powerful support for the task of teaching girls to resist White perceptions of Black womanhood while appearing to conform to them. In contrast to the isolation of middle-class White mother/ daughter dyads, Black women-centered extended family networks foster an early identification with a much wider range of models of Black womanhood, which can lead to a greater sense of empowerment in young Black girls.

Social Learning Theory and Black Mothering Behavior

Understanding this goal of balancing the needs of ensuring their daughters' physical survival with the vision of encouraging them to transcend the boundaries confronting them sheds some light on some of the apparent contradictions in Black mother-daughter relationships. Black mothers are often described as strong disciplinarians and overly protective parents; yet these same women manage to raise daughters who are self-reliant and assertive.[34] Professor Gloria Wade-Gayles offers an explanation for this apparent contradiction by suggesting that Black mothers "do not socialize their daughters to be passive or irrational. Quite the contrary, they socialize their daughters to be independent, strong and self-confident. Black mothers are suffocatingly protective and domineering precisely because they are determined to mold their daughters into whole and self-actualizing persons in a society that devalues Black women."[35]

Black mothers emphasize protection either by trying to shield their daughters as long as possible from the penalties attached to their race, class, and gender or by teaching them how to protect themselves in such situations. Black women's autobiographies and fiction can be read as texts revealing the multiple strategies Black mothers employ in preparing their daughters for the demands of being Black women in oppressive conditions. For example, in discussing the mother-daughter relationship in Paule Marshall's *Brown Girl, Brownstones*, Rosalie Troester catalogues some of these strategies and the impact they may have on relationships themselves:

> Black mothers, particularly those with strong ties to
> their community, sometimes build high banks around
> their young daughters, isolating them from the dangers
> of the larger world until they are old and strong enough
> to function as autonomous women. Often these dikes are
> religious, but sometimes they are built with education,
> family, or the restrictions of a close-knit and homogene-
> ous community . . . this isolation causes the currents
> between Black mothers and daughters to run deep and
> the relationship to be fraught with an emotional inten-
> sity often missing from the lives of women with more
> freedom.[36]

Black women's efforts to provide for their children also may affect the emotional intensity of Black mother-daughter relationships. As Gloria Wade-Gayles points out, "Mothers in Black women's fiction are strong and devoted . . . but . . . they are rarely affectionate."[37] For far too many Black mothers, the demands of providing for children are so demanding that affection often must wait until the basic needs of physical survival are satisfied.

Black daughters raised by mothers grappling with hostile environments have to confront their feelings about the difference between the idealized versions of maternal love extant in popular culture and the strict, assertive mothers so central to their lives.[38] For daughters, growing up means developing a better understanding that offering physical care and protection is an

act of maternal love. Ann Moody describes her growing awareness of the personal cost her mother paid as a single mother of
three children employed as a domestic worker. Watching her
mother sleep after the birth of another child, Moody remembers:

> For a long time I stood there looking at her. I didn't
> want to wake her up. I wanted to enjoy and preserve
> that calm, peaceful look on her face, I wanted to think
> she would always be that happy . . . Adline and Junior
> were too young to feel the things I felt and know the
> things I knew about Mama. They couldn't remember
> when she and Daddy separated. They had never heard
> her cry at night as I had or worked and helped as I had
> done when we were starving.[39]

Renita Weems's account of coming to grips with maternal
desertion provides another example of a daughter's efforts to
understand her mother's behavior. In the following passage,
Weems struggles with the difference between the stereotypical
image of the super strong Black mother and her own alcoholic
mother, who decided to leave her children:

> My mother loved us. I must believe that. She worked all
> day in a department store bakery to buy shoes and
> school tablets, came home to curse out neighbors who
> wrongly accused her children of any impropriety (which
> in an apartment complex usually meant stealing), and
> kept her house cleaner than most sober women.[40]

Weems concludes that her mother loved her because she provided for her to the best of her ability.
    Othermothers often play central roles in defusing the emotional
intensity of relationships between bloodmothers and their daughters and in helping daughters understand the Afrocentric ideology of motherhood. Weems describes the women teachers,
neighbors, friends, and othermothers that she turned to for help
in negotiating a difficult mother/daughter relationship. These
women, she notes, "did not have the onus of providing for me,
and so had the luxury of talking to me."[41]
    June Jordan offers one of the most eloquent analyses of a
daughter's realization of the high personal cost Black women
have paid as bloodmothers and othermothers in working to provide an economic and emotional foundation for Black children.
In the following passage, Jordan captures the feelings that my
Black women students struggled to put into words:

As a child I noticed the sadness of my mother as she
sat alone in the kitchen at night . . . Her woman's work
never won permanent victories of any kind. It never enlarged the universe of her imagination or her power to
influence what happened beyond the front door of our
house. Her woman's work never tickled her to laugh or
shout or dance. But she did raise me to respect her way
of offering love and to believe that hard work is often
the irreducible factor for survival, not something to
avoid. Her woman's work produced a reliable home
base where I could pursue the privileges of books and
music. Her woman's work invented the potential for a
completely different kind of work for us, the next generation of Black women: huge, rewarding hard work demanded by the huge, new ambitions that her perfect
confidence in us engendered.[42]

Jordan's words not only capture the essence of the Afrocentric
ideology of motherhood so central to the well-being of countless
numbers of Black women. They simultaneously point the way
into the future, one where Black women face the challenge of
continuing the mothering traditions painstakingly nurtured by
prior generations of African-American women.

NOTES

1. The definition of culture used in this essay is taken from Leith Mullings,
"Anthropological Perspectives on the Afro-American Family," *American Journal of Social Psychiatry* 6 (1986): 11–16. According to Mullings, culture is
composed of "the symbols and values that create the ideological frame of
reference through which people attempt to deal with the circumstances in
which they find themselves" (13).

2. For analyses of the relationship of the cult of true womanhood to Black
women, see Leith Mullings, "Uneven Development: Class, Race and Gender
in the United States Before 1900," in *Women's Work, Development and the
Division of Labor by Gender*, ed. Eleanor Leacock and Helen Safa (South
Hadley, MA: Bergin & Garvey, 1986), pp. 41–57; Bonnie Thornton Dill,
"Our Mothers' Grief: Racial Ethnic Women and the Maintenance of Families,"
Research Paper 4, Center for Research on Women (Memphis, TN: Memphis
State University, 1986); and Hazel Carby, *Reconstructing Womanhood: The
Emergence of the Afro-American Woman Novelist* (New York: Oxford University
Press, 1987), esp. chapter 2.

3. Contrast, for example, the traditionalist analysis of Selma Fraiberg, *Every
Child's Birthright: In Defense of Mothering* (New York: Basic Books, 1977) to
that of Jeffner Allen, "Motherhood: The Annihilation of Women," in *Mothering, Essays in Feminist Theory*, ed. Joyce Trebilcot (Totawa, NJ: Rowan &

Allanheld, 1983). See also Adrienne Rich, *Of Woman Born: Motherhood as Experience and Institution* (New York: Norton, 1976). For an overview of how traditionalists and feminists have shaped the public policy debate on abortion, see Kristin Luker, *Abortion and the Politics of Motherhood* (Berkeley, CA: University of California, 1984).

4. Mullings, "Uneven Development"; Dill, "Our Mother's Grief"; and Carby, *Reconstructing Womanhood*. Feminist scholarship is also challenging Western notions of the family. See Barrie Thorne and Marilyn Yalom, eds., *Rethinking the Family* (New York: Longman, 1982).

5. Since Black women are no longer heavily concentrated in private domestic service, the Mammy image may be fading. In contrast, the matriarch image, popularized in Daniel Patrick Moynihan's, *The Negro Family: The Case for National Action* (Washington, D.C.: U.S. Government Printing Office, 1965), is reemerging in public debates about the feminization of poverty and the urban underclass. See Maxine Baca Zinn, "Minority Families in Crisis: The Public Discussion," Research Paper 6, Center for Research on Women (Memphis, TN: Memphis State University, 1987).

6. For an alternative analysis of the Mammy image, see Judith Rollins, *Between Women: Domestics and Their Employers* (Philadelphia: Temple University, 1985). Classic responses to the matriarchy thesis include Robert Hill, *The Strengths of Black Families* (New York: Urban League, 1972); Andrew Billingsley, *Black Families in White America* (Englewood Cliffs, NJ: Prentice-Hall, 1968); and Joyce Ladner, *Tomorrow's Tomorrow* (Garden City, NY: Doubleday, 1971). For a recent analysis, see Linda Burnham, "Has Poverty Been Feminized in Black America?" *Black Scholar* 16 (1985):15–24.

7. Mae King, "The Politics of Sexual Stereotypes," *Black Scholar* 4 (1973):12–23.

8. Barbara Christian, "An Angle of Seeing: Motherhood in Buchi Emecheta's *Joys of Motherhood* and Alice Walker's *Meridian*," in *Black Feminist Criticism*, ed. Barbara Christian (New York: Pergamon, 1985), p. 214.

9. See Christine Oppong, ed., *Female and Male in West Africa* (London: Allen & Unwin, 1983); Niara Sudarkasa, "Female Employment and Family Organization in West Africa," in *The Black Woman Cross-Culturally*, ed. Filomina Chiamo Steady (Cambridge, MA: Schenkman, 1981), pp. 49–64; and Nancy Tanner, "Matrifocality in Indonesia and Africa and Among Black Americans," in *Woman, Culture, and Society*, ed. Michelle Rosaldo and Louise Lamphere (Stanford, CA: Stanford University Press, 1974), pp. 129–56.

10. Christine Oppong, "Family Structure and Women's Reproductive and Productive Roles: Some Conceptual and Methodological Issues," in *Women's Roles and Population Trends in the Third World*, ed. Richard Anker, Myra Buvinic, and Nadia Youssef (London: Croom Helm, 1982), pp. 133–50.

11. The key distinction here is that, unlike the matriarchy thesis, women play central roles in families and this centrality is seen as legitimate. In spite of this centrality, it is important not to idealize African women's family roles. For an analysis by a Black African feminist, see Awa Thiam, *Black Sisters, Speak Out: Feminism and Oppression in Black Africa* (London: Pluto, 1978).

12. Sudarkasa, "Female Employment."

13. John Mbiti, *African Religions and Philosophies* (New York: Anchor, 1969).

14. Niara Sudarkasa, "Interpreting the African Heritage in Afro-American Family Organization," in *Black Families*, ed. Harriette Pipes McAdoo (Beverly

Hills, CA: Sage, 1981), pp. 37–53; and Deborah Gray White, *Ar'n't I a Woman? Female Slaves in the Plantation South* (New York: W.W. Norton, 1985).

15. The terms used in this section appear in Rosalie Riegle Troester's "Turbulence and Tenderness: Mothers, Daughters, and "Othermothers" in Paule Marshall's *Brown Girl, Brownstones,*" *SAGE: A Scholarly Journal on Black Women* 1 (Fall 1984):13–16. [Reprinted in this collection.]

16. See Tanner, "Matrifocality"; see also Carrie Allen McCray, "The Black Woman and Family Roles," in *The Black Woman,* ed. LaFrances Rogers-Rose (Beverly Hills, CA: Sage, 1980), pp. 67–78; Elmer Martin and Joanne Mitchell Martin, *The Black Extended Family* (Chicago: University of Chicago Press, 1978); Joyce Aschenbrenner, *Lifelines, Black Families in Chicago* (Prospect Heights, IL: Waveland, 1975); and Carol B. Stack, *All Our Kin* (New York: Harper & Row, 1974).

17. Martin and Martin, *The Black Extended Family;* Stack, *All Our Kin;* and Virginia Young, "Family and Childhood in a Southern Negro Community," *American Anthropologist* 72 (1970):269–88.

18. Stack, *All Our Kin.*

19. Ellen Cantarow, *Moving the Mountain: Women Working for Social Change* (Old Westbury, NY: Feminist Press, 1980), p. 59.

20. Thordis Simonsen, ed., *You May Plow Here, The Narrative of Sara Brooks* (New York: Touchstone, 1986), p. 181.

21. White, *Ar'n't I a Woman?;* Dill, "Our Mothers' Grief"; Mullings, "Uneven Development."

22. Simonsen, *You May Plow Here,* p. 86.

23. Mamie Garvin Fields and Karen Fields, *Lemon Swamp and Other Places, A Carolina Memoir* (New York: Free Press, 1983), p. xvii.

24. Ibid, p. 195.

25. Cheryl Gilkes, " 'Holding Back the Ocean with a Broom,' Black Women and Community Work," in *The Black Woman,* ed. Rogers-Rose, 1980, pp. 217–31, and "Going Up for the Oppressed: The Career Mobility of Black Women Community Workers," *Journal of Social Issues* 39 (1983):115–39.

26. Gilkes, " 'Holding Back the Ocean,' " p. 219.

27. Fields and Fields, *Lemon Swamp,* p. xvi.

28. Charles Johnson, *Shadow of the Plantation* (Chicago: University of Chicago Press, 1934, 1979), p. 173.

29. Pamela Reid, "Socialization of Black Female Children," in *Women: A Developmental Perspective,* ed. Phyllis Berman and Estelle Ramey (Washington, DC: National Institutes of Health, 1983).

30. For works in the feminist psychoanalytic tradition, see Nancy Chodorow, "Family Structure and Feminine Personality," in *Woman, Culture, and Society,* ed. Rosaldo and Lamphere, 1974; Nancy Chodorow, *The Reproduction of Mothering* (Berkeley, CA: University of California, 1978); and Jane Flax, "The Conflict Between Nurturance and Autonomy in Mother-Daughter Relationships and Within Feminism," *Feminist Studies* 4 (1978):171–89.

31. Ann Moody, *Coming of Age in Mississippi* (New York: Dell, 1968).

32. Ladner, *Tomorrow's Tomorrow;* Gloria Joseph, "Black Mothers and Daughters: Their Roles and Functions in American Society," in *Common Differences,* ed. Gloria Joseph and Jill Lewis (Garden City, NY: Anchor, 1981), pp. 75–126; Lena Wright Myers, *Black Women, Do They Cope Better?* (Englewood Cliffs, NJ: Prentice-Hall, 1980).

33. Elsa Barkley Brown, "Hearing Our Mothers' Lives," paper presented at fifteenth anniversary of African-American and African Studies at Emory College, Atlanta, 1986. This essay appeared in the Black Women's Studies issue of *SAGE: A Scholarly Journal on Black Women*, vol. 6, no. 1:4–11.

34. Joseph, "Black Mothers and Daughters"; Myers, 1980.

35. Gloria Wade-Gayles, "The Truths of Our Mothers' Lives: Mother-Daughter Relationships in Black Women's Fiction," *SAGE: A Scholarly Journal on Black Women* 1 (Fall 1984):12.

36. Troester, "Turbulence and Tenderness," p. 13.

37. Wade-Gayles, "The Truths," p. 10.

38. Joseph, "Black Mothers and Daughters."

39. Moody, *Coming of Age*, p. 57.

40. Renita Weems, " 'Hush. Mama's Gotta Go Bye Bye': A Personal Narrative," *SAGE: A Scholarly Journal on Black Women* 1 (Fall 1984):26.

41. Ibid, p. 27.

42. June Jordan, *On Call, Political Essays* (Boston: South End Press, 1985), p. 145.

P A R T 2

PIECING BLOCKS: IDENTITIES

The way that I pieced...sewed rag, needlepointed...are another hand-me-down from my mothers and grandmothers.

AMINAH ROBINSON

What these mothers passed on would take you anywhere in the world you wanted to go.

MARY HELEN WASHINGTON

It was Alice Walker, in her landmark essay "In Search of Our Mothers' Gardens: The Creativity of Black Women in the South," who reminded us of the gifts which her mother bestowed on her: stories, a typewriter, sewing machine, flowers, a love of beauty, and respect for strength.[1] The most memorable tribute to her mother is contained in the simple, yet powerful statement, "I consider her a great role model, a sister warrior."[2] In this much anthologized essay, inspired by the creativity of her artist/ mother, Minnie Lou Walker, and other nameless Black women of the South, is perhaps the most poignant and eloquent analysis of the legacy Black mothers and grandmothers left to their daughters, their families, their communities.

The theme of "mothering the mind," which alludes to the various ways creativity is nurtured, also permeates this section.[3] In selection after selection, daughters acknowledge how their mothers provided road maps and patterns, a "template," which enabled them to create and define themselves as they moved from childhood through adolescence to adulthood.[4] Though daughters must forge an identity which is separate from their mothers, they frequently acknowledge that a part of themselves is truly their mother's child. Within African-American communities, this psychic bond frequently transcends the personal relationship between a mother and her daughter. A nurturing female community of grandmothers, aunts, and friends often encircles their "daughters," in order to ensure some familiarity in their journey into a world characterized by uncertainty and even hostility.

The heading for this section is reminiscent of a particular type of needlework—the pieced or patchwork quilt which is created by arranging and sewing contrasting pieces of plain and/or patterned cloth in geometric patterns or mosaiclike designs. Another kind of patchwork is the appliqué quilt, which is a top made from a large piece of fabric to which smaller pieces (cut into particular shapes) of contrasting fabric have been applied. The patchwork or appliquéd quilt is an appropriate metaphor for the socialization process that often characterizes Black mother-daughter relationships. Mothers, like seasoned quilters, knew the basic patterns, but child-rearing, like patchwork, also required creativity and improvisation. The process by which quilting mothers handed down these patterns to their daughters is analogous to the process by which successive generations were taught how to rear their daughters.

Quilts, like good mothers, keep you warm and protected. The artistry required for making the extraordinary quilts African-American women have constructed for hundreds of years has only recently been acknowledged. This section contains similar testimonies about the gifts of our mothers in all their various textures and designs.

Beverly Guy-Sheftall

NOTES

1. Alice Walker's "In Search of Our Mothers' Gardens" appeared first in *Ms.* (May 1974):64–70, 105.

2. Mary Helen Washington, "Her Mother's Gifts," *Ms.* (June 1982):38.

3. Ruth Perry and Martine Watson Brownley, eds., *Mothering the Mind* (New York: Holmes & Meier, 1984). This collection of essays, containing twelve studies of writers and their silent partners, illuminates the concept of "mothering the mind," which refers to the processes by which people help to create the conditions for another's creativity. In the case of three African-American women writers—Alice Walker, Paule Marshall, and Dorothy West—it was definitely their mothers, according to Mary Helen Washington, who sparked and helped to sustain their creative urges. See her essay, "I Sign My Mother's Name," pp. 144–63.

4. In quilting lexicon, a template is a pattern for each individual part of the pattern block. Template patterns can be used for both machine and handwork.

THE POWER OF NAMES

Irma McClaurin

I slip my mother's name on like a glove
and wonder if I will become like her
absolutely.
Years number the times I have worn her pain
as a child, as a teenager, as a woman—my second skin—
or screamed her screams
as she sat, silver head bowed
silent
hedging the storm.

Her name, at times, does not fit me.
I take it, turn it over on my tongue—
a key.
Shape my lips around its vowels
hoping to unlock elusive doors,
understand the instincts
my body follows.
The family named her Pearl,
a first among them;
yet others have owned this name.
They haunt me.
I follow their destiny.

Each year I return home,
a salmon caught in an act of survival.
I search my mother's face
neatly carved in obsidian
and wonder
how much of myself I owe this woman
whose name I have swallowed like a worm.
Her inner soul transferred through the eating.

I slip my mother's name on
with wonder
and become like her
absolutely.

TOUCHING/NOT TOUCHING: MY MOTHER

Toi Derricotte

I.

That first night in the hotel bedroom,
when the lights go out,
she is already sleeping (that woman who has always
claimed sleeplessness), inside her quiet breathing
like a long red gown. How can she
sleep? My heart beats as if I am alone,
for the first time, with a lover or a beast.
Will I hate her drooping mouth,
her old woman rattle? Once I nearly
suffocated on her breast. Now I can almost
touch the other side of my life.

II.

Undressing
in the dark,
looking,
not looking,
we parade before each other,
old proud peacocks, in our stretch marks
with hanging butts. We are equals. No
more do I need to wear her high heels to step
inside the body of a woman.
Her beauty and strangeness no longer seduce
me out of myself. I show my good side, my
long back, strong mean legs, my thinness that
came from learning to hold back
from taking what's not mine. No more
a thief for love. She takes off her
bra, facing me, and I see those gorgeous

globes, soft, creamy,
high; my mouth waters.
How will I resist
crawling in beside her, putting
my hand for warmth
under her thin night dress?

ON THE SPIRT OF
MILDRED JORDAN

June Jordan

After sickness and a begging
from her bed
my mother dressed herself
grey lace-up oxfords
stockings baggy on her shrunken legs
an orange topper
rhinestone buttons
and a powder blue straw
hat with plastic
flowers

Then
she took the street
in short steps toward the corner

chewing gum
no less

she let the family laugh
again

she wasn't foxy
she was strong

From *Things That I Do in the Dark* by June Jordan (New York: Random House, 1977).

MOM DE PLUME

SDiane Bogus

Dear Mama,

I realize that this letter-writing-business is silly, especially since we haven't been in touch for all these years, and I really don't expect an answer, but who's a lesbian supposed to talk to if not her mother?

She talks to her lover, or mate. Of course this is true, but what I have to say involves my mate, and well, frankly, I wouldn't want to bring it up and have her misunderstand.

You may wonder how that leaves you with an ear to hear. Well, what I have to say involves you, too, so let me explain.

When I was a child, I know you couldn't have helped but know how much I adored you. You did know, didn't you?

Well, I guess it was no prodigious wonder then, especially since my resultant emulation of you was indistinguishable from my role socialization. Who would have thought that, out of love, I consciously copied everything that you did; unlike some little girls who do so, I did not thoughtlessly act like my mother. I did so with a self-indulging awareness, and I loved every xeroxed minute of it. No, it's no wonder at all that I learned your walk, talk, gestures and nurturing laughter. At that time, Mama, had you swung from bars, I would, to this day, be hopelessly, imitatively, hung up.

But, I think the major expression of my "daughter-see, daughter-do" love act lay in how carefully I noted your every motherly task. From counselling, discipline to cooking, and diaper changing, I grokked it all. Not only did I watch with duplicative eyes, but practice made irrevocable perfect in the husbandless world of my playtime imagination.

Here my doll children were chastised, encouraged, and dressed, doted upon, spanked and prayed for. No less did I do for them, Mama, than you did for my brothers and me.

So, you see, Mama, having no way to get in touch with my latent but definite woman-loving feelings, I assumed your wom-

Originally published in *Lesbian Tide* (Nov.–Dec. 1977), Los Angeles, CA.

aness, your motherness. Like a mirror-sponge, I saw and soaked in all that you were, and today I represent the greater part of you. Yet, while I am fully the woman you were, I'm nobody's mother.

Well, that's not exactly true. I hold three mothering positions, yet I'm nobody's mother who calls me mother.

First of all, I spend daily chunks of my time with children, who for all purposes intended, are mine. I often stop the flow of an explanation to have Arnold close his fly, or button his shirt. I may even take Rachel aside to remind her of the importance of good personal hygiene, but come three o'clock and the sound of the last class bell, my "children" say, "Goodbye, Teacher,"—not "Mother."

Likewise, I am mother-of-a-kind to children who, like this letter, were not procreated, but simply created. They are the word products of this my literary wedlock. Nevertheless, I put each of these prosaic babies up for public adoption, whereupon I am read and called, not mother, but writer.

It is not that I long to be a natural mother, for by close definition I am, and while I have not actually given birth to a child, I am one mother among what may be a myriad cache of "mothers" (some of whom are men, in a reversed situation).

You see, Mama, there are godmothers, where mothers may be; there are foster mothers where mothers cannot be, and there are stepmothers where mothers have been, but where there are two parents of the same sex nurturing and rearing one or the other's children, only one of them can conceptually be called "Mother," while the other is none of the above.

The fact is, Mom, were the opposite sex involved, my dilemma would be nonexistent for it stands heterosexually solved. If one of the parents is the "mother," the second, quite obviously, is the "father."

As you may already have guessed, my complaint is that I hold the unnamed parental place within F's and my family unit. Because I don't want her to feel that I want to usurp her biological first place, or make her think that I wish I had my own children or cause her to think that I am ungrateful for the total sharing of her children, I have not brought the issue to her. What's more, Mama, other than you, there are very few people who will understand what it is that I am saying. For while I love children, I chose not to have any of my own (in deference to my writing career, not sex with a man), yet with all of your motherness embedded within me, to not have entered a child-blessed relationship would have been to alienate a part of myself from myself. It would have been, more seriously, a denial of my love for you, and that love remains ever deep.

So here I reside: Fran, me, and our two children. When she is unable to, or too tired, I deign to fill out our kids' school forms which inevitably have heterosexual blanks that disallow any possibility other than the designated "mother," "father," or "guardian." And try as I might, I cannot stifle the anger that I feel toward a definitionless society which makes me unavoidably neither.

Or, upon taking the kids on an outing, where we invariably encounter new acquaintances, there's always that someone who, having given the kids a praiseworthy once-over, asks "now, which one of you is the mother of these fine looking youngsters?" Were it that an established concept of the relationship could be conveyed!

What am I to do, Mama, when I'm living a sane, but socially unincorporated, lifestyle in so conceptually limited a society?

So, now you see why I'm writing you. All of this time I've been happy enough to leave you in peace, feeling, too, a little hesitant to tell you about such things as my early, unspoken love for you, only to have grown into a lesbian woman, who claims that she is formed in your image.

This is especially contradictory since I know that you neither had nor wanted a woman to love, even though you lived painfully without the man you chose. And although we both loved him, we knew also that your man was a capricious husband and father, and served as such by spells, leaving you to implement a struggling self-reliance.

So, I watched how you managed this married/single state. Unaware that you were sick and growing sicker, I saw you work full time, cook, clean, see after my brothers and me, and fill us with an indelible mother-wit. It is from here, then, that my nameless, boundless adoration, my emulation grew. Maybe during those few, but intensely loving, copyist years, I xeroxed a subliminal image of you which I have since applied toward my own happiness. Maybe, then, my lesbianism is no more than your manless self-reliance turned into itself.

Maybe, Mama, your unexpected death caused me to doubly cherish you, caused me to seal your essence and image tightly within me, made me forever a woman of like feathers, a "mom de plume."[1]

Can this also serve as the name for a second lady parent?

NOTE

1. Plays on the French expression *nom de plume*, a pen name (originally, *Nom de guerre*).

LESSONS

Pearl Cleage

My mother put tap dancing in the same category as cheerleading and pierced ears. It was something you did only if you didn't know any better. It was something some black people did, but that we did not do because we were aware of things they didn't know yet.

Not yet, my mother would say. She was tired of having this "can't we puh-leez take tap instead?" discussion every time she dropped my sister and me off for ballet at Toni's School of Dance Arts. We knew she was tired before we asked the question, but we had to ask it every time. We didn't want her to change her mind without telling us. We didn't want her to turn to us, years later when we tried to prove that she was responsible for our current, sorry adult state, and say, "I changed my mind about that whole thing. I even remember when. It was that week it rained so much. But you never asked me again. Why should I have been the one to bring it up? I thought if it was really important to you, you'd mention it. But you didn't, did you?"

We didn't want her to smile that smile, proving to us once again that she had been more than just a *good* mother. She had been a smart one.

So we asked, and she denied, and our lust intensified and turned in on itself until tap dancing took on the importance of sacred ritual in our lives. We would stand in the hallway and watch the tap dancing class go through their latest routine with a reverence that I have felt for few things since (Bob Marley being a notable exception).

"Tap, tap, slap! Tap, tap, slap!" Toni would be screaming from the front of the room, her back to the class, her eyes riveted to the reflected feet in the mirrors. "Tap, tap, slap!" And she would wave her long arms, clapping in time with the rhythm of all those shiny black shoes.

"Smile," she would say, insistent and breathless as a lover. "Smile," as if secrets would be revealed, boulders would roll from tombs, lives would be saved, and orgasms eternally achieved if they could only learn to *smile*.

Those who had momentarily forgotten would hear her voice through their brow-furrowed concentration and drag up the corners of their mouths, skin their lips back over square, white, middle-class teeth, and just smile awhile.

A few minutes later in ballet class, Toni acted like she didn't even know the word for the phenomenon known as smiling. She left her volume in the tap class and brought with her only a hiss: "Straighten that back!" Or: "Watch that turn-out!" Never: "Smile!"

She probably knew it would have been useless in ballet class anyway. Those of us in ballet had parents who were concerned about culture and propriety and keeping our dresses below our knees. They had spent many hours teaching us not to smile at strangers and white folks. Our rapid generalization of this command accounted for the sullenness which was our usual expression. Smiling was not a priority.

But the tappers' parents knew where the goat was tied. They were raising children who could keep a smile in place during the most intricate maneuvers. The more advanced among them had even learned to complete complex multirhythmic steps without once licking their lips.

I used to wonder if any of the girls in the tap class would care if they found out what my mother was saying about them being invisible. My mother claimed they were all invisible and would probably remain so. "Their parents have never read Ralph Ellison," she would say. "Doomed to repeat history time after time, straightened head marching after straightened head, because they will not read Ellison."

We were older, of course, before we realized that Ralph Ellison was regarded by most people who took notice of him at all as a fine writer about whom it was often said, "too bad he never wrote another novel," but by only a very minute group as the most neglected prophet of his time and potential savior of The Race. My mother fell into, perhaps totally comprised, the latter group.

After she said that his book, *The Invisible Man*, had taught her everything she knew, I scanned its pages for weeks looking for some prohibition against tap dancing and pierced ears before realizing that once she had gotten the basics down, my mother was prepared to improvise on the details.

But she was convinced of the tappers' invisibility just as she was convinced that pierced ears led to dope smoking and indiscriminate kissing after school. My sister and I had no evidence to refute her. We did have strong evidence that, invisible or not, the tappers had style, a style I was convinced would sustain them even in the face of their own invisibility.

I wondered if they would be frightened or concerned. They didn't look to me like they would ever be frightened or concerned about anything. I can assume now that my impression had more to do with gross misinterpretation than with any kind of collective optimism, but, admittedly, that is hindsight. At the time, I was convinced that they smiled because the joy of "tap, tap, slap" was far greater than that to be found in an equal number of pliés or grand jetés. I believed that their sheer smiling pleasure in doing what they were busy doing in that hot little room was proof that this kind of dancing was worth the risk. Invisibility seemed a small price to pay.

My father took this desire to tap dance as evidence of weakness in my genetic makeup, inherited, of course, from the nameless white ghosts skulking in our blue-veined past. Maybe he was right, or that may have been his way of trying not to blame himself. My father is, after all, maybe even above all, A Race Man.

My mother blamed it on the forces of invisibility and refused to look any closer than that. My mother was also the first person to make the distinction for me between truth and foolishness, and she, certainly, was no fool.

MOTHERS OF MIND

Elsa Barkley Brown

Several years ago, having been asked to address the National
Multicultural Curriculum Development Conference in Oswego,
New York, I wrote what I considered an appropriate speech
discussing the theoretical, methodological, and political issues
important to the study of African American women. The conference lasted for several days and my address was to be on the
last day. As the conference proceeded and I tried to grapple
with the issues raised by the other presenters and the ensuing
discussions, I began to rethink my presentation and to be concerned about how it was that I could get across the ideas which
I thought important but which seem so evasive in our intellectual
training. The night before the presentation I went to bed still
uncertain but assumed I would give the paper that I had brought
with me. Somewhere in the middle of the night I awoke, took
out the ever-present steno pad and tape recorder, and began to
write and talk until dawn. The next day, without time to even
read what I had written, I presented to the conference the pen-
ciled recordings in that steno pad. That talk represents in many
ways my most cogent presentation of the issues involved in
researching, writing, and teaching about African American
women. Entitled "With Whom Do We Entrust Our Mothers'
Lives," it dealt with work, female networks and relationships,
and women's struggle—but most importantly, it talked about my
mother.

Following that presentation I found myself many times wondering why I had chosen (but if we really understand the forces
operating that night, then we know that I did not choose) to talk
about my mother. And I began to realize (but not clearly comprehend) my mother's impact on my thinking, my understandings, my historical perspective. I have spent the last several
years, off and on, trying to grapple with that influence—trying
to really understand it. I am still involved in that process but
as I research and write my own work—on the African American
community in Richmond, Virginia—I am increasingly aware of
the influence of my mother on that study. This paper therefore

represents my thoughts in midsentence—it is an ongoing process of trying to understand the work in which I am engaged. My academic training has been designed to teach me paradigms for and theories about African American people and historical development and to teach me to use them as the basis of my analysis of the people whose lives I study. But I, like many African American scholars before me, have often had to question that training; it has, after all, been designed to teach me how to interpret an Afrocentric community in terms of a Eurocentric worldview. And, as I question the applicability of my historical training, I have to look for other ways to analyze my community. It is in this discovery of new directions that my mother has influenced my work, and thus what follows could most appropriately be subtitled "How My Mother Taught Me to Be a Historian in Spite of My Academic Training."

We are generally familiar with acknowledgments by noted writers of the ways in which their mothers influenced their works. Alice Walker's tribute is probably the most often quoted:

> . . . our mothers and grandmothers have, more often
> than not anonymously, handed on the creative spark,
> the seed of the flower they themselves never hoped
> to see: or like a sealed letter they could not plainly
> read . . . so many of the stories that I write, that we all
> write, are my mother's stories. Only recently did I fully
> realize this: that through years of listening to my moth-
> er's stories of her life, I have absorbed not only the sto-
> ries themselves, but something of the manner in which
> she spoke, something of the urgency that involves the
> knowledge that her stories—like her life—must be
> recorded.[1]

Paule Marshall has also explored the relationship between her work and her mother: ". . . I grew up among poets. Now they didn't look like poets . . . They were just a group of ordinary housewives and mothers, my mother included . . . Nor did they do what poets were supposed to do . . . They never put pen to paper."[2] After spending their days toiling as domestic workers, these women regularly stopped off at Marshall's home for tea, cocoa, and "talk":

> For me sitting over in the corner . . . it wasn't only
> what the women talked about—the content—but the
> way they put things—their style. The insight, irony, wit
> and humor they brought to their stories and discussions

and their poet's inventiveness and daring with language . . . They had taken the standard English taught
them in the primary schools . . . and transformed it into
an idiom, an instrument that more adequately described
them—changing around the syntax and imposing their
own rhythm and accent so that the sentences were more
pleasing to their ears. They added the few African
sounds and words that had survived . . . And to make it
more vivid, more in keeping with their expressive quality, they brought to bear a raft of metaphors, parables,
Bible quotations, sayings and the like . . . using everyday speech, the simple commonplace words—but always with imagination and skill—they gave voice to the
most complex ideas.[3]

And although Marshall did graduate "from the corner of the
kitchen to the neighborhood library, and thus from the spoken
word to the written word," receiving other literary mentors along
the way, her dream always was "that I might someday write . . .
with something of the power with words my mother and her
friends possessed." Thus she acknowledged that the influential
"usual literary giants" in her career

were preceded in my life by another set of giants whom
I always acknowledge before all others: the group of
women around the table long ago. They taught me my
first lessons in the narrative art. They trained my ear.
They set a standard of excellence. This is why the best
of my work must be attributed to them: it stands as testimony to the rich legacy of language and culture they
so freely passed on to me in the wordshop of the
kitchen.[4]

The notion that the prevailing scholarship and its conceptual
frameworks do not reflect the communities which African American scholars and artists know has also become a familiar refrain
by now. Ralph Ellison noted the ways in which scholarship
conflicted with the reality he knew:

I simply don't recognize Harlem in [the sociological for-
mulas]. I certainly don't recognize the people of Harlem
whom I know. Which is by no means to deny the rug-
gedness of life there, nor the hardship, the poverty, the
sordidness, the filth. But there is something else in
Harlem, something subjective, willful, and complexly
and compellingly human. It is 'that something else' that
challenges the sociologists who ignore it, and the society which would deny its existence.[5]

Ralph Ellison argued that if the African American writer accepts "the cliches . . . if he believes . . . that "Harlem is a 'Negro ghetto' . . . —well, he'll never see the people of whom he wishes to write . . ."[6] In reviewing sociological and historical works about African Americans, Ellison found himself asking whether they could possibly be true:

> . . . can a people . . . live and develop for over three hundred years simply by *reacting?* Are American Ne- groes simply the creation of white men, or have they at least helped to create themselves out of what they found around them? Men have made a way of life in caves and upon cliffs, why cannot Negroes have made a life upon the horns of the white man's dilemma?[7]

But African American scholars always have had to contend with stereotypical notions and with the reluctance of the schol- arly world, and certainly the publishing world, to have any other images. Zora Neale Hurston expressed particular concern about "What White Publishers Won't Print": "It is assumed that all non-Anglo-Saxons are uncomplicated stereotypes . . . For var- ious reasons, the average, struggling, non-morbid Negro is the best kept secret in America."[8] And it was the "lives and emo- tions" of this average nonmorbid Negro that Hurston herself set out to chronicle. She discovered that her Barnard College train- ing as an anthropologist, while giving her certain skills and understandings, did not equip her with the "right approach" for doing research in the African American communities of the South.

However, she did become an excellent anthropologist and she did write what still remain among the best studies of African American folklore, but only when she overcame certain aspects of her training—only when she realized that "in a way it [the collecting of folklore] would *not* be a new experience for me. When I pitched headforemost into the world I landed in the crib of negroism."[9]

And when she realized this, the first place she went to collect material was home to Eatonville, Florida—the all Black town in which she grew up and where she knew the people would not tolerate her Barnardese anthropology. She had learned by then that "Folk-lore is not as easy to collect as it sounds." Her understandings of the people with whom she had grown up had told her that Black folk were "most reluctant at times to reveal that which the soul lives by." She therefore understood that much that passed for folklore represented merely the Black folks' tactics of "set[ting] something outside the door" of their minds for researchers "to play with and handle" but never to allow them really to read their minds. She realized that even she would have some hindrance to overcome. "But . . . I thought about the talks I had heard as a child. How even the Bible was made over to suit our vivid imagination." And she relied upon her experiences in Eatonville both to help her overcome the hindrance and to understand the inner lives and emotions which she desperately wished to capture in nonstereotypical ways. There was much that she believed had "never been written and it is waiting for me to write it." Much of that sense of mission came out of her belief that she was to be the voice of her community, particularly of her mother. "[S]he looked at me, or so I felt to speak for her. She depended on me for a voice."[10]

Zora Neale Hurston is not the only African American female social scientist to acknowledge the need to break out of the traditions in which she was trained. Nor is she the first to note the influence of her community on her ability to develop works more clearly reflective of the true experiences of African American people. This has especially been the case when African American female social scientists have been writing about African American women. Joyce Ladner's introduction to *Tomorrow's Tomorrow* is often quoted in this regard. It was in fact her years "growing up in rural Mississippi and experiencing all the tensions, conflicts, joys, sorrows, warmth, compassion and cruelty that was associated with "becoming a Black woman" that shaped the perspective which she brought to her research on what approaching womanhood meant to poor Black girls in the city. But that study brought its own conflicts: on the one hand, an academic training which used Euro-American "standards as the *ideal* by which others are to be judged," and, on the other hand, "the *reality* and *validity*" of the lives of the girls she studied. "If I had continued within" the Euro-American academic context, "I would have concluded the same thing that most social scientists who study Black people concluded: that they are pathology-ridden. However, this role was difficult, if not impossible for me to play because all of my life experiences invalidated" that perspective. What Joyce Ladner at some point came to grips with was the fact that it was her mother, Annie Ruth Perryman, who really taught her what it meant to become a Black woman and it was these teachings which she had to rely

upon if she was to produce a credible study of approaching
Black womanhood. [11]

Similarly, Elizabeth Clark-Lewis, writing a study of African
American domestic workers in Washington, D.C., found that
"Often, what I read conflicted with what I lived." While studies
of these women depicted them as "sad, passive reactors . . .
who seemed to exist in discordant emptiness," Clark-Lewis's
experience contradicted these generalizations:

> The lives of the African-American household workers in
> every community I had ever seen bore very little resem-
> blance to the creations I encountered in the works of
> scholars.
>
> I wondered how I could convey the fullness of these
> women's lives—their exemplary family contributions,
> energetic community service and visible presences
> everywhere in national life?
>
> Very quickly I realized only the women themselves
> could provide the corrective to the many misconceptions
> that existed. [12]

Clark-Lewis had come to understand the necessity of learning
to see in a different way from the historical and sociological
studies which were supposed to be her guides.

Thus I follow a long tradition of African American scholars
who understand the limitations of the paradigms and underlying
assumptions that pervade Western educational institutions and
bookshelves and who draw upon our own communities—and for
African American women especially, the women in our communities—to help us understand and depict the lives of African
American people in a way that they/we would recognize as reality. I build upon the experience of my scholar/mothers in rec-
ognizing the difference between the two views and noting the
important role that my community, especially the women in it,
has played in my development. What I have tried to do, however,
is to go beyond mere acknowledgment to analyze the precise
ways in which my mothers have influenced my historical understandings. In so doing I have had (to quote Sherley Anne
Williams's paraphrase of Alice Walker) to go in search of my
mothers' gardens "not really to learn who trampled on them or
how or even why—we usually know that already," but rather to
learn what my "mothers planted there, what they thought as
they sowed, and how they survived the blighting of so many

fruits."[13] And thus to go further I must tell you something of my mother.

My mother was born in 1916, the youngest of eight children—six of them girls—to Kentucky farmers. She was fortunate to be the youngest. Two of the three eldest sisters passed quickly through the rural elementary school, married, and moved to the city to work as domestics. More importantly for the other four daughters, their homes became one by one their sisters' homes as they came to the city to attend the colored high school. The next eldest, having finished high school and normal school, became a teacher and opened her home to her younger sisters. As was the tradition among African American families, the two brothers remained on the farm, but it was important to provide the daughters with as much education as possible so that they might escape the plight of domestic work and particularly the sexual violence and abuse. The fourth and fifth sisters then went beyond high school and normal school and were certified as teachers, the pride of the family and its collective struggles.

My mother's turn came. She too went to the city, lived in her sisters' homes, graduated from the colored high school in 1934. A new development in Louisville, Kentucky, was the opening of Louisville Municipal College for Negroes.[14] It was now possible for African Americans to attend college in the city. It was a difficult decision for a Black family, even one as large as this in the midst of the Depression, but it was in keeping with their traditions, their belief in education, their faith in each other that they decided that this daughter/sister would go to college. As a matter of fact, as my mother describes it, it was not a decision at all—they just assumed that she would go. They all had gone as far as was possible and for her there was a new level of possibility. Four years later, when she graduated as a mathematics major, her achievement represented the culmination of generations of struggle.

The question was, what was this African American female mathematician, pride not only of her family but of her communities—both rural and urban—going to do? Teach? Her temperament ruled that out. But there were surely other possibilities. And so she went, diploma, pride, and courage in hand, in search of her future. It took some time but finally she did find a job, with an employer who was suitably impressed with all that this young African American girl had accomplished; yes, it would be so refreshing to have an intelligent maid for a change.

And so my mother, unwilling to accept the only profession open to African American women—teaching—hung her sheepskin in other women's kitchens as she cooked and washed and cleaned and tended their children.

She soon married, and as they planned their future the one thing of which she and her husband were certain was that she had not struggled all those years never to have a life of her own; and so she chose, as many other African American women did, despite economic hardship, to leave the world of Black women's work inside the household outside her home and raise a family which would have her time and attention. For her, as for many other women, the decision to be a wife and mother first in a world which defined African American women in so many other ways, the decision to make her family the most important priority was an act of resistance to a system which would define her place for her in terms of its own economic and racist needs.

Thus, the maintenance of her children and family became the priority of her life. She taught her three daughters that they should get good educations, including college degrees. There were more opportunities then and a degree would allow them to be something other than a domestic. But first and foremost they must maintain their family. Unless it was an economic necessity, they should never work if they had children.

Two of her daughters listened and learned and obeyed, at least for a number of years. They went to college, married, and raised their families. But one—you can probably guess which one; as my mother says, "I don't know where I got that child from"—was more restless. And so she went to college, married, had two daughters, and worked while her husband went to graduate school. One day she wrote her mother a letter telling of her own ambitions—and her frustrations. While she did not mind working while her husband went to school, what she did mind was all the talk in the family/community about his education and future and none about hers.

Mother read this letter and worried and pondered. A month later she replied in a letter which once again told her daughter that raising a family was and should be all that she concentrated on. Future schooling and careers should not be in her immediate plans. A Black woman's responsibility was to maintain her family. Enclosed in that same envelope with that letter was a check in the amount of tuition for graduate school—an enormous sum for the mothers/sisters/aunts who had pooled all and sold some to raise it—an act of faith in another generation of African American women.

When this daughter reached the stage of Ph.D. candidacy exams, this mother came and stayed a month to care for the two granddaughters. Every night at dinner she gave her daughter a lecture on the evils of pursuing a career and neglecting her children and begged her to give this up and be a proper Black mother. And every morning she got the children up quietly and tiptoed 'round the house all day so her daughter's studying would not be interrupted. When time came to take the oral exams, the sisters/aunts/mothers sent an appropriate suit for their child to wear. And the mother loudly proclaimed the evils of such careerism and neglect of family priorities as she cooked a very special dinner to celebrate.

There is much more to my mother's story but this represents the basic outline of those things with which I wish to deal.

First is simply a matter of understanding the information you have. A number of years ago, Carter G. Woodson wrote a moving tribute to Negro washerwomen in which he acknowledged their importance in the maintenance, nourishment, and development of the African American community.[15] Scholars since have noted its existence, commented on its sentimentality, and moved on to their own analysis of the African American female labor force and particularly African American washerwomen. In my study of Richmond, Virginia, I was apt to do the same; the historical studies which I had read and my own statistical evidence taught me that women's paid employment was an important economic resource to the African American community, that being a washerwoman was a preferred occupation for women with husbands and children, as it allowed them to bring in an income and at the same time care for their own homes. I could also clearly see, as Woodson had pointed out, that these washerwomen were important to the institutional development of the community. But, like many other scholars, I was prone to assume that their importance lay in the economic resources they could bring to those institutions—it was their money which enabled many a church, mutual benefit society, and later bank to develop. While all of that is true, it is my mother who taught me to see more than that when she talked to me about my grandmother, a washerwoman.

We have traditionally assumed, since taking in laundry was an activity that women did individually and since one of the

primary reasons for preferring this occupation was caring for
one's home, that washerwomen spent much of their day in isolation—inside their homes trying to do this washing, ironing,
picking up, and delivering of clothes at the same time as they
cleaned, cooked, and cared for their own. When my mother
spoke of her mother and the other washerwomen in her neighborhood I came to understand something about washerwomen's
culture and community; I also came to understand washerwomen
as entrepreneurs.

My grandmother took in washing on a daily basis, but she and
the other women in her neighborhood, rather than being confined
to their individual homes for a day of drudgery, took their laundry
to the home of the woman with the largest kitchen. There they
collectively scrubbed, rinsed, starched, ironed, and folded the
pounds of laundry as they also talked, much in the way of Paule
Marshall's mother and her friends. They created a community
and a culture among themselves, turning what could have been
a solitary act into a collective effort. Furthermore, they eventually organized themselves in a more formal fashion—so that
the woman with the largest kitchen actually contracted all of the
work and hired many of the other women to work for her as
laundresses. She had moved from washerwoman to entrepreneur,
in much the same fashion as contemporary market women have
in Lagos, Nigeria.

These are at one level interesting tidbits about the women, at
another, meaningful insights about the organization of work and
daily activities. But for me, in the context of my research, there
was something far more. For it was not until my mother told me
this that I came to understand the real connection between
washerwomen and institutional development in the African
American community. It was not merely the economic resources
that the washerwomen wielded; I came to realize that those
mornings spent scrubbing were also spent organizing. I discovered that a number of churches grew out of the discussions
among washerwomen about the need for a place of worship in
their own neighborhood; schools and recreational centers also
had similar origins. When these women moved into developing
mutual benefit societies and their affiliates, it was with clear
planning and organizational skills that they had developed over
the washtub—it was with a commitment to each other which
had been born in mounds of suds. And so it was clear why and
how it was washerwomen and washerwomen's daughters who

organized the branches of the Independent Order of Saint Luke, one of the most successful and prominent mutual benefit societies of the early twentieth century. They had the skills and they had long before dreamed the dreams and laid the plans together. And when they moved from there to organize a bank and a department store, and then to dream of beginning a factory, it was with the assurance and the skills that came from already having been entrepreneurs.[16] Thus Woodson was right about the debt the community owed to the washerwomen: their roles were ones which went far beyond economic resources.

What my mother did was tell me about the washerwomen she knew, and what she told me did not fit the historical studies. What she told me required me to look for something more. In other words, it was my mother who taught me how to ask the right questions—and all of us who try to do this thing called scholarship on a regular basis are fully aware that asking the right questions is the most important part of the process. It was when I began to ask the right questions that I not only knew that washerwomen were members of the major organizations, but I began to discover their roles as organizers, planners, policy makers, leaders, and developers of the community and its institutions.

My mother also taught me to understand theoretical concepts and to develop new frameworks. Several years ago Bonnie Thornton Dill wrote about "The Dialectics of Black Womanhood" and has since refined those ideas to give us a good basis for understanding the relationship between African American women and the society in which we live. What Dill argues is that Black women in the United States have lived in a society which defined womanhood in one way while they have been required to live lives that were in reality totally different from that definition. For example, "true women" did not work outside the home at a time when the majority of African American women were employed. And in that process, as Dill argues, African American women were forced to define themselves and to develop new definitions of womanhood—those definitions coming out of the dialectics of their lives.[17] African American women have lived lives filled with contradictions and have formed a meaning for themselves and their people out of those contradictions.

My mother best explained that contradiction to me: when she was in college—majoring in mathematics—she worked as a live-in servant. In the mornings she rose early enough to clean house, cook breakfast, and prep the baby before she went off to classes; at noon she hurried back to the house to fix lunch and walk the dog; afternoons to class and then home to cook dinner and perform any other unfinished chores before she began a night of study. It was not just a full schedule in terms of hours taken up; but it was also a life that was built around coming to terms with contradictions. She lived a life which defied in very basic ways both the notions of the proper role of women and the proper place of Blacks. She lived a life which simultaneously conformed to notions of the proper place of Black women and defied those notions. To be a domestic worker is in many ways to be all that the larger society assumes about African American people and particularly African American females: it is to do the work that the majority women believe beneath them and fit only for those of lower status and intellect. It requires certain attitudes and actions, deferences and subserviences even in the most defiant. It requires in many ways submission to a set of notions. To be a Black female college student in the early 1930s—and to major in mathematics—was to defy notions in the larger society about both women and African American people. To do both of these simultaneously is to live a life inherently contradictory. In the process, one has to define one's self through the interrelationships of *both* of those lives. It is the dialectical process at its core which was my mother's life.

My mother's seeming contradictions don't end there. Her letter and the accompanying check for my graduate education demonstrated her understanding of the need to socialize me to live my life one way and, at the same time, to provide me with all the tools I would need to live it quite differently. When I finally comprehended that, I understood much about the unique and essential dynamics of Black mother-daughter relationships. Moreover, it helped me understand much that seems conflicting when I study the Richmond, Virginia, Black community. Historians frequently have assumed that the seeming contradictions between the rhetoric and the actions, or differing sets of actions, of the African-American community or of some of its leaders is evidence of duplicity; "wearing the mask"; of massive confusion and disorientation; or of accommodation. Some of these interpretations may in some instances be true. But what I came to understand on a concrete level through my mother was the possible necessity of the simultaneous promotion of two contradictory sets of values. *Both* were essential to the survival—of me as a person in the society in which we lived, and of the African American community as a whole. That understanding has greatly enhanced my comprehension of political developments in Richmond and elsewhere.[18]

Perhaps most obviously, but not always so, my mother has enhanced my understanding of familial relationships. Historians and other social scientists have difficulty grappling with the basic conceptions of African American families. There is either the tendency to try to fit them into Eurocentric notions of family, or, as Niara Sudarkasa has noted, even when it is recognized that they are not Eurocentric, Eurocentric terminology and definitions are employed to characterize them and so their difference is described in distorting ways.[19] I understood that most clearly when a friend of mine, with whom I often share notes on teaching and writing, called me one night to say that she had been trying to talk about families in her women's studies class and that she had tried to do it in a way which did not assume Eurocentric family norms. So, having explained the differing notions of family, she asked her students to talk about their families. Teaching in a southern California university, she has a number of racial/ethnic groups in her classroom, and her students began, having heard her lecture and understanding that they could speak of more than their parents and siblings, to describe their nuclear and extended family networks. All of them spoke until she got to the one African American woman in the class, who was an older woman returning to school. The woman looked at my friend and said quite clearly, "I don't understand— I just got family." My friend Lillian came to understand what she was saying, that even in attempting to recognize that there might be a different conception of family, she had imposed a way of defining it on her students—so they could talk about whoever was their family but they still had to divide it up according to Eurocentric distinctions among who is nuclear and who is extended, who is blood kin and who is fictive kin. And this Black woman refused to try to dissect her family along Eurocentric lines, for all she had was family.

A notion of family which transcends Eurocentric notions about relationships and roles is what my mothers have clearly passed to me. Perhaps the most cogent expression of that was on my wedding day. One of my mothers/aunts sat me down to talk about many things. All that I explicitly remember is her depiction of our relationship, for she said to me, "Your mother is my sister, my daughter, my mother, my cousin, and to you I have been and always will be your aunt, your mother, your grandmother, your sister; your children will have an aunt, a grandmother, a great-grandmother, a mother, a sister, a cousin." I understood it then in sentimental ways. I comprehended it years later when I couldn't, using the paradigms I had, accurately describe the family relationships in the community which I was studying. Often as I have tried particularly to discuss relationships among African American mothers and daughters in my research and in my classroom, I have been drawn back to my mother/aunt's statements. And I have understood the fallacy of trying to impose ideas that those doing African American family studies have often tried to impose—they have required their subjects to define their relationships with the other women/people in their family by Eurocentric notions and have marveled at the difficulty.

Sometimes, however, one's academic training is overwhelming—and it is then that my mother brings me back to reality. Several weeks ago she was talking to me and she said something about my sister; she was speaking of the woman who in Eurocentric terms is her sister and my aunt. And I, in one of my "let's get this accurate" modes, commented on her having misspoken since clearly she meant her sister. Without a moment's hesitation she said, "you are often my sister and her sister"—and went on with her conversation. Nothing more was said, but I understood quite clearly that she was telling me that I could let my scholarly training impose new definitions on my life but I would not impose them on hers.

And I realize more and more that that does happen if we don't guard against it. Several years ago I read a discussion of southern women—Black and White—which argued that family/kin relations overwhelmed them and that female relationships/friendships did not develop as they did among northern women. For African American women in particular, according to this argument, "while supportive female relationships existed, Black women were likewise primarily oriented toward family and kin . . . Afro-American culture placed emphasis on family rather than on female friendships."[20] When I initially read this I thought that the analysis failed to understand the connection between community and family in an Afrocentric community—that community is family—and thus had somehow tried to divide community and family in artificial ways. But I also thought back to an incident in my youth which in some ways perhaps on the

surface substantiated the idea of "family" networks superseding
the development of "friendships." When I was in high school,
some of the great fun of my brother's and my life was teasing
my mother, who had for the first time to our knowledge a "roady"
as they were called then, a best friend. All of the women whom
we understood previously and since then to be my mother's
closest confidantes, her support network, were her sisters and
cousins and aunts. Thus, I initially thought that perhaps the
article on southern women captured some element of African
American women's networks but failed clearly to comprehend
that element in light of the differing conceptions of family and
of community in the African American and Euro-American communities. It was not until I sat down to write this article that I
realized the fallacy in my own thinking, even about my mother's
life. Of course my mother's female network consisted almost
exclusively of family members—because all those women who
had become part of her support network had also become part
of her family—so much so that my brother and I had recognized
them only as family. So much so that when I had attempted to
really think about the female networks in my mother's life I had
been unable to separate "friends" from "family" but, knowing
them all to be family, had assumed my mother had had no need
for "friends." An equally telling example of the incorporation
of "friend" into "family," offered by one of my students, demonstrates the ways in which Eurocentric notions can becloud
and distort the lives of African American women. When her
mother was hospitalized and needed a blood transfusion, members of the family, including her aunt—her mother's sister, were
called in to provide blood. Not until the family members learned
with surprise that the tests proved this aunt's blood to be incompatible for transfusion, did they realize/"remember" the process by which she joined the family—i.e., that she was fictive
kin. The bonding had been such that not even the closest of
family members, or the aunt herself, consciously recognized this
woman as anything but the sister of the hospitalized woman.
This sister was also best friend. This demonstrates as well the
difficulty of writing accurately about African American women
without establishing a firm basis in Afrocentric values and culture to which one can always be drawn back when one is about
to tumble over in the world of scholarly training.

All of this is to say that my mother has required me to deal
up front with Eurocentricity and its influence on my education

and my scholarship. She has required me to reject the notion that one can or should remain "objective," a truly Eurocentric notion which says that you can divorce yourself from your scholarship and from your community. Any true Afrocentric scholarship has to be based on placing oneself inside one's community and inside one's scholarship rather than standing in an "objective"/outside position to each. Black studies (and to some degree women's studies) began from an understanding of the necessity of connecting the people doing the research and the people who were the subjects of the inquiry—to have the academy informed by those whose very lives spoke to that about which we intellectualize. However, in the struggle to be seen as "legitimate" academic disciplines, many of these programs have retreated from the community base which was their initial core and support. The effect of that has often been to disconnect the study of African American people from that experiential basis. Afrocentric scholarship requires understanding on a concrete level that "I am because We are; and because We are, therefore I am." There can be no I unless there are We. And it requires more than Western thought and sensibility with its emphasis on the rational, objective, and logical. Afrocentric scholarship proceeds from a worldview which incorporates both "rational" analysis and "intuitive, subjective, and communal" analysis.[21] Thus, W.E.B. Du Bois wrote of his development into a scholar-activist once he realized the impossibility of being "a calm, cool, and detached scientist while Negroes were lynched, murdered and starved";[22] Joyce Ladner also had to come to terms with this notion:

> Although I attempted to maintain some degree of objectivity, I soon began to minimize and, very often, negate the importance of being 'value-free,' because the very selection of the topic reflected a bias, i.e., I studied Black women because of my strong interest in the subject. I decided whose side I was on and resolved within myself that as a Black social scientist I must take a stand and that there could be no value-free sanctuary for me.[23]

Vincent Harding began his "experiment in history, solidarity, and hope" by:

> Affirming objectivity and subjectivity as equally necessary to any compassionate rendering of our flawed and

splendid human strivings . . . identifying fully with the
subjects of my study and the substance of their hope. I
have freely allowed myself to celebrate. For I could not
possibly remain silent and unmoved in the presence of
the mysterious, transformative dance of life that has
produced the men and women, the ideas and institutions, the visions, betrayals, and heroic dreams renewed
in blood that are at once the anguish and the glory of
the river of our struggle in this land.[24]

Students and scholars sometimes question how much value
we should give to African American women's personal accounts
of their lives. My mother has taught me the arrogance of such
a question and she regularly combats any signs of my suc-
cumbing to the Eurocentric tendency to assume that those of us
who have been trained to analyze people's lives are better able
to understand them than the people whose lives they actually
are. I have come to have great respect for people's abilities to
understand their own lives. And I have learned to listen, not
just to what they tell me about the particulars of their lives, but
also to the ways in which they define them for themselves.

Yet, for all my efforts to understand my mother's influence on
my scholarship, I have only very recently come to realize the
real nature of this relationship. Limited by disciplinary and
professional blinders, it has taken me years to be able to see
my mother as a historian—that, in fact, I am a historian because my mother was one before me. As with Paule Marshall's
mother, my mother did not do what historians do, or so it might
on the surface appear. She did not write an article or teach a
class. What she did do was record in her mind all the facts
about the people and community of Black Louisville and tell
those to me on a daily basis. I grew up knowing the names of
all the Black teachers and principals from the first decades of
the twentieth century on. I knew what they did in their school
and their community. I knew what they said publicly and what
they did privately. I knew about African American ministers,
barbers, beauticians, washerwomen, household and factory
workers, librarians, chauffeurs, and postal clerks. I learned the
history of institutions—schools, churches, families—and of
neighborhoods. I knew the interrelated and sometimes turbulent
relations between urban and rural persons. When my mother
now says to me, "You remember Mrs. Dowery," I say, "yes."
I have never even seen Mrs. Dowery; she died before I was

born, but I know how many husbands she had and the many
ways in which she motivated her students in her classes. I
learned about the outspoken Mr. Meyzeek and others who the
history books now categorize as accommodationists. But when
I learned about them from my mother they were all far more
complex persons.

Like any good historian, my mother looked at the people's
words and their actions—public and private. She analyzed them
and preserved them. And, in fact, she taught both the facts and
the form of analysis in her class, even if it had only one pupil,
her daughter.

When I entered graduate school and began to read the historical books on the African-American community, the picture
presented there did not merely contradict the lives of the people
I know personally, but, what I realize now was the biggest
problem for me—and what sent me on my continuing search for
new methodologies and theoretical perspectives—is that they
contradicted the historical documents my mother had daily laid
before me, her record of people's speeches, ideas, and actions.
She taught me the importance of preserving the historical record
of the community as the people within it understood it and thus
grounded me in a far different historiographical tradition than
the one I encountered in my academic training. The manner in
which I practice the historical craft is far different from my
mother's, but the fact that I do it and the assumptions that guide
me are firmly grounded in her historical practice. She preserved
in her mind and in her conversations with her namesake a history
and a way of historical understanding that I now attempt to
preserve in my writing and in my classroom.

With my mothers' understandings to guide me, I am slowly
becoming a historian in spite of my academic training.

NOTES

1. Alice Walker, "In Search of Our Mothers' Gardens," in *In Search of
Our Mothers' Gardens* (New York: Harcourt Brace Jovanovich, 1983), p. 243.

2. Paule Marshall, "From the Poets in the Kitchen," *The New York Times
Book Review*, January 9, 1983, p. 3.

3. Ibid., p. 34.

4. Ibid., p. 35.

5. "A Very Stern Discipline," interview with Ralph Ellison, *Harper's Magazine*, March 1967, p. 76.

6. Ibid.

7. Ralph Ellison, "An American Dilemma," in *Shadow and Act* (New York: Random House, 1967), pp. 315–16.

8. Zora Neale Hurston, "What White Publishers Won't Print," *Negro Digest,* April 1947, pp. 85–89.

9. Zora Neale Hurston, *Mules and Men* (New York: J.B. Lippincott, 1935; New York: Harper and Row, 1970), p. 17.

10. Ibid., pp. 17–20; Zora Neale Hurston, *Dust Tracks on a Road* (New York: J. B. Lippincott, 1942), p. 24.

11. Joyce Ladner, *Tomorrow's Tomorrow* (Garden City, N.Y.: Doubleday & Co., Inc., 1971), pp. 1–14.

12. Elizabeth Clark-Lewis, "Clearinghouse Column: Domestic Workers," *The Newsletter: Center for Research on Women,* Memphis State University, 4 (Fall 1985). Clark-Lewis's research on African American domestic workers is published as *"This Work Had A' End": The Transition From Live-In To Day Work,* Southern Women: The Intersection of Race, Class and Gender, Working Paper No. 2, Center for Research on Women, Memphis State University.

13. Sherley Anne Williams, "Foreword" to Zora Neale Hurston, *Their Eyes Were Watching God* (Urbana: University of Illinois Press, 1978), pp. vii–viii.

14. Louisville Municipal College for Negroes opened in February 1931 with junior college accreditation. It quickly developed a four-year curriculum and by 1936 had received accreditation as a standard four-year college from the Southern Association of Colleges and Secondary Schools. George C. Wright, *Life Behind a Veil: Blacks in Louisville, Kentucky, 1865–1930* (Baton Rouge: Louisiana State University Press, 1985), pp. 272–73.

15. Carter G. Woodson, "The Negro Washerwoman, A Vanishing Figure," *Journal of Negro History* 15 (1930):269–77.

16. For a discussion of the Independent Order of Saint Luke, see Elsa Barkley Brown, "Womanist Consciousness: Maggie Lena Walker and the Independent Order of St. Luke," *Signs: Journal of Women in Culture and Society* 14 (Spring 1989):610–33.

17. Bonnie Thornton Dill, "The Dialectics of Black Womanhood," *Signs: Journal of Women in Culture and Society* 4 (Spring 1979):543–55; "The Dialectics of Black Womanhood Revisited," presented at Georgia State University, "Black Women: Images, Styles, and Substance" Conference, March 22, 1985. The dynamics between societal pressures "to cultivate the traits that lend themselves to femininity, i.e., dependency, passiveness, submissiveness, etc.," and "the political-economic system and survival needs of the Black community to develop those traits that are contrary to the ideas of womanhood as prescribed by the sex role standard, i.e., independence, self-assertion, persistence, etc.," have also been explored by Algea O. Harrison, "The Dilemma of Growing Up Black and Female," *Journal of Social and Behavioral Sciences* 20 (Spring 1974):28–40.

18. Elsa Barkley Brown's, "Africanamerican Women's Quilting: A Framework for Conceptualizing and Teaching Africanamerican Women's History," *Signs: Journal of Women in Culture and Society* 14 (Summer 1989):921–29, develops a nonlinear framework for interpreting these seeming contradictions.

19. Niara Sudarkasa, "African and Afro-American Family Structure: A Comparison," *The Black Scholar* (November/December 1980):43–44. Lerone Bennett has spoken of the necessity to develop new frames of reference which transcend the limits of Eurocentric concepts. "By and large, reality has been

conceptualized in terms of the narrow point of view of the small minority of white men who live in Europe and North America. We must abandon this partial frame of reference of our oppressors and create new concepts which will release our reality, which is also the reality of the overwhelming majority of men and women on this globe. We must say to the white world that there are things in the world that are not dreamt of in your history and your sociology and your philosophy." "The Challenge of Blackness," in *IBW and Education for Liberation*, Institute of the Black World, Black Paper No. 1 (Chicago: Third World Press, 1973), p. 3.

20. Jean E. Friedman, "Women's History and the Revision of Southern History," *Sex, Race, and the Role of Women in the South,* ed. Joanne V. Hawks and Sheila L. Skemp (Jackson: University Press of Mississippi, 1983), pp. 3–12.

21. Vernon J. Dixon and Badi G. Foster, *Beyond Black or White: An Alternate America* (Boston: Little, Brown and Company, 1971); Johnnella E. Butler, *Black Studies: Pedagogy and Revolution: A Study of Afro-American Studies and the Liberal Arts Tradition Through the Discipline of Afro-American Literature* (Washington, D.C.: University Press of America, 1981). It is what Patricia Hill Collins has persuasively described as a simultaneous reason/emotion/ethics validation process in "Critical Issues in Black Feminist Thought," presented at Summer Research Institute on Race and Gender, Center for Research on Women, Memphis State University, June 1986.

22. W.E.B. Du Bois, *Dusk of Dawn: An Essay Toward an Autobiography of a Race Concept* (New York: Harcourt, Brace & World, Inc., 1940; New York: Schocken Books, 1968).

23. Ladner, *Tomorrow's Tomorrow,* pp. 7–8.

24. Vincent Harding, *There Is A River: The Black Struggle for Freedom in America* (New York: Harcourt Brace Jovanovich, 1981), p. xi. Harding refused to use the third-person but places himself squarely inside the community about which he writes.

BLACK MOTHERS AND DAUGHTERS: TRADITIONAL AND NEW PERSPECTIVES

Gloria I. Joseph

"What your mother tells you now,
in time you will come to know."

Black women in the U.S.A.—our histories and contemporary lives are still in need of demystification. Our beliefs, attitudes, conflicts, joys, pain, and desires, in light of ongoing social, economic, and political adversities, must be made explicit. Our voices through our literature must clarify and validate our existence and our roles in history.

It is rewarding to note that in the past decade there has been an increase in Black women researchers, novelists, poets, writers, and editors who have produced important and valuable material focusing on the experiences of Black women in their personal and collective struggles for livelihoods free from debilitating oppression. Within this body of works there still remains a critical dearth of resources on mother and daughter relationships. This article will specifically address traditional Black mothers and daughters; Black adolescent/teenage mothers and daughters; and Black lesbian couples and daughters. The focus will be on their interactions and relationships and their functions as role models.

The flourishing of sociological, psychological, and anthropological studies on the role of mothering, which was spurred by the second wave of feminism in the U.S.A., produced literature which in general was/is inapplicable to the relationships between Black mothers and daughters. For example, note the findings and conclusions of the following authors:

> Girls are still trained to be wives and mothers first. Parents still teach them to be modest, unassuming and retiring; to please men rather than to satisfy themselves, to put others' needs and interests before their own.[1]

> The oppression of women has created a breach among us, especially between mothers and daughters. Women

cannot respect their mothers in a society which de-
grades them; women cannot respect themselves. Mothers
socialize their daughters into the narrow role of wife-
mother; in frustration and guilt, daughters reject their
mothers for their duplicity and incapacity—so the alienation grows in the turning of the generations.[2]

Consider the assumption of Nancy Chodorow in her very popular book, *The Reproduction of Mothering: Psychoanalysis and
the Sociology of Gender* (1978), that the mothering role is the
root cause of female dependence and of subordination to men.[3]

These findings are in direct contrast to the results of research
conducted by Black women on Black subjects:

Black females are socialized by adult figures in early
life to become strong, independent women, who because
of precarious circumstances growing out of poverty and
racism, might have to eventually become heads of their
own households. Black mothers teach their female offspring to perform adult tasks, such as household chores,
when they are still in their pre-adolescent years.[4]

The socialization process was also responsible for deter-
mining two seemingly incompatible facts: (1) the Black
woman defining herself, and her existence in relation to
Black men; (2) while simultaneously seeing herself as
an independent being. This duality may seem incongruous but only if "womanhood" in Black mothers and
daughters is compared to white patterns of womanhood.
The white pattern regards love and economic interest as
mutually incompatible.[5]

This finding is not unmindful of Black lesbians who may
maintain personal relationships with men. Like most Black
women, their lives include males on some level—father, son,
nephew, brother, uncle, or grandfather.

In *Common Differences: Conflicts in Black and White Feminist
Perspectives* (1981), Gloria Joseph's original research on Black
mothers and daughters produced data concerning the daughters'
feelings and attitudes towards their mothers.[6] The daughters
showed tremendous respect, concern, and love for their mothers. The positive feelings that were expressed did not imply
that all was sweet, kind, and loving between them. Rather,
what was expressed was an undeniable respect and admiration
for their mothers' accomplishments and struggles against overwhelming odds; their economic ability to make ends meet; their
personal relationships with men; for having raised their families

as a single parent or head of household and having encouraged them to be independent and to get an education. The mothers were role models for their daughters. Data from research on socialization among Black mothers and daughters regarding the institution of marriage verified previous findings on Black heterosexual women. Two seemingly incongruous facts were dramatically and graphically disclosed. The messages that the majority of mothers gave their daughters about men were in the "abusive and unreliable" category. At the same time the mothers assumed and accepted as a given fact that their daughters would marry these men. The methodology for obtaining the data was as follows.

The question was asked: "What stands out in your mind most clearly with regard to what your mother told you about men?" The categorical results were:

(1)	Abusive comments and warnings of potential of being abused	43.9%
(2)	Unreliable, undependable and ways to avoid dependency	33.1%
(3)	A few good ones	5.5%
(4)	Other	17.5%

Examples of category (1), abusive comments and warnings of potential abuse (43.9%):

"They're dogs. Always in heat, move from one woman to another without a thought in their minds."	(age 19)
"Every man has some dog in him."	(age 20)
"Never allow yourself to be used."	(age 20)
"He who lies with dogs shall rise with fleas."	(age 20)

This question was followed by: "What stands out most clearly in your mind as to what your mother told you about marriage?"

Category (1)	Responses with an explicit or an underlying assumption favoring marriage. This category was subdivided into four groupings:	
	(1) Not to marry at too early an age	17.6%
	(2) Encouraged marriage without qualifications	9.6%
	(3) Marry but maintain independence	5.6%

(4)   Don't have sex before
       marriage   3.7%

These four categories accounted for 36.5% of the responses:

Category (2)	Mutual struggle to make it work (implicit encouragement)	30.6%
Category (3)	Discourage	10.2%
Category (4)	Other	22.7%

Examples of encouragement (36.5%):

"Everyone in the *world* should get married
and have children. Marriage is
fulfillment."   (age 19)

"Marriage is needed for the raising of
children."   (age 20)

"Always maintain your personal financial
stash—don't give up everything."   (age 21)

"It's important to be married in order to have
children."   (age 21)

"Be sure, don't rush, you've time."   (age 21)

"Get married as opposed to living together
because she feels that the woman had the
most to lose in the long run if the living-in
arrangement fails."   (age 21)

"Marriage is an *important* step in your life.
It shouldn't be rushed; but it is a natural
must."   (age 21)

Examples of discouragement (10.2%):

"Don't."   (age 20)
"My mother told me not to get married."   (age 32)
"Avoid it."   (age 34)
"Don't do it."   (age 75)

It is actually misleading and dysfunctional to engage in a discussion of Black mothers and daughters patterned along the
lines of white theoretical writing, which focuses on specific psychological mechanisms operating between mothers and daughters, unless the relevance of racial oppression and cultural
differences are considered as critical factors. To date, with few
exceptions, few white theoreticians and authors take into account
these factors.

In discussing Black mothers and daughters, it is absolutely
essential to speak of their roles and functions within the Black
community and the community's relation to the dominant white

society. Moreover, the mother/daughter interaction *must be* discussed within the context of the Black family network.

At this particular time, 1984, we must be aware of changing and different mother/daughter patterns in the Black family network. This is due to a startling increase in adolescent/teenage mothers and the recognition of lesbian couples and their children. (There has also been an increased number of polygamous [U.S. style] families, but due to insufficient material at this writing, this category will not be discussed.)

Black adolescent/teenage mothers pose a most serious situation that the Black community and families must be concerned with for the health and welfare of the present and future generations. Black adult lesbian mothers who are out to the public bring no special problems to the community. It is society's oppression of homosexuals that is responsible. Attitudes of family and community toward lesbian mothers play a major role in the difficulties they face. Hostile and opprobrious attitudes and' actions have forced Black lesbian mothers to seek support from lesbian friends and communities (most of the latter being white). (Since 1984, there has been an increase in Black lesbian Mother Community and support groups.)

The psychological, mental, and physical hardship that Black women have had to endure as a result of racist and economic oppression has not changed dramatically over the past three generations. Black granddaughters face the same obstacles as their grandmothers and mothers faced. It is a cyclical pattern. Granddaughters still share the portrayals popularized by social science feminist literature of Black women in stereotypical conflicting images. On the one hand, they are portrayed as strong, competent, self-reliant, and dominant; and on the other hand, they are viewed as victims suffering from double or triple jeopardy, lacking the gumption to remove themselves from the bottom of the occupational and economic ladders. Grandmothers, mothers, and daughters routinely face objectifying sexist behavior from Black men as well as from patriarchal society at large. The truth of the matter is that the social history of Black women in North America has been one of suffering under severely adverse economic conditions, and today they continue to live under oppressive conditions. By necessity, not choice, Black women have had to be resourceful, assertive, and self-reliant in order to survive. They could not routinely depend on Black men to lend or give the needed economic or emotional support. The same system that victimized and dehumanized Black men also victimized and dehumanized Black women. Black women are simply responding to adverse conditions. Over the generations, theirs is a characteristic response to an exploitive, oppressive system.

It was and remains necessary for Black mothers and daughters to collaborate in their fight against powerful societal conditions that continue to force fathers out of home and out of work; that push brothers and boyfriends and sons into prisons and/or to drugs; that make it necessary to raise babies without support from the fathers; that encourage by "sanctioning" beating/battering of women (encourage in the sense that the law and courts which are the domain of white males do little to discourage battering); and similarly encourage lesbian baiting and victimization. This mother/daughter collaboration is reflected in the ways Black mothers teach their daughters highly adaptive mechanisms designed to promote physical and mental survival. Without such teaching the mental and physical survival of Black women would be impossible.

As we discuss the new population of adolescent mothers we must keep in mind the existing hardships Black women as mothers face, and the importance of their roles.

ADOLESCENT MOTHERS

The new population of adolescent mothers presents a definitely growing contemporary social reality with alarming ramifications for the present and following generations. This population of mothers, ages twelve to seventeen, has unique characteristics and needs. Adolescence in our society is characterized by conflicts, unrest, insecurities, and the acting out of unconscious wishes and needs in a struggle for a sense of identity and autonomy. It is also a time of high dependency needs, low frustration tolerance, poor judgment, and heightened narcissism. The adolescent is dealing with high-powered physiological, psychological, and social forces that significantly influence her behavior.

To what extent can the adolescent be expected to bring a sound developmental foundation to motherhood? What capacity can she have to use the experience of motherhood for her own good? The quality of parenting and the ability to sustain a stable, harmonious mother/infant relationship are incompatible with adolescent needs and traits. It is recognized that there is a wide variance among the population of teenage mothers, with some being at the psychologically and physically healthier end of the continuum and others being on the borderline or psychotic end. Some of the young mothers may have help from the extended family and access to counselling and health care. But regardless of the range, as a population these young mothers must be identified as limited in their ability to bring to motherhood the quality of parenting needed to ensure the healthy development of infants, particularly during the initial formative years. Children cannot be expected to assume adult parenting responsibilities. Many of these adolescents are themselves in need of mothering and are using pregnancy as a means of meeting their unmet needs. As the primary caretakers, their limitations and inadequacies are directly related to the mothering they give to their babies. Adolescent mothers who bring developmental lesions to the task of motherhood are already at risk, and they bring these risks to their infants.

What is the nature and quality of the mother/child-daughter relationship? What can reasonably be expected from these adolescent mothers? Some of the young mothers have mothers or other relatives who are able to provide both the adolescent and the infant with critical caring and mothering skills. And some young mothers do a reasonably good job of caring for their babies. The majority however, follow a typical pattern of what can, with candor, be called, "Doll Playing." The babies are serving as object replacements. The infant is used as a doll— a toy—to gratify the needs of the child/mother. The adolescent mother's needs may be so great and demanding that they distort her perception of her infant's needs. She is unable to differentiate her needs from her infant's. The adolescent's desire to have something of her own, something that is always there, is met by having the baby. The child/mother has a cute, cuddly, tiny object to possess. She can shower attention on the infant and feel wanted and needed. She can dress the baby up and show it off as her prize possession. Some of these infants could win the best-dressed infant of the year award! The mother's behavior is very much akin to a child playing with a doll. Change the clothes frequently; hug it; hold it close; show it off; feed it; and put it to sleep in keeping with the mother's wishes and needs. The "doll's" needs may become secondary to the mother's.

As the infants enter different stages of development, however, when separation and differentiation begin, and they are no longer tiny, cuddly "dolls," the child/mothers lack the emotional stability and know-how to cope with their babies' changing needs. As the children enter toddlerhood, become more mobile, and begin to crawl and toddle, the mothers are less able to care for the children physically and emotionally. They want the children to "not get into everything and not be so much trouble." Typically, the mothers attempt to restrict the children's movements, and expect them to stay off of and out of cabinets, drawers, and trash baskets at the time when the children's need to explore is heightened. If the children persist, as most will, the low frustration and tolerance level, the narcissistic needs of the adolescents prevail and the children are in line for being yelled at, screamed at, slapped or beaten. The toddler's behavior is often dissonant with the child/mother's needs, as was the case during infancy. Far too often when the babies reach the toddler stage, the young mothers become pregnant again in order to once again have something, someone, that is theirs—that they own—that no one can take away. They want another "doll."

As the children of the adolescent mothers grow older, what messages can the mothers give their daughters about marriage; about men; about getting ahead in the world and getting an education? These are the major lessons that traditional Black mothers give to their daughters, and they are important ones. The teenage mothers are preoccupied with the tasks facing post-adolescent females and need socialization from adult females.

In her research on the transmission of knowledge, skills, and role models from Black mothers to their daughters, Suzanne C. Carothers, on reflecting on her family life, recalls her mother as a role model and as being "sensitively human, independent and a doer." Most women in the neighborhood, as mothers, workers in the home, workers away from home, and active participants in community and church affairs are women who share with, look out for, and help each other.[7] Black mothers have traditionally served as role models for their daughters. The young adolescent mothers will likely serve in some respects as role models for their daughters but in ways that may be detrimental. The situation will be one of mothers, ages for example twenty-three to twenty-seven, serving as role models for daughters ages ten to thirteen. The young mothers lack the experience and developmental consolidation necessary for raising adolescent daughters. The daughters may be seen as competitors for the mothers' personal space and time and even in dating situations.

The *New York Times Magazine*, September 9, 1984, ran a cover story on "The Working Mother as Role Model." Shamefully and disgracefully, throughout the entire feature never once was a Black woman mentioned nor shown in any of the pictures. A subcaption stated, "As more and more women enter the work-force, researchers are beginning to study the psychological and social effects this may have on their children." A look at the pattern of labor force participation shows that Black women show a pattern similar to males, both Black and White. In the case of working mothers as role models, the *New York Times* treated Black women as INVISIBLE! Black mothers as working mothers have traditionally served as valuable role models for their daughters.

As is customary in American society, problems such as drugs, single mothers, and absentee fathers either go unrecognized or are regarded as a malignancy, a Black genetic inferiority, or as a blight on the surface of White respectability until sufficient numbers of Whites are affected and involved. The involvement of Whites as victims or participants changes the entire com-plexion of the picture. In the case of drugs it became a national problem with the establishment of treatment centers and at-tempted control of drug traffic. Single parenting became sanc-tioned and legitimized as an alternative family style; "new" research shows that the absence of a father in the home does not seem to have any more adverse effects on the children as long as there are other male models. This has been the case in Black extended families for generations, yet research has con-stantly been negative about Blacks in this regard.

Adolescent mothers must have services available to help them and their daughters. Such services must reflect the range and diversity of needs among adolescent mothers. It is of utmost importance that services be available since it is unlikely that there will be a substantial reduction in Black adolescent preg-nancy for quite some time. In many of the cases of adolescent pregnancy, a lack of sex education is not the cause. Emotional, psychological, and social factors are the major underlying causes. For the Black female, racism and poverty are strong factors that contribute to her being denied needed material con-ditions for adequate development. Unless substantive changes are made in society, adolescent mothers will be raising daughters and giving them dysfunctional and inappropriate messages, and the daughters will be earmarked for impending disasters.[8]

BLACK LESBIAN MOTHERS

The relationship between Black lesbian mothers and daughters will be discussed within the context of lesbian households. Throughout the United States and internationally, increasing numbers of lesbian couples are having babies. The director of a sperm bank in California reported that about 40 percent of the recipients were lesbians, most of them couples. Historically there have always been homosexuals in heterosexual marriages or unions, and children have been a part of the family structure. Currently, with the momentum of the gay and lesbian movement, there is a marked increase in women electing to have children, not in a heterosexual arrangement but within a lesbian relationship. Through artificial insemination, adoption, and intercourse with a selected male, lesbian couples are having children.

Myths abound about homosexuals regarding their interrelationships and family relations, such as their being anti-family and narcissistic and their trying to "convert" children to homosexuality. Recent research dispels these myths and calls for new directions in research on lesbians. The research conducted on lesbians and their children is sparse, and what exists predominantly concerns white lesbians. What must be realized is that there is a growing number of Black women who are developing and establishing intimate relations with other women. Despite repression, discrimination, and hostility, Black lesbian families will continue to develop as a divergent family/life pattern.

Lesbian mothers have been an invisible part of society, and Black lesbian mothers are a shadow of the invisibility. The truth of the matter is that lesbians, Black and White, have historically, like millions of other unmarried women, been caretakers and nurturers within their families, and lesbian mothers have always existed. A rose by any other name is still a rose. The actual number of lesbian mothers in the United States is uncertain, with estimates ranging from two hundred thousand to three million. Researchers have found as broad a range of personalities and attitudes about child-rearing among lesbians as among heterosexual women, the same degree of ambivalence about their children, and as wide a range of life styles, from traditional to open. Similarities between lesbian mothers and heterosexual mothers far outweigh the differences.

Black lesbian mothers, like Black heterosexual mothers, bring to the task of motherhood risks that can be measured in terms of the degree of their stabilized adult behavior. The quality of mother/daughter relationships is largely determined by the extent to which the mothers have established satisfactory development in the areas of intimacy/relationship; work/career; proven competency/self-worth. Black lesbian mothers have the added obstacles of overcoming negative, oppressive, hostile attitudes from both the larger world and the Black community. They are aware that they are exposing their daughters to potential conflict as the community becomes aware of the lesbian coupling. Knowing this, the fear of disclosure and threat of discrimination for many lesbian mothers greatly affect the way they manage their daily lives. The degree of heterosexist oppression is directly related to the amount of realistic fear and struggle needed for survival.[9] Hence, a relatively large number of Black lesbian mothers in the middle to upper income brackets display high levels of independence, are self-employed, and own their own homes, such that their economic security serves in some measure to buffer some of the realistic fears. Lesbian mothers who have a positive acceptance of self, and no guilt about their lesbianism affecting their children's growth (knowing that it is society's attitudes and behavior that are responsible for the oppression) have reported that lesbianism and parenthood are intrinsically compatible.

Recent research has disclosed that most children of lesbians were accepting of their mother's lifestyle but concerned about reactions and pressures from outside, i.e., peers, classmates, neighbors.[10] In a study by J. B. Miller (1982), it was actually reported that lesbian mothers were more child-oriented in their responses to their children than married heterosexual mothers, and noted that generally these mothers are exceptionally concerned about the long range development of their children.[11]

Black lesbian mothers have reported that in their decision to have a child (unlike the case of an unwanted pregnancy), both partners want the child and do not feel that a close father relationship is necessary for their daughters' development. They also express a desire for their daughters to have positive relations with men and women. For those lesbian mothers who have internalized guilt about their lesbianism, who have arrested development and bring severe emotional problems to motherhood, the prognosis for a good mother/daughter relationship is very poor, as would be the case for heterosexual mothers. However, for lesbian couples the decision to have a child requires certain preconditions which foster more favorable outcomes. To begin with, most couples are in their late twenties or early thirties when development is solidified and the capacity for mature judgment is present, and, secondly, it is definitely a planned affair.

Black lesbian mothers, like Black heterosexual mothers, are aware of the problems their daughters have to face coping in a racist, sexist, heterosexist society, one in which every twelve seconds a woman is beaten; where every three minutes, a woman is raped (90 percent of rapes of Black women are committed by Black men); in which thousands of Black children have no economic support from their fathers. The Black lesbian mother has the additional burden/hardship/obscenity of having to face horrendous, hostile, heterosexist oppression. The Black community must prepare to accept lesbian couples and their children. The trend is upward.

Black families and communities have been protective and caring of children and respectful of differences. We have historically cared for and nurtured White and mulatto children even as we were discriminated against and oppressed. Given this tradition it is incumbent upon us to be no less humane to Black lesbian mothers and daughters. Black adult mothers will continue being key figures in the maintenance and continuance of Black life in families and communities.

NOTES

1. Stella Chess and Jane Whitbread, *Daughters: From Infancy to Independence* (New York: Doubleday, 1978).

2. Judith Arcana, *Our Mothers' Daughters* (Berkeley: Shameless Hussy Press, 1979).

3. Nancy Chodorow, *The Reproduction of Mothering: Psychoanalysis and the Sociology of Gender* (Berkeley: University of California Press, 1978).

4. Joyce Ladner, *Labeling Black Children: Some Mental Health Implications*, vol. 5 (Washington D.C.: Institute for Urban Affairs and Research Howard University, 1979), p. 3.

5. Jualynne Dodson, *To Define Black Womanhood: A Study of Black Female Graduate Students* (Atlanta, GA: The Institute of the Black World, 1975).

6. Gloria Joseph and Jill Lewis, *Common Differences: Conflicts in Black and White Feminist Perspectives* (New York: Doubleday and Co., 1981).

7. Suzanne C. Carothers, "Generation to Generation: The Transmission of Knowledge, Skills and Role Models from Black Working Mothers to their Daughters in a Southern Community." Unpublished dissertation, 1980.

8. Throughout this section, reference to daughters does not mean that male children are being ignored. Much of what has been said applies equally to sons. However, this article is focused on the mother-daughter relation. The same consideration prevails for the section on lesbian mothers. Black male children are co-partners in this adolescent adversity. Adult Black males must assume their responsibility in socializing Black male children. Too much is at stake here, and the gravity of the situation requires a shared Black mother-father partnership.

9. The author prefers the use of the more accurate and valid word, heterosexism, rather than homophobia.

10. K. G. Lewis, "Children of Lesbians: Their Point of View," *Social Work* 25 (1980):198–203.

11. J. B. Miller, "Psychological Recovery in Low-Income Single Parents," *American Journal of Orthopsychiatry* 52 (1982):346–52.

P A **3** R T

STITCHING MEMORIES:
HERSTORIES

The quilt, the central trope for this volume, finds some of its finest articulation in this section—"Stitching Memories." A recurring pattern in this patchwork quilt of mother/daughter relations is memory. Like the quilt which is pieced from scraps of old family clothes, "Stitching Memories" comprises recollections of mother/daughter relations from childhood through adulthood. The selections represent—in both form and content—discrete "pieces" of memory, including loving memories, memories edged with ambivalence and anger, and memories of maternal sacrifice and support, among others, together forming a composite reflection on the relationship between mothers and daughters. Whether in their roles as mothers, domestics, or professionals, the women in "Stitching Memories" reflect upon their own mothers in similar or contrasting postures. These women also gesture toward understanding their connection with, ambivalence toward, and alienation from their mothers.

The writers in this section provide multiple perspectives on the mother/daughter relationship. Belvie Rooks's "Precious Memories" recalls early childhood experiences with her mother and juxtaposes them with her immediate concern for her own daughter. Remembering her experience as a two-year-old protected by her mother from natural storms, she contemplates her present posture as a mother concerned to shield her daughter from the storms of racism and human violence.

Dolores Kendrick's "Something Domestic" and Louise Robinson-Boardley's "Mother, in Sunlight," rehearse the labors of those caring mothers whose influence is both immediate and far-reaching. Gloria T. Hull's "The Taste of Mother Love" is a daughter's admission of being influenced by and yet different from her mother. Pinkie Gordon Lane's "Old Photo from a Family

Album: 1915" contrasts the beauty and "innocent hope" of the woman who would become her mother with the "gross figure" whose "angry defiance" the daughter came to recognize in the flesh. June Jordan's "Ah, Momma" and Renita Weems's "Hush. Mama's Gotta Go Bye-Bye" resonate with evocations of love and loss.

Miriam DeCosta-Willis's "Smoothing the Tucks in Father's Linen" delineates the ambivalence of Rosetta Douglass Sprague toward her mother. DeCosta-Willis argues that Sprague's *My Mother as I Recall Her* is a belated gesture at trying to protect her mother's reputation by valorizing her "submerged life" and countering the gossip surrounding Frederick Douglass's alleged affair with Julia Griffith. DeCosta-Willis further asserts that Sprague, while openly protective of her mother, was in actuality her father's ally.

Shaped by multiple and varied memories, "Stitching Memories" forms an essential block in the larger quilt that configures the relations between mothers and daughters.

Lucie Fultz

SOMETHING DOMESTIC

Dolores Kendrick

He had heard her complain about how hard
the white folks worked her; she had told
him over and over again that she lived
their lives when she was working in their
homes, not her own.
        RICHARD WRIGHT, *Native Son*

She had worked for a million years,
worked in the kitchens of the rich,
feeding them their white food from her
Black hands
resting their pale rest
in her dark dreams,
catering to butlers and bells and pantries
and ringed fingers
and cigarette butts smashed in cold soufflés
and voices coming from airy rooms and tight eyes
that practiced squeezing the last paytime
from her fleshy footsteps;
worked for a million tears in-maid and out,
millionaire's cook; and laundress where there the
bloodletting steam stomped upon the women's faces
and pressed them like so many solid sheets
into a vat where the eight-hour day
would clean and wash them dry;

        worked for a day in the sun that never came,
        worked for an hour of pension and pennies
        that slipped into her dress pocket
        with the daily carfare, worked for—
        the Black girl who stood before her,
        words sticking like pastry to her college mouth.

        The Turkish pastry was a bit too sticky tonight,
        Rose. Watch that next time, will you?

Originally published in *Through the Ceiling* (London: Paul Bremon, Ltd., 1975).

Words sticking to the sound of a new voice
and the wetness of rain that now came
full onto blood-bought windows
cleansing them.

Be sure the crystal is spotless tonight, Rose,
there were a few watermarks on one of the luncheon
glasses. Mrs. Yemen's. We caught it just in time.

Remember?

Sticking to Remember,
remember the child studying
in the middle of another's strange kitchen
that warmed her appetites mixing with smells
and sounds of frying pans and caviar
and duckling and cold cutlery;
sticking to the child who warmed inside
while her Proust made compromise with watercress
and tea-trays,
the Black girl now bred in choice
beyond the one who chopped the chicory,
the woman stretched to laundry trees
and dining room tables,
whom for now the child frees
the millionth word,
unleashed to a servant telling of a tale:

The certain child whose first tried love
is now ordinary
rolled in sheepskin
delicate
does not squander words to nonbelievers
but keeps them frugally for a rainy day;
for a doctor's calling
that she alone decided that she degreed
could answer
brings deafness instead
and she for something to like
will sit at a secretary's living
nothing more—now.

No response.

"We have a million lives," the girl whispers.
"Mother! Mother!" in the bright white kitchen.

She gave a servant answer,
she never said a word.

MOTHER, IN SUNLIGHT

Louise Robinson-Boardley

I tugged at your skirt, and you smiled.

You stood in sunlight
Near the coal stove
A black iron heating,
A black iron slicking wrinkles
On percale dresses and starched white shirts.
You stood in sunlight
Sweat dripping down your brow.

I think of the hours you spent
To make our world sparkle.

THE TASTE OF MOTHER LOVE

Gloria T. Hull

I. DIALOGUE: A QUESTION AND AN ANSWER

Q. How come my food don't taste like yours?
A. That's the mother love in it, honey.

II. THE FACT

Make no mistake about it:
Mother love has taste.

That's what
        seasons the beans
        and salts the roast
        and makes the cabbage taste good
        (even when they're just cooked in bacon grease).

It's what
        you yearn for on separated holidays
        rush back to on vacations
        and what makes you fat
        (when you stay there too long).

It's why
        you beg for a bite off mama's plate
        (right after you finish cleaning your own)
        and why home for you will always be
        your mother's yellow, broken-backed kitchen.

From *Healing Heart*, by Gloria T. Hull (Latham, NY: Kitchen Table: Women of Color Press, 1989).

III. LEARNING EXPERIENCE

I sit in my mama's kitchen, watching her cook.

Did you brown the meat before you set it in the oven?
How much onion did you put in that dressing?

Do you use milk or water in your cornbread? any eggs?
And how many spoons of sugar did it take to make the potatoes
this sweet?

What made your stew go from thin to thick like that?
Sometimes mine never does, no matter how long and slow I cook
it.

My mother is a patient woman;
she cooks and answers,
sometimes even in measurements and minutes—
if I keep pinning her down.

Later, I stand in my own kitchen, trying to cook.
I do it just so, remembering and following exactly everything
mama said.

BUT THEN, MY FOOD JUST WON'T TASTE LIKE HERS.

That's why when anybody says
cooking is a science,
I know better.

Ever been served contentment in a laboratory?
And any fool can tell you:
Real mother love don't grow on trees.

OLD PHOTO FROM A
FAMILY ALBUM: 1915

Pinkie Gordon Lane

for my mother, Inez Addie West Gordon

This lovely young woman,
with the elegant hat
and dress of flowing gauze,
sits in a chair (a rocker)
contemplating a feather
poised in two fingers
of her right hand

What photographer arranged
this photo in a studio
with the tapestried background
draped like a mural? See
how he catches
the pensive gaze,
face soft, unsmiling,
full of innocence and hope.

She sends the picture
to her lover:

> *Dear William, again*
> *I make another attempt*
> *—Please send me*
> *one of yours . . . or*
> *else you can come*
> *and make one*
> *at our house*

Her body curved, relaxed, slender—
the eyes returning into themselves

From *I Never Scream*, by Pinkie Gordon Lane (Detroit: Lotus Press, Inc., 1985).

She is contained in her
assurance that leads
into the future

Nothing in this photo
resembles the gross figure
the angry defiance
the abused spirit
of the woman I knew

The enlarged hand,
fingers swollen from years of work,
would no longer hold a bird's feather
but a torch to light
her way back to corridors
of love expected
of fury diffused to a spiral
of smoke, and a gown
that (shroud of her life)
she might have placed
upon her unmarked
grave

AH, MOMMA

June Jordan

Ah, Momma,
Did the house ever know the night-time of your spirit: the flash
and flame of you who once, when we crouched in what you called
"the little room," where your dresses hung in their pallid col-
orings—an uninteresting row of uniforms—and where there were
dusty, sweet-smelling boxes of costume jewelry that nevertheless
shone like rubies, gold, and diamonds, once, in that place where
the secondhand mirror blurred the person, dull, that place without windows, with doors instead of walls, so that your small-
space most resembled a large and rather hazardous closet, once,
in there you told me, whispering, that once, you had wanted to
be an artist: someone, you explained, who could just boldly go
and sit near the top of a hill and watch the setting of the sun.

Ah, Momma!
You said this had been your wish when you were quite as young
as I was then: a twelve- or thirteen-year-old girl who heard your
confidence with terrified amazement: what had happened to you
and your wish? Would it happen to me too?

Ah, Momma:
"The little room" of your secrets, your costumery, perfumes and
photographs of an old boyfriend you did not marry (for reasons
not truly clear to me as I saw you make sure, time after time,
that his pictures were being kept as clean and as safe as possible)—"the little room" adjoined the kitchen, the kitchen where
no mystery survived, except for the mystery of you: woman who
covered her thick and long, black hair with a starched, white
nurse's cap when she went "on duty" away from our home into
the hospital I came to hate, jealously, woman who rolled up her
wild and heavy, beautiful hair before she went to bed, woman
who tied a headrag around the waving, kinky, well-washed
braids, or lengthy, fat curls of her hair while she moved, without

From *Things That I Do in the Dark* by June Jordan (New York: Random House, 1977).

particular grace or light, between the table and the stove, between the sink and the table, around and around and around in the spacious, ugly kitchen where she, where you, never dreamed about what you were doing or what you might do instead, and where you taught me to set down plates and silverware, and even fresh-cut flowers from the garden, without appetite, without excitement, without expectation.

It was not there, in that obvious, open, square cookery where you spent most of the hours of the days, it was not there, in the kitchen where nothing ever tasted sweet or sharp enough to sate the yearnings I began to suspect inside your eyes, and also inside the eyes of my father, it was not there that I began to hunger for the sun as my own, legitimate preoccupation; it was not there, in the kitchen, that I began, really, to love you.

Ah, Momma,
It was where I found you, hidden away, in your "little room," where your life and the power, the rhythms of your sacrifice, the ritual of your bowed head, and your laughter always partly concealed, where all of you, womanly, reverberated big as the whole house, it was there that I came, humbly, into an angry, an absolute determination that I would, one day, prove myself to be, in fact, your daughter
Ah, Momma, I am still trying.

PRECIOUS MEMORIES

Belvie Rooks

Some journal reflections and entries about:

MY MOTHER:
October 1987

I have often wondered what it was about royal crown grease that made me love the taste of it so. Crave it with such determined and willful passion. Was it some vitamin or nutritional deficiency? Or was it a lingering remembrance of the way your hair smelled; freshly pressed no doubt—as I snuggled in the hollow of your neck. My two-year-old arms wrapped tightly around your neck.

You were all I had . . .

. . . And another memory, that I'm not supposed to have because, "you were so young, barely two." But I remember a terrible, terrible storm. It must have been a hurricane or a tornado. We barely made it to the storm shelter. But we made it. I remember how dark it was. There was a man with us and once we were safely inside the underground shelter, he closed and bolted the door, and lit a lantern. I remember the warm yellow glow, the towering, frightening shadows, the wonderful underground smell of moist earth. You held me tightly as the storm raged above our heads; the wind threatening to lift the tiny overhead door off its hinges. How the wind made the shadows dance. The loud, crashing sounds of uprooted trees all round us. The thunder. The lightning. How scared I was. My small two-year-old arms tightened around your neck.

You were all I had . . .

MY DAUGHTER:
March 2, 1968
Santa Fe, New Mexico

Another perfect morning!!! Silence, 900 acres of sunshine. The Sangre de Cristo Mountains, and lots of wonderful fluffy white clouds for miles. From the sun's position on the Sangre de Cristo's, it must be around 7 o'clock. Real mountain time.

What a joy and wonder Noliwe is! What an imagination. Driving into town yesterday morning—to her playgroup—she made up the most incredible cloud story. Wish I had had a tape recorder. As we drove along Tano road I was absorbed in the constantly changing world of interesting cloud formations—miles and miles of them—and my own thoughts. Noliwe was, as usual, a constant stream of chatter, questions, insights, and explanations—none of which I was paying any attention to as indicated by my occasional, "uh huh, uh huh"; a sure sign to us both that I wasn't really listening, and had not been for the last two or three miles. Feeling guilty and selfish at shutting her out, I suggested that she tell me a story (an increasingly desperate act of survival that usually works)—about clouds; that way, at least, we would both be in the same universe. Without a moment's hesitation or pause, she looked up at the sky and launched into a wonderful story about white clouds and black clouds.

At some point in the story, the black clouds were all eaten by the white clouds. Naturally all my racial antennas shifted to full alert, since she is the only Black child in this playgroup we were driving to. "Why did the white clouds eat the black clouds?" I asked, as casually and nonchalantly as I could manage. "I *told* you, the black clouds were running away!" (Not quite the answer I was getting at.) "Well, did the white clouds eat the black clouds because they were being mean?" (There, I said it!) Her puzzled four-year-old expression told me I had completely missed the point; it also told me that she suspected that I hadn't really been listening to the complex intricacies of detail and plot. "No-o-o!" (as in I told you this already), "the white clouds were trying to hide the black clouds!" Well as it turned out the black clouds were being chased by dinosaurs. Friendly dinosaurs who just wanted to play—but, of course, the black clouds didn't know that. (It was a game in which everybody was having fun.)

Clearly I had missed a lot. I even found myself leaning over the steering wheel and looking up at the clouds anew. This time trying to see these vast new kingdoms—inhabited by dinosaurs, butterflies, and the like—that were being described with such familiarity. What a relief that her world seems so alive—so friendly; that there were no monsters and the dinosaurs (as big as they were and as clumsy as it must have been for them) chased clouds because they just wanted to play. Thank God for no t.v.!!!

April 4, 1968
Santa Fe, New Mexico

There are millions of stars here tonight, and lots of tears. "Martin Luther King, Jr. is dead."

April 5, 1968

"Martin Luther King, Jr. is dead." I keep hearing Harry Edwards's voice, over and over again, "Martin Luther King, Jr. is dead." I had been anticipating last night for weeks. I was excited all day yesterday; Harry Edwards was coming to Santa Fe to talk about racism in general, and the world of sports, in particular.

The auditorium at Santa Fe Junior College was packed. Nobody in the audience seemed to mind that he was a few minutes late. As he walked slowly onto the stage, with his head down, we all applauded enthusiastically. I was applauding his presence and his courage. He stood quietly at the podium for a few minutes, before making the announcement that, "Martin Luther King, Jr. is dead." There was a collective gasp. "He was shot and killed a few minutes ago in Memphis."

I can't stop crying today. Several times last night I had to stop on the road trying to get home. Poor Noliwe is having such a hard time trying to understand what is going on. How could any four-year-old? I tried to explain that she couldn't go to school today because we were mourning Dr. King's death. How to explain mourning? Finally—"we are trying to be very, very quiet and think about Dr. King. To remember his life and all he tried to do" (which was why she was not going to school and why her father was not going to work). She just came in a little while ago and wanted to know if, "Mar-t-i-n-e Lu-ter King would mind if I played with my doll." Through more tears, I explained that he was our friend and that it would make him very happy. I *feel so sorry for us all*.

MY MOTHER:
October, 1987

. . . My final "early childhood" memory of you, has over the
years, proven to be the most difficult; the most painful . . . as
the void—of what would become our final separation—became
a reality. Even though *again* I was not supposed to, I remember
a bus. A large bus. I think blue and white. And I am sitting on
the back row with someone—waving goodbye to you. Taken
away. Sent away. Forever. But how does a three-year-old
grasp—FOREVER. Was it a sunny day? Did I get caught up
in allowing myself to be fooled? Pretending, too, that I would
see you tomorrow. It was such a big journey. Did I get bravely
onto the bus? Insist on taking each of the steps—alone . . .
unassisted . . .

I've recently come to wonder what that day was like for you.
How you felt? What you remembered? Did you remember what
color dress I wore?

You were all I had . . .

"HUSH. MAMA'S GOTTA GO BYE-BYE"

Renita Weems

Karintha is a woman. Men do not know that the soul of her was a growing thing ripened too soon. They will bring their money; they will die not having found it out.... Karintha at twenty, carrying beauty, perfect as dusk. When the sun goes down. Karintha....

JEAN TOOMER, "Karintha," *Cane* (1923)

Although Jean Toomer wrote these words about the women of Sparta, Georgia more than four decades ago, some ten years before my mother was born, I still cling to them, believing that somehow they hold the mystery to the women born in my mother's hometown.

My mother was born in 1932, and after thirty years of being her eldest daughter, I must admit that I know very little about the sullen woman from Sparta, Georgia who brought me into the world.

My mother's mother, Willie Lou Clark, was short, round, and dark, with jet black hair down her back. She had, I am told, an appetite for loving that embarrassed my grandfather. She was a Spartan woman who measured her pain with song. Like any "growing thing ripened too soon," to quote Toomer, my grandmother eventually had to give up a part of herself before it was time. She gave up lust, though not her music, and lived to make a man out of my grandfather and a home for their seven children—four boys and three girls. One of those girls was my mother, Carrie Baker.

One Mother's Day in 1947, after Sunday-morning service, my grandmother was killed by a bullet intended for one of her sons. Shortly thereafter, my mother dropped out of school to help her elder sister care for their brothers and baby sister. About my mother's past, this is all I have been able to piece together.

My mother is an alcoholic. These words are as hard for the relatives as they are for the victims. She has been an alcoholic at least since I was a little girl. My most poignant memories of my childhood are of my older brother and me conspiring among ourselves for one of us to stall the bill collector at the door or my father on the telephone while the other tried—usually in vain—to wake Mama. After years of my embarrassment and being caught in lies, it was one of my mother's girlfriends—a drinking buddy and reputed licensed practical nurse—who showed me how, in emergencies, to wake my mother. "Stick ice cubes on her chest," she demonstrated. I can hear my mother crying and pleading with me, as I massaged her chest, to leave her alone. "Hush now," were her words, "I'll be back in a little while."

It has been said before and deserves to be said again: When one person in the family has a drinking problem, the whole family has a drinking problem. One person contracts the disease and everyone else dies from it. Children grow old before their time. They must learn to lie well to the outside world, to other members of the family, and to themselves. Parents fight with words and screams too bitter for children to be able to decide who is wrong and who has been wronged. Everyone must take sides, however. The whole nightmare is kept going by an endless succession of lies where the difference between what is real and what is not slowly pales.

When I am in physical pain, I think a lot about my mother. The unexplainable headache. The unusually tender breasts. The annoying pelvic exam. The sore pimple. I see her clearest when I stand in front of the mirror, which holds the jagged reflection of us both. Hers is the color of unground pepper, mine the brown of old honey. No matter where I might go, she has made sure to remind me that I, too, am a woman from Sparta. There are those hips much too wide for the thin, slightly bowed legs. Her big feet, one turned east and the other west, are mine, as are the long fingers that have never known the discipline of an instrument. But it is neither the hips nor the feet that make my mother's friends slap their knees when they see me and say in a declarative tone, "Lord, you must be Carrie's girl." "Yes," I smile. It's the large oval eyes that confess that they've seen more than it's moral to tell and the grin that is somewhere between shy and sly that make them say that. The only difference between us, as I see it, is that I have my father's nose and, my mother adds, my father's ways: stubborn and self-righteous. That, according to her, made me the girl who was "almost" her daughter. She did not seem to find any comfort, either, in the fact that although my sister looked like my father, she had my mother's temperament. In 1966, when my mother gathered up her nerve and her drawers and walked out on my father and their five children, I suppose I always suspected that she was leaving me, her second child and eldest daughter, who favored her but denied her immortality.

My father, whose testimony is not unimpeachable, says that it was after the birth of the first child that he first realized that my mother had a drinking problem. Nineteen years old, new to the big city of Atlanta, married to a gifted but poor young colored man, stuck in the basement of his doting aunt's house and burdened with the care of a newborn, my mother had more than enough to make her look for a melody in a bottle. It is the fact that she was only nineteen that keeps me awake at night. At nineteen, I was in astronomy classes at an Ivy League women's college in New England, tracing the course of the galaxy and talking myself out of marrying a premed student from Long Island because his moon was in the wrong house. Nineteen years old. There must have been something more, I tell myself. "Believe me—being Black, female, poor, married with a new baby and living with in-laws—that's enough to make you drink," says a girlfriend who ought to know. Actually, any two of the six is enough to make you stand on the corner and talk to yourself.

Less than a year after my mother left, my father remarried. Before he and Miss Nancy (this is what we called her, because she was our Sunday school teacher before she was our father's wife) could get back to my great-aunt's house to pick up the furniture he and my mother had shared, my mother had been there and gone. I can still see my father, brothers, and stepbrothers unloading the shredded green French provincial sofa along with the deeply slashed coffee and end tables. My sister and I turned our heads in horror. My father mumbled obscenities and my stepmother bit her lip and muttered, "Lord have mercy." Neither the assorted throw covers that were purchased over the years to drape the sofa nor the pints of finish used to stain those tables could hide, much less blot out, the fierceness of my mother's rage on the day she found out that my father would not come to get her. Because we could not afford to buy new furniture or have what was left professionally reupholstered, the sliced sofa and scratched tables served as permanent reminders of what my stepmother's happiness cost another woman. It was a long time before I could sit on the sofa again.

My mother loves us. I must believe that. She worked all day in a department-store bakery to buy shoes and school tablets, came home to curse out the neighbors who wrongly accused her children of any impropriety (which in an apartment complex usually means stealing), and kept her house cleaner than most sober women. When money permitted, which was rare, or when she didn't give a damn about which bill collector had called that morning asking for "Willie" or "Carrie," she'd bring home a German-chocolate cake, her favorite, for dinner. The sight of her coming across the parking lot smiling slyly, her dark calloused hand swinging the white square box with the skinny string around it, sent us kids into a chorus of giggles, and we raced to see which one would get to her first to relieve her of such a delightful burden. Yes, my mother loved us. She bore us. She nursed us. She worked for us. She cried over us. She stayed up all night holding us when we were sick. Yes, my mother loved us. Even though she left us. I am her eldest daughter. I look just like her, and although I have never been married, have no children, and have never needed anything more than a cold Coke to quench my thirst, I know without ever being told that her leaving us had nothing to do with her love for us. She exercised an option usually reserved for men. She loved us and she left us—for her own reasons. I just regret that she left before we could get to know each other. I had so many things to say to her, like how I was sorry for scratching the only record that made her smile: "Blowing in the Wind" by Stevie Wonder. Mama, if you ever read this, I'm sorry.

It was the not being known that pained me the most when I was a little girl. Known the way I thought all my girlfriends' mothers knew them: "This is Patricia. She is moody and reflective and needs more attention than my other children." I could live with my mother's drinking. And I did. I could live with the haunting sounds of her and my father's battles (they fought unapologetically before us all) that drove me into the bathroom to play church and pull out my hair. I can now forgive her for teaching me how to lie with a straight face to my father, to neighbors, to creditors, and to my playmates. (It was a lesson that took years to unlearn.) I could live with these horrible memories and more. And I have. But it was the not being known for who I singularly was that sent me into the arms of women teachers, neighbors, friends' mothers and perfect strangers— women who did not have the onus of providing for me, and so had the luxury of talking to me.

What my mother was not able to give me, I learned to steal emotionally from other women. I longed for my own private smile from my mother. When it did not come, I learned to be smart enough to be refreshing and witty enough to be charming for others. Being the top student in my class was my way of securing the teacher's attention and affection. I fought anyone who tried to take that away from me. To those beautiful colored women from Albany State, Alabama State, and Fort Valley State who took the time to rebraid a loose plait and spread Jergens lotion across my ashy face, my answers were bright instead of sassy and my opinions thoughtful instead of womanish. They loved me enough to beat me, but not for the same reason as my mother. They beat me believing that there was a limit to who I could become. My mother beat me because she was afraid of what I might become. At night, lying scared and restless in my bed, I dreamed of those sweet-smelling colored women from state colleges. I also dreamed of a woman in a distant room, listening to sad, sad music and the bottomless sound of liquid splashing into a glass. I longed for that woman, singing her sad song, to come tuck me in and reassure me that the shadow across the ceiling was not Billy Goat Gruff who'd come to terrorize me for my sins. I tried to imagine her coming into the room with a broom in one hand and rocking me until I was exhausted with love with the other hand.

Next in significance to those lovely colored teachers, Miss Susie Skinner and Mrs. Daisy Henderson, and the women in the neighborhood who sent me to the store for Kotex, were my paper dolls. Those pale, thin White girls, in pretty lace underwear and contrived smiles, depended on me to speak for them, dress them, fight for them, love them, and give their cardboard lives meaning. In exchange for giving them life, they taught me two things: how to love, and how to heal myself. When their heads fell off, which was often, there were always the ladies in the Sears and Roebuck catalogs. Then there were the dolls made from Coke bottles. The coarse rope that tied store-bought collard greens became their hair.

I now remember how much delight my mother took in buying these things for me. Perhaps she knew. (My God, did she know?) Her buying me paper dolls and ordering catalogs from which she never made purchases and spending money she didn't have on Sally, the pink plastic doll with omniscient eyes who came to my shoulder and danced with me—was this my mother's way of creating a world she was unable to give me? Is this why she never laughed when I'd spend the entire day in the closet with my dolls, and later turned her head when I grew to be a woman and still had long eloquent conversations with myself? In her liquor bottle she found what she must have hoped I would find in my dolls.

Of all those educated colored teachers whom I knew and loved, it was my mother, the skinny bowlegged girl from Sparta with a ninth-grade education, who was the first feminist I ever knew. Everywhere we moved until I was twelve (which was, at last count, thirteen times), no matter how short our tenure, my mother always surrounded herself with women. They drank together, played cards together, danced together, laughed together, fished together, fought one another, scratched one another's heads, and always protected one another from the wrath of husbands, lovers, and boyfriends. For sure, she loved men—my brothers, her brothers, Jackie Wilson, Solomon Burke, and sometimes my father. But she needed women. "She is my girlfriend," she'd blurt out in defense whenever my father accused her of hanging out with "them women" more than he thought she should.

When they were not drinking, my mother and her girlfriends busied themselves with the ceremonies of womanhood—shucking corn, snapping beans, shelling peas, kneading dough, mending hems, folding clothes, and fanning themselves with the hems of their dresses. Invariably, a little girl, like my sister or myself, could be found kneeling between some woman's legs getting her hair combed. "Girl, hush." "Child, please." "Heifer, no." One woman would yell across the room to another over the noises of children and a scratched record. Their words sashayed over our heads—dancing, curtsying, bowing, and finally embracing one another in holy communion. Love of women and appreciation for the sound of a woman saying, "Go on, girl, with you' bad self"—these were my mother's exquisite gifts to my sister and me.

Over the years I tried to forget my mother. There are many Black women who have not been able or eager to talk about our less-than-perfect, our outrageous mothers. It's like playing the dozens on your own self. It's counterrevolutionary, in fact. We have simply sat and nodded while others talked about the magnificent women who bore and raised them and who, along with God, made a way out of no way. We recited their poems. We bought their novels. We paid to hear them lecture about the invincible strength and genius of the Black mother, knowing full well that the image can be as bogus as the one of the happy slave. But we smiled, clapped, and shouted too, because we knew that what our mothers were forced to become was not what they had dreamed for themselves, that part of the healing is learning how to rejoice over other folks' blessings and that our mothers would have wanted us to know that there was another way.

The easiest thing in the world would be to romanticize my mother's drinking, see it as the muted need of a repressed artist who seeks to drink in the fullness of life. That would make a great sermon or poem and would certainly help me get some sleep at night. The next easiest thing would be to blame my father for my mother's illness. This I have done. But the truth is never that simple. Besides, both have a way of overlooking the very real fact that there was an element of choice. Notwithstanding culture and circumstance, my mother chose to drink and retreat, rather than remain sober and fight. No, she did not intend to become an alcoholic. I know that now. She just wanted to get through another day. She did not intend to leave her five children. She just had to get out of that house. My stepmother would always say, "Neetie, I love being a mother. I just get tired, however, of mothering. Sometimes I want to walk out that door and never look back." But she didn't. My mother did. I've had enough experience with depression and madness to know that no matter how absolute the loneliness or the madness, there is always that one final moment—however fleeting—when one can still choose not to let go. It is the difference between Zora Neale Hurston and Virginia Woolf. And mothers are different, too.

I cannot forget my mother. Though not as sturdy as others, she is my bridge. When I needed to get across, she steadied herself long enough for me to run across safely. For that I am grateful. She left before she could crumble before my eyes. Sometimes, when I visit her, I catch myself studying her out of the corner of my eye, wondering what really drove her to drink. The poet in me searches frantically for the subtle turn in the drama. But the woman in me tells me that if what I do know is enough to keep me awake, then I cannot begrudge my mother the desire to sleep through it all.

My mother still lives alone in Atlanta. Her life is filled with her grandchildren, soap operas, her girlfriends, a man friend, and fishing. Our lives have taken radically different courses. I am fulfilled by my ministry and my writing. She is plagued by failing health. When I am depressed, I pray and write poems. When she is depressed, she drinks and waits for a disability check that never comes. When I am happy, I strut and write sermons. When she is happy, she fishes, makes centerpieces of pinecones and needles—and takes a little nip. I have tried giving her my God. And being the well-bred southern lady that she is, she never refuses a gift given from the heart. She simply smiles and nods her head and puts the God I have offered in the shoe box she keeps on the shelf of her closet where she stores her insurance policy and scraps of material for a future quilt. My professional ministry is mainly to women. I preach to them. I cry, shout, pray, and laugh with them. I encourage them to believe that their lives and their situations can be changed. But many times, when I am in the presence of my own mother, I cannot say a mumbling word. Songs, poems, and sermons escape me. "I am a feminist and a minister," I say to myself, "but I cannot reach my mother." But she never holds that against me.

Now I am thirty and she is fifty-two. Both of us are those strange Baker girls from Sparta, Georgia. When it hurts too much to be mother and daughter, we try being girlfriends. In a few weeks I will go home to see her, and this time I think I'll tell her about the Stevie Wonder record. I will call to her through the screen door and watch her saunter across the room with a broom in her hand. There will be a shy grin etched on her face and I'll hear her say, "Girl, hush." A voice inside of me will whisper, "Child, that's your mama." I'll giggle, as I always do, for I know that there is still a chance that the shadow on the wall will be chased away.

MY MOTHER, CARRIE BAKER WEEMS, died in Atlanta just before this article was first published in late 1984. She died from complications due to alcoholism before I could tell her about the Stevie Wonder record, but not before I could ask her to forgive me and tell her that I'd forgiven her.

SMOOTHING THE TUCKS IN FATHER'S LINEN: THE WOMEN OF CEDAR HILL

Miriam DeCosta-Willis

In her biographical sketch of Anna Murray Douglass, *My Mother As I Recall Her*, Rosetta Douglass Sprague portrays the archetypal Black woman of the nineteenth century—wife, mother, worker, and antislavery advocate—while in her letters to Frederick Douglass, Rosetta alludes to problems in her parents' marriage, the marriage of an uneducated, working-class woman to a distinguished man of letters. Originally written as a speech, *My Mother As I Recall Her* was published by Rosetta's daughter, who writes in the foreword, "I am publishing this little booklet that the world may learn some thing [sic] of the noble woman who was the wife of a great man . . . and the mother of his children."[1] The sketch is clearly a defense of the submerged life—a life spent in submission and service to men—for as Anna's grandchild explains:

> Too often are the facts of the great sacrifices and heroic
> efforts of the wives of renowned men overshadowed by
> the achievements of the men and the wonderful and
> beautiful part she has played so well is overlooked.
> (p. 4)

Anna Murray Douglass, whom her granddaughter calls "The Mother of Cedar Hill," grew up in rural Maryland, the child of slaves, Mary and Bambarra Murray.[2] Born around 1813, she was the eighth of twelve children, and the first freeborn.[3] At age seventeen, she went to Baltimore to work as a domestic, spending two years with the Montells and seven years with the Wells family on South Caroline Street. While living in Baltimore, she met and fell in love with Frederick Bailey, a slave, whom she introduced to a circle of free Blacks who belonged to the East Baltimore Improvement Society.[4] With Anna's encouragement, financial support, and assistance (Anna even made the sailor suit that Douglass wore during his escape), Frederick fled North in 1838, reaching New York on September 3. In his

Narrative, Douglass (who by that time had changed his surname) fails to acknowledge the support of Anna Murray (indeed, he mentions her only twice in the 1845 narrative), but Rosetta is proud of the role that her mother played in her father's escape.

> She had lived with the Wells family so long and having been able to save the greater part of her earnings was willing to share with the man she loved that he might gain the freedom he yearned to possess. (p. 9)

A few days after his arrival in New York, Frederick sent for Anna.

> At this time, Anna, my intended wife, came on; for I wrote to her immediately after my arrival at New York, (notwithstanding my homeless, houseless, and helpless condition,) informing her of my successful flight, and wishing her to come on forthwith.[5]

There were many differences between the newlyweds: she was born free, while he was an escaped slave; she was twenty-five, and he was twenty; she was illiterate, but he had learned to read and write; she had money, earned during nine years in service, but he was penniless; she had personal possessions ("a feather bed with pillows, bed linen, dishes, knives, forks and spoons, besides a well filled trunk of wearing apparel for herself," including a "new plum colored silk dress [that] was her wedding gown"), while he had nothing but the clothes on his back.[6] Soon after their marriage, they set out for New Bedford, Massachusetts, where he found work loading boats, shoveling coal, and sweeping chimneys, while his wife labored in their two-room home. Rosetta writes that the "early days in New Bedford were spent in daily toil, the wife at the wash board, the husband with saw, buck and axe" (p. 10). And then the children came: Rosetta in 1839; Lewis in 1840; Frederick, Jr. two years later; Charles in 1844; and, finally, in 1849, Annie, who died at age ten. Soon, Frederick began lecturing at antislavery meetings. Eventually, his work took him away from home for extended periods, and, in 1845, soon after the publication of his slave narrative, he fled to Europe, remaining there for two years. These were difficult years for his wife, who worked as a shoe binder to support her small children (aged one, two, four, and six). Douglass had taken the oldest child, Rosetta, to Albany, where she was cared for during his absence by Abigail and Lydia Mott, two abolitionists and the cousins of Lucretia Mott. Meanwhile, Anna, who was then living in Lynn, Massachusetts, joined the Anti-Slavery Society and sewed articles for the Anti-Slavery Fair at Faneuil Hall in Boston. A hard-working, frugal woman, she managed to support her family, donate some of her earnings to the abolitionist cause, and save what Frederick sent her. Rosetta recalls:

> One day while talking over their affairs, mother arose
> and quietly going to a bureau drawer produced a bank
> book with the sums deposited just in the proportion
> father had sent, the book also contained deposits of her
> own earnings—and not a debt had been contracted dur-
> ing his absence. (p. 13)

Soon after his return to this country, Douglass moved his family to Rochester, New York, where he founded the *North Star*, later called *Frederick Douglass' Paper*. The move was difficult for Anna because, according to her daughter, she had to leave a circle of friends that included Wendell Phillips, William Lloyd Garrison, and their wives, to live in a place where people were less cordial, and where, in the early 1840s, prejudice was rampant. In Rochester, she became reclusive, drawing "around herself a certain reserve" because she was distrustful of others. Dorothy Sterling suggests, however, that Rosetta Douglass was not completely candid in ascribing Anna's unhappiness to her social isolation; Sterling attributes Anna's difficulties, in part, to her husband's relationship with an Englishwoman, Julia Griffiths, who lived with the Douglasses for three years, helping him to edit the *North Star*.[7] Julia's friendship with Douglass continued even after her return to England, where she sent him long letters describing the antislavery activity in that country, while the gossip about "Fred and Julia" spread even onto the pages of Garrison's *Liberator*.[8]

Apparently, her husband's relationships with abolitionists (particularly the women), his frequent absences from home, and his increasing stature as a publisher and orator, only intensified Anna's adoration of and admiration for her husband. According to their daughter, "Father was mother's honored guest." The word *guest* suggests that the Douglasses had a formal, unequal, and distant relationship, for a guest is a stranger to whom one extends hospitality. Further evidence of the social distance between the couple is the fact that Anna always addressed her husband as "Mr. Douglass," while he frequently called her "Mother," indicating that she was important to him primarily as the mother of his children.[9]

Although by this time she had a laundress to help with her large family's wash, Anna Douglass attended to her husband's laundry personally, managing to keep his linen immaculate: "she must with her own hands smooth the tucks in father's linen and when he was on a long journey she would forward at a given point a fresh supply" (p. 16). Rosetta paints an idealized portrait of her mother, describing her as an untiring worker, a warm hostess, a Christian woman, a virtuous and temperate person, and a stern disciplinarian. Only once does she suggest that Anna and Frederick disagreed on her function as a wife:

> Mother occasionally traveled with father on his short
> trips, but not as often as he would have liked as she
> was a housekeeper who felt that her presence was nec-
> essary in the home . . . (p. 14)

In her letters, however, she reveals that all was not well in the Douglass household.[10] In 1862, she wrote to her father, "I often think of your loneliness for I well perceive the necessity of congenial companions," implying that there was little companionship between Douglass and his wife, who was also described as unhappy.[11] Clearly, Rosetta adored and admired her father, explaining to him that "most of my ideas of morality and uprightness of character I have learned from you father."[12] She attributes her intelligence to her father—to their "table talks" and his encouragement of her reading, adding, almost as an afterthought, that "for smaller things mother has given some counsel."[13] Evidently her father had chastised her for spreading "family differences," but she denied telling people "things with which they have no business."[14]

In 1869, when she was a mature young woman of thirty, a wife (albeit an unhappy one), and a mother, Rosetta wrote to her father very explicitly about the alienation within the family:

> You say you are a lonely man. No one knows it better
> than myself and the causes. I have felt it for years for I
> have been in a measure lonely myself but would not al-
> low myself to analyze my feeling as I was the daughter
> and had duties to fulfill in that relation. I knew where
> my sympathies were . . . I never dared to show much
> zeal about anything where you were concerned as I
> could very readily bring a storm about my ears if I en-
> dorsed any of your sentiments about matters pertaining
> to the household.[15]

Such sentiments indicate that she identified with and sympathized with her father, for she was like him in many ways. In contrast to her mother, Rosetta Douglass led a somewhat privileged life. As a child, she went to Albany, New York, to live with Quaker sisters in a White, middle-class, cultured environment. Later, her parents moved to Rochester where her family, somewhat affluent by then, moved into a two-story, nine-room brick house.[16] Because the Rochester public schools did not admit Blacks until 1857, Rosetta attended the fashionable Seward Seminary until her father discovered that she was forced to sit in a separate room away from the White students.[17] For a while, she studied under a White governess, and then spent a year in the preparatory department at Oberlin College Academy studying business. Rosetta then returned home to help her father with his correspondence, and, in the spring of 1862, moved to Philadelphia in an unsuccessful attempt to obtain a teaching position. She taught for a short time in a country school, and then, in the fall of 1862, went to teach in Salem, Massachusetts, one of the few cities that hired Blacks in its public schools.[18] While there, she embroidered garments, knitted edgings, and taught classes on Tuesday, Wednesday, Thursday, and Friday nights to supplement her income. In 1863, Rosetta married Nathan Sprague, an untrained, poorly educated ex-slave, who served during the Civil War with the Massachusetts 54th in South Carolina. After the birth of their first baby, she returned to Rochester to live with her parents. Her husband's business ventures, launched with the assistance of Frederick Douglass, all failed, and he was sent to the penitentiary for stealing money from the post office. In 1876, Rosetta Sprague sold her personal property—49¾ yards of Brussels carpet, two marble top stands, a small rocking chair, and other luxurious furnishings—as well as two pieces of real estate for $3,700, then moved to Washington to join her parents at Cedar Hill.[19] In Washington, she supported her six children (the seventh died) by working with her father and clerking in various government offices.

Rosetta and her mother shared similar experiences: they worked for a time before marriage (Anna for nine years, Rosetta for one); married in their mid-twenties; had several children (Anna five, Rosetta seven); were separated from their husbands for long periods; had to support their children during those absences; and participated in nineteenth-century social reform movements (Anna in the antislavery cause, Rosetta in the women's club movement). Rosetta, however, led a sheltered life as the child of a prominent, Black, middle-class family, who could offer her a superior education, emotional support during times of crisis, and financial assistance throughout her life. Rosetta returned often to live with her parents (in 1862, 1870, and 1876), first as a single woman, and then as a wife and mother. Apparently, Rosetta and Anna were supportive of each other as adults. On March 26, 1867, Rosetta wrote her father, "Mother came down one day and helped me to get somewhat put to rights,"[20] and, two weeks later, she added, "I ran up to the house yesterday to see mother. She was not well at all. She complained of dizziness in the head. I gave her some pills and tomorrow I am going up again."[21] In 1875, Anna Douglass left her husband behind in Washington and went to Rochester to help her daughter in the difficult period following the death of Rosetta's little girl Alice.[22]

The daughter also served as the family secretary and as her mother's amanuensis. Anna Douglass never learned to read and write, although "her husband hired a tutor for her and the children, but she gave up quickly, protesting that she was too old to learn."[23] In 1851, she dictated a letter to her eleven-year-old daughter that Dorothy Sterling describes as "in sharp contrast to Frederick Douglass's eloquent and polished writing."[24] Although Anna Douglass was an unlettered woman, she supported her children in their educational pursuits, agreeing with Frederick that Rosetta should withdraw from a segregated school, and encouraging her youngest daughter, Annie, to study German when she was only ten years old.[25]

In spite of the symbiotic relationship with her mother, Rosetta Douglass Sprague is clearly her father's daughter, as she reveals in correspondence with him that began in 1846, when she was only seven years old, and ended only with his death in 1895. What motivated her, then, to write *My Mother As I Recall Her* when she felt such a strong attachment to her father—a distinguished statesman, prominent man of letters, and patriarch of Cedar Hill? It is possible that she wrote the sketch after her father's death in reaction to Douglass's association with other women, particularly White women like Julia Griffith and Helen Douglass, her father's second wife. Indeed, Douglass's remarriage to a much younger White woman was deeply resented by some members of the Black community, although Rosetta wrote a letter of thanks to John E. Bruce on March 27, 1895, and signed it "from Helen, Rosetta, Lewis and Charles Douglass."[26]

Still, the biography of her mother can be read as "A Defense of the Black Wife and Mother."

Another possibility is that the *Sketch* is a manifestation of Rosetta's feminist consciousness, a consciousness that was elevated by her participation in the Black women's club movement during the last decade of the nineteenth century. Although not an activist, nor a major figure in the movement, Rosetta was called on to address public assemblies, like the first convention of the National Association of Negro Women, after her father's death. This was the age of race women like Mary Church Terrell, Anna J. Cooper, Fanny Jackson Coppin, Fannie Barrier, and Ida Wells-Barnett, who underscored the role of Black women in the moral, spiritual and educational advancement of the Negro race. Influenced by the uplift movement, first articulated by Maria Stewart in 1832, Rosetta Sprague must have realized that her mother, like so many wives of prominent men, had never received recognition for the role that she played in making a public life possible for her husband. Anna Murray Douglass, wife and mother, is ennobled ("the noble woman"), enlarged, and elevated in a process of deification that transforms her from woman to Woman, metaphor of a race of superwomen. As her granddaughter explains, "she stretches out her *motherly* arms and gathers to her grateful bosom the *daughters of her race*" (p. 4, italics added).

Finally, it is possible that Rosetta Sprague, like many Black men and women, was influenced by the nineteenth-century Cult of True Womanhood, whose believers maintained that the home is woman's "proper sphere" in her role as wife, mother, and homemaker.[27] This emphasis on woman's domestic role undergirded and supported the uplift movement, whose adherents— writers, teachers, ministers, and even women reformers— stressed the sanctity of the home and the wife/mother's sacred mission in that domain. Thus, Rosetta Douglass Sprague's sketch is much more than a portrait of her mother. It is also a figuration of the archetypal nineteenth-century Black woman.

NOTES

1. Rosetta Douglass Sprague, *My Mother As I Recall Her* (n.p., 1900), p. 4. Subsequent references to this work are noted in the text of the paper. Grammatical errors in the original text have not been corrected.

2. The Douglass home in Anacostia, Washington, D.C.

3. Rosetta D. Sprague writes that the exact date of her mother's birth is unknown, but Dorothy Sterling, in *We Are Your Sisters* (New York: W.W. Norton, 1984), p. 133, lists a birthdate of 1813.

4. Sylvia Lyons Render, "Afro-American Women: The Outstanding and the Obscure," *The Quarterly Journal of the Library of Congress* 32 (October 1975):p.308.

5. Frederick Douglass, *Narrative of the Life of Frederick Douglass, An American Slave* (Boston: The Anti-Slavery Office, 1845; reprinted New York: Dolphin Books, 1963), p. 108.

6. Sprague, *My Mother*, p. 9.

7. Sterling, *Your Sisters*, p. 135.

8. Ibid., pp. 136–37.

9. Render, "Afro-American Women," p. 310.

10. Most of the letters referred to here are those published in Sterling's *We Are Your Sisters*.

11. Sterling, *Your Sisters*, p. 142.

12. Ibid.

13. Ibid.

14. Ibid.

15. Ibid., pp. 420–21.

16. Render, "Afro-American Women," p. 308.

17. Sterling, *Your Sisters*, p. 138.

18. In 1856, immediately after graduation from the Salem Normal School, Charlotte Forten was hired to teach at the Epes Grammar School of Salem with a salary of $200 a year. See Charlotte Forten, *The Journal of Charlotte Forten* (New York: W.W. Norton, 1953), p. 24 and p. 230, n. 57.

19. Sterling, *Your Sisters*, p. 421.

20. Ibid. pp. 418–19.

21. Ibid. p. 419.

22. Render, "Afro-American Women," p. 309.

23. Sterling, *Your Sisters*, p. 135.

24. Ibid.

25. Render, "Afro-American Women," p. 309.

26. Bruce Collection (Box 2, file 3, Ms. 162), Schomburg Center for Research in Black Culture, New York.

27. Barbara Welter, "The Cult of True Womanhood: 1820–1860," *American Quarterly* 18 (Summer 1966):151–74.

P A R T

4

FRAYING EDGES: TENSIONS

It is critical that we do not romanticize the struggles of Black mothers by failing to acknowledge and understand fully the psychological and physical costs of their survival.

BEVERLY GREENE, 1990

Historically, one of the most pervasive images of Black women in America has been that of the "superstrong, resilient mother who is devoted, self-sacrificing, understanding and wise," her love "enduring, unconditional and without error."[1] In this section, portrayals of our "less than perfect" mothers underscore the difficulties of motherhood and the sometimes problematic relationships between Black mothers and their daughters. There are unconventional images of Black mothers here—women who defy the stereotype of the all powerful, nearly perfect matriarch. There are moving narratives which convey the anguish of daughters attempting to come to terms with their far from perfect relationships with their mothers. An incest survivor painfully recalls her mother's refusal to protect her from a sexually abusive father. Another daughter writes poignantly about her mother's preference for her curly haired brother.

We hope that this more balanced view will deepen our understanding of the complex experience of African-American motherhood. An appreciation of the turbulence *and* tenderness which sometimes characterizes relationships between Black mothers and daughters is necessary for a fuller understanding of both the strengths and weaknesses of Black families. We acknowledge in this anthology the struggles of *all* our mothers, even the less sturdy ones, whose flawed attempts to ensure the survival of their daughters in a sometimes hostile environment can not be overlooked. Renita Weems reminds us: "I cannot forget my mother. Though not as sturdy as others, she is my bridge. For that I am grateful."[2]

Like the worn quilt with tattered edges, Black mothers and daughters have weathered enormous difficulties, struggled to overcome many tensions. Ultimately, we must both forgive the other for not being what is impossible—perfect.

Janet Sims-Wood

NOTES

1. Gloria Wade-Gayles, "The Truths of Our Mothers' Lives: Mother-Daughter Relationships in Black Women's Fiction," *SAGE: A Scholarly Journal on Black Women* 1 (Fall 1984):8.

2. See Renita Weems's essay in this collection, pp. 123–30, for a discussion of our "outrageous" mothers. See also Beverly Greene's essay "Sturdy Bridges: The Role of African-American Mothers in the Socialization of African-American Children" in a special issue of *Women and Therapy*, "Motherhood: A Feminist Perspective," 10, nos. 1/2 (1990):205–25.

BEATRICE'S NECK

Ann T. Greene

My mother was
is
the darling of her hometown.
She and Miriam
her girlfriend then
laughed in the pews at Mt. Zion.
Their silky brown
in summer auburn heads bent
shoulders heaving
tongues battling illicit giggles
incited by another look at Beatrice.

Beatrice with her skinny neck
sitting a pew (or two)
in front of Mother and Miriam
whose curly locks freed from the
paper bag knots of the night before
danced.

Two colored Shirleys
Shirley Temples
with their saucy curls
unneeding heat.
Blessed brown girls of natural beauty
brown curled daughters
of the colored gentry
finger the lace hankies
Aunt Mamie starched and pressed
into their expectant hands.

Hankies full of pennies
copper pennies for Sunday collection at
Mt. Zion Church of God
where they would see Beatrice's neck
black

snow-capped by a pimple on the leathered skin
made by the tracks of Sun's rays
on her cotton picking back.

Oh how their eyes traveled
the creases of Beatrice's neck.
Oh how they filled with mirth
having seen the tell tale scars
the meniscus of pinked underskin at the hairline's edge
where Beatrice had touched up her naps.

Miriam laughed (between the Psalms)
and my mother hit her their heads bounced together
colliding stars
these colored Shirleys
Shirley Temples
beloved daughters of the negro gentry
pretty girls with good hair
disturbing knotted hankies
of copper pennies
sated with the knowledge of Beatrice's shame.

My mother darling
of her hometown married my father.
It was spite
she confessed as she furrowed my scalp.
She gave him four children
nappyheaded every one.
She sighed as if to say
Do I deserve this?
Four?

She followed me around the kitchen
we waltzed across the living room
the hot comb in her hand.
The smoke swirled leaving behind
the stink of my hair my burned ear.
All it took was that first touch
when
after she had sipped from her glass of gin
gin like heavy water where I glared distorted
half-done

one side in plaits
still throbbing from their shackling
the other oiled
aroused upright before being rolled in
paper strips and tied down
with a scarf of romping deer.
Then tied in a nylon net
and forbidden
although there was still
Saturday's light
to go outside.
Forbidden to play
almost to breathe
admonished to keep still sleep tight.

She sipped her gin and arched that red hot comb
before my eyes
I saw the burning before I felt it
and I ran half-crazed
half-done
away from her kitchen through the house
everywhere.
I was so ugly anyway
what difference did it make?

My mother
darling of her hometown
followed my father
before he was my father
out of Carolina and colored doorways.

And away from Mt. Zion
to the passionless droning of white
psalmody
where I and my brothers would be made to sit
with my father every Sunday morning.
He glistened with sweat and we
his copper pennies wrapped in the starch of
our mother's fury
buttoned and laced into silence we would sit
visible as all Hell
absent as nothingness

and my brothers with their shaven scalps
would point to me
my burns the pinked rims of my tender ears
slathered with vaseline and radiating blood
for anyone to see.
My brothers would
heads together
sparks flying
from the friction of their hairs
blow snot between their fingers and choke into their palms
as their eyes slid sideways to look at me.
My father, whom I was made of,
could hear their laughter
and feel my eyes beg for sanctuary.
Oh Daddy please make them stop.
It's not my fault.

But he was quiet
My Father said little to anyone, ever.
He had not spoken to my mother since my youngest brother
came who was not black like the rest of us.
He looked unlike my father and had my mother's hair.

So that she loved him more than life itself
she told me
and it was with him to him
that her unginned attention went.
It was his head not mine
not Daddy's
which lay between her milkless breasts and
her steady hands would walk through his scalp
and she would sing to him
my baby
my pretty baby.

In the summer it was that one
her favorite her curly-headed darling
that went home with her to Mama's house
and stayed inside
so as not to get darker
while I stayed behind reluctantly growing up
to starch and iron my father's shirts

and cook his pork chops which he ate in silence
with no grace.
Until the moment
the only moment we had together he took me in his
green De Soto to the beauty parlor
and stepped inside with his hat in hand.

Into the women's lair
with their naked heads prior to perfection.
(Before beauty, absolution.)
And he said to the beautician,
brownskinned, with Spanish curls divining her face,
Can you do something with it?

The beautician took my motherless hair
unwashed
unpressed
in one hand.
Dismay darkened her pretty face and she told my
father
This will take a while.
And he nodded relieved that it was not too late
after all.
She took me in the back and pushed me in a chair
and said
Velma see if you can do something with this girl's hair.

So that when my father arrived
(the setting sun backlighting his return)
and saw what Velma had done for me
he almost smiled.
He walked around my slatted body
he stood behind me in the mirror
and gave Velma a handful of dollars.
He offered me his arm and I
the woman to the green De Soto strolled
towards home.

SUCCESSIONS

Valerie Jean

Like my mother did, I yell
at my daughter, watch her rage
a back-talk I could never
speak. As a child, the words
my mother's hands refused
to hear got snapped, or broken
in the frenzied marks left
burning on my face and legs.
It makes me crazy, sometimes,
hearing words I had to swallow,
come out bold and equal in
their intensity to my own
talk. Trying to make sense
to a grown-up-child, a woman
must be strong, like my mother
was. But often, when my anger
lashes quick, it strikes hard,
threatening to expose how close
to surfaces old wounds heal.
My daughter does not know
of leather straps or branches
stripped and thinned for
whistling deep and lasting
scars, like my mother must have
gotten. Losing her mother
at ten, then being shifted from
one aunt to another, she was
taken in, after three years,
by her father's people, this
his only contribution to her
growing, and she had to learn
to keep her mouth in check,
like her mother never taught

her to. The things my mother
learned of rage and silence,
she taught me, what my daughter
does not know. The way we roar
our thunder, we shout loud,
insistent words between us.
Now, I have to fight to hide
a violence in my hands and
in my blood, while I struggle
to maintain this delicate
balance I have forged between
my mother's distant scream
and the other voice I recognize
as mine, but spilling from
the open lips of my daughter.

STEPMOTHER

Irma McClaurin

She cannot see herself in me
I am not the daughter of her flesh
only the shadow of his last wife.
Inside the rolls of flesh,
a body no one wants
beats itself by eating more.
She does not understand this stringbean
of a stepdaughter is hungry too.
We both wait inside his house
for a man neither of us knows.

From *Pearl's Song* (Detroit: Lotus Press, 1988); reprinted by permission of the author.

REFLECTIONS OF A
"GOOD" DAUGHTER

Bell Hooks

I am most passionate in my relationship with mama. It is with
her that I feel loved and sometimes accepted. She is the one
person who looks into my heart, sees its needs, and tries to
satisfy them. She is also always trying to make me be what she
thinks it is best for me to be. She tells me how to do my hair,
what clothes I should wear. She wants to love and control at the
same time. Her love is sustained and deep. Sometimes I feel
like a drowning person, saved by the pulling and tugging, saved
by the breath of air that is her caring. I want to tell her this but
the gifts we buy on Mother's Day, at Christmas, on birthdays
seem only to make a mockery of that love, to suggest that it is
something cheap and silly, something that is not needed. I do
not want to give these gifts. I do not want to take these times
to show my care, times someone else has chosen. She interprets
my silence, my last minute effort at a gift, as a sign of the way
I am an uncaring girl. The fact that I disappoint her leaves me
lying awake at night sobbing, wanting to be a better daughter,
a daughter that makes her life brighter, easier. I am a pain to
her. She says that she is not sure where I come from, that she
would like to send me back. I want so much to please her and
yet keep some part of me that is my self, my own, not just a
thing I have been turned into that she can desire, like, or do
with as she will. I want her to love me totally as I am. I love
her totally without wanting her to change anything, not even the
things about her that I cannot stand.

Whenever I try to speak to her about the things that weigh
deeply on my heart, that press it down so that I feel as though
a huge stone has fallen and is crushing me, she changes the
subject. I think it is because she cannot bear to hear about a
pain that she cannot understand, that she cannot make better.
She has no time for pain. There is so much work for her to do.
When I use the word lonely she does not say anything. She
closes her ears. Although she does not know I can see, it is as
if the second pair of hands—the pair she stows away in pockets,

closets, and drawers to get all the work done that there is no time to do—those invisible hands cover her ears. She does not want to hear the word loneliness. She does not want to remember because they are tired. I tell her that I want to die before her, that I cannot live without her. She is angry. She thinks these are too strange words for a daughter to say. She tells me to shut up saying foolish things. She tells me that of course she will die before me, that she is older. She says such thoughts will drive me crazy, that I should be outside playing, outside being young and happy.

They can tell that their mama is not like other mothers. They can see that she is working hard to give them more than food, shelter, and clothes to wear; that she wants to give them a taste of the delicious, a vision of beauty, a bit of ecstasy. Even so, she is obsessed with the latest products. Even so, she is moving away from her awareness of the deeper inner things of life and worrying more about money. I watch these changes in her and worry. I want her never to lose what she has given me—a sense that there is something deeper, more to this life than the everyday.

When she speaks of dying I do not want to listen. I do not want to ever imagine a world in which she is not. She tells us that we must know the possibility that is her death. She tells us where everything important is. She tells us about the clothes she would like to be buried in, about where in her chest of drawers we can find things. She wants to make us close to one another—a family that can go on even if she is no longer with us. We are not sure what all this talk of death means. We know it must mean something. She tells us finally that she is very sick, that she must go into the hospital to have an operation. We know that it is serious because she does not go to the Black hospital but across town, to the one we cannot walk to, where we know no one. When we want to know what is wrong, what is really wrong, she does not say. This is one of her ways that I cannot stand. Trying to protect us, she makes us very afraid, so afraid we are silent. Words like cancer, tumor, hang suspended in the air like rain in dark clouds waiting to soak us at any moment. It is the uncertainty that makes me hide in books. She sees it as another sign that I am uncaring, without feeling, hateful. I see the invisible hands cover her eyes so that she does not have to see our fear. Since she cannot say there is nothing to worry about, do not be afraid, she refuses to acknowledge our fear.

She does not think about being sick. She is busy planning, shopping for the food, planning meals, making lists, tiring herself out. She has no space during the day to be afraid. I lie awake at night listening, wondering if she is lying in the dark crying, wondering if she is clutching her body trying to ward off the coldness of death. I hear nothing but the sound of her footsteps as she walks from the front of the house to the back, finishing some chore she cannot leave until morning. We want to know if we will be able to visit her in the hospital. It is then that we see the fear in her lips, the trembling, the hesitation. Again she wants to protect us, again she is hiding. I walk away. I cannot stand the hiding. I cannot stand all the secret places I have had to make inside myself. No one comes to stay with us, not like the old days. We are big. We are able to follow orders. We fear punishment if we disobey. To come home from school and find her not there is already a hint of loss. We feel the emptiness, the cold place that her heart warms. We go from room to room to see if everything is still there, in place.

They say she is near death, that we must go and see her because it may be the last time. I will not go. I have my own ideas about death. I see her all the time. I see her as she moves about the house doing things, cooking, cleaning, fussing. I refuse to go. I cannot tell them why, that I do not want to have the last sight of her be there in the white hospital bed, surrounded by strangers and the smell of death. She does not die. She comes home angry, not wanting to see the uncaring daughter, the one who would not even come to say goodbye. She is in control. She is not yet ready to love. She does not understand. Upstairs in my hiding place I cry. They tell her I am upstairs crying and will not stop. She sends me orders—to stop crying right this minute, that I have nothing to cry about, that she should be crying to have such a terrible daughter. When I go to her, sitting on the bed, with my longing and my tears, she knows that she breaks my heart a little. She thinks I break her heart a little. She cannot know the joy we feel that she is home alive.

A DAUGHTER
SURVIVES INCEST:
A RETROSPECTIVE ANALYSIS

Linda H. Hollies

There has been a gigantic mountain in my life since the age of twelve or thirteen. This mountain could not be moved, and it was too overwhelming for me, a child, to attempt to climb. I didn't have the faintest idea that a mountain could be chipped away at, or even tunneled through. So, what did I do with this mountain? I tried to ignore it! I was positive that no other individual could have a mountain like this in her life. This type of mountain didn't have a name; it was never mentioned in my world. The mountain didn't have a face; it appeared in the night, simply as an ugly mess. Now, if it had no name or face, how could I describe it to anyone? If I didn't talk about it, maybe it would just go away.

My father brought this mountain into my world, for, you see, I am the victim of incest. He was a very angry man. He was called "Thor, god of thunder" by his children. He yelled, screamed, and hurled insult upon insult at us. His demeanor was seldom pleasant, either at home or away; he was a strict disciplinarian and quick to whip with the handy strap. He was emotionally, physically, and mentally abusive to me and my seven siblings; his behavior toward my mother was the same. I cannot remember one kind or encouraging remark my father ever made to me; my accomplishments were usually belittled or ignored.

The act of incest alone is enough to cause one psychological trauma and lifelong emotional damage, but when coupled with heavy theological ramifications, one is in double-trouble! My father was the assistant pastor of the small, family-type, Pentecostal church I was raised in and where God's love was constantly preached; respect for parents was another favorite topic. But the most popular theme was the sinner and the sinner's abode in hell. Well, I had problems. I could not love this man who came into my bedroom and did unmentionable things to me; I could not believe that God could love me and yet allow this to continue. I surely had no respect for my father as a parent. Therefore, I was a sinner, right?

Another dynamic at play was the fact that my father found scripture to justify the liberties he took with me (the story of Lot and his two daughters, who had sex with him after they made him drunk, to perpetuate the lineage). Now, if this was a Biblical injunction, sanctioned by Scripture, why was I threatened and physically abused when I was told not to talk about this to anyone, and especially not my mother? Of course, my father had an answer: "Your mother has had one heart attack, and if she really doesn't understand the Bible, this might kill her,"—a typical threat. I did not know that this was just another lie, but I did know that I didn't want my mother to die. What would happen to me then?

Now, when I was growing up, there were no "Just Say No" programs, no television coverage, no Oprah Winfrey show— there was no one to talk to about this mountain that I faced. I wondered what I had done to invoke this invasion of my person, this assault against what I had been taught was good and decent behavior? Was I really going to hell? I could not receive any clarification or reassurance because there was no one to talk to about this ugly mess. I felt I should love my parents because "this is the first commandment with the promise of long life," and I surely wanted to live long. What was I to do? Ignore the mountain? Try to push it out of my mind? Pray about it? Have faith? Would it disappear?

As I have since learned, my rationalizations were typical of someone raised in a dysfunctional family: don't talk about the issue; don't feel; be loyal to the family and do not allow outsiders to know what's going on. I knew outsiders should not be brought into this mess, but why couldn't my mother see, hear, and know what was going on? Couldn't she notice my anguish—intuit my grief—how could she not be aware of my pain?

My mother was the "total woman." She was always well groomed, in a starched house dress, and she would never wear curlers or sleepwear around the house. She was a good cook and an immaculate housekeeper. She was the "perfect" wife; whatever her husband said was LAW! She related to all of us as the woman who carried out her husband's orders and commands. My siblings and I went almost everywhere she went, because my father was "too much of a man" to babysit! He was "too saved" to allow her to use any form of birth control, and she was "too saved" to disobey. She never made any decision without consulting him. Although we spent a great deal of time with her, she was not emotionally available to any of us; seldom did she smile or display affection toward us, except for the perfunctory good morning, good-bye, hello, and good-night kisses that my father demanded from all of us. She was repressed, afraid of conflict and rejection and never knew what "living" was all about. Her husband would not allow her to work because that might invoke rebellion—with her role as wife; her function was to be mother to his children.

As I reflect on the experiences and traumas of my childhood, I am amazed and grateful that I have sanity today, but I realize that I have the natural instincts of a survivor. The atmosphere in our home was perhaps similar to a slave labor camp, with father as master and mother as general overseer. There were no loving relationships; we related to my father out of fear and to my mother out of respect. My father used the word love to justify his cruel behavior—"it's because I love you that I must whip you." I recall the one time he asked me if I loved him and I honestly replied, "No." He tried to slap the "hell" out of me. "Little saved girl, you MUST love your father and respect him as well!" I was an adult, married and pregnant with my first child, when I challenged my mother and heard her say to me, for the very first time, "I love you." And they were my primary caregivers, nurturers, protectors from the outside world? From them I was to learn trust and intimacy?

I married my childhood sweetheart immediately upon graduation from high school. He was shy, introverted, and had a horrible relationship with his parents. He was just what I needed, a man who was an emotional mess, who wouldn't make too many demands upon me. We were together long enough to have two sons and to make life miserable for each other. He is a decent human being; I simply refused to be "wife." My earliest prayer was never to be like my mother, the "total woman."

The most significant incident in this lifelong struggle involved my sister, Jacqui. She was "my" baby. She is three years younger and I looked after her (as a matter of fact, with mother's constant pregnancies, I looked after all of my siblings and my mother as well!). After I moved out of the house, my father approached my sister to molest her. The same pattern and the same threat were involved, but my sister didn't accept this "strange" behavior. She called me.

I approached my husband, who was somewhat aware of my personal history. I had explained to him why I would not visit my mother except when my father was at work and why I would not allow my sons to stay overnight. When I told him about the situation, we went to see an attorney. His advice was to consult with my mother, have a warrant sworn out and have my father arrested. My husband even told my mother that we would move into her home and take over financial responsibility. She absolutely refused. However, she did confront my father and the molestation of my sister ceased.

I felt relieved for Jacqui, but I became very angry with my mother as I thought about her behavior when I finally told her what was going on with me at the age of sixteen. This was after enduring three years of hell all alone, not having a big sister to turn to, and not trusting that my mother would believe my word against my father. She was wise enough to "set" my father up— she walked in and "caught him in the very act." He cried, asked forgiveness, and of course she forgave him. When I asked to move out of state in order to reside with her brother, she replied, "You have to stay here. Your father loves me, nothing will happen to you again!" When the molestation and rape resumed, there was no reason to return to her. My back was against the wall. My mother was no protection for me; she could not provide the emotional nurturing I needed for growth and development.

After the break-up of my first marriage, I was a single parent, a working adult and enjoying a measure of success, yet the mountain was still in control. My sense of worth was steadily diminishing; nothing covered my deep sense of shame. The "filth" of my secret was eating me up and there was no one to confide in. I desired intimacy, but I was afraid to allow anyone, male or female, to come close to knowing me. I had no experience in relating in honest relationships. The demands that I placed on myself to "be perfect" did not allow for leisure, nor did I have the patience with others who wouldn't or couldn't measure up to my specifications.

I was a very unhappy woman. I remarried. This time I selected a man who was twelve years my senior. He too was from an unstable home and had been in a bad marriage and was an active alcoholic. Once again I selected a man who would need me and yet was emotionally unavailable to me. To further complicate matters, we had a daughter.

My sons did not prevent me from working long hours (my job was in the steel mills), as long as I provided the monetary benefits, but having a daughter meant to me that some major lifestyle changes were necessary. So, I went back to school to complete degree requirements and to get a professional position so that I would have quality time to spend with my little girl. My husband's insecurities caused him to challenge this desire for additional education, and since I refused to compromise (or be controlled) I left him, moved to a city miles away, and enrolled.

While living with a friend and her family, I began to attend church services at the United Methodist Church. Their theological stance was broadly based; their "God" was not so restrictive. And in this setting I again considered my personal relationship with God. This God loved me, just as I was; this God invited me to come and receive the abundant life. This was appealing to a survivor—I wanted to know what "authentic" living was all about. But, the mountain was still there, and I was not able to talk to anyone. I still hated my father; I went to talk with him and apologized for hating him all those years. He did not understand my pain nor my anger. Forgiveness was supposed to follow my repentance, but I never felt forgiven, for I honestly could not forgive him! Most importantly, I could not forget! But, this newfound relationship with God and a new community was too delightful to turn my back on. Once again I felt that if I could just pray correctly and ignore this mountain, it would go away.

Finally, the burden of carrying this secret became too much, so I went to the pastor to "confess." With much emotion, I told my story and he listened attentively, after which he advised me to "agree with him in prayer." When I left, I had two secrets: one from my childhood, and the newly found secret that my "new" relationship with God did not perform the miracle of wiping my memory clean or restoring love for my father within my heart. The fault/blame had to be mine; this was the only logical conclusion. The mountain was yet in control.

Where was the peace in my life? My other endeavors, such as working with the Christian Education Department and the young adult ministry in the local church, completing university requirements, and reuniting with my husband after two years did not bring release from the mental and emotional bondage to "the mountain." The cycle continued—better jobs, more material gains, even professional positions and recognition—but the shame and humiliation which caused me to doubt my self-worth and faith, remained.

The Christian experience challenged me to grow and expand my horizons. I felt "called," but I did not feel worthy and I certainly was not ready! I decided to continue work in the church, but I would keep my full-time, well-paid position as supervisor at General Motors. On the other hand, I was getting more and more involved in the life of the local congregation. Could God actually require more? Besides, my father is a minister and I have no trust in him. Would I be accepted/trusted if the story of the mountain was known? For surely I had a great part in the mountain, right? If I was going to minister to others, I had to look good—act as if I had it all together and had MOST of the answers.

At the age of forty, I met Dr. Lee M. Jones, a United Methodist pastor. He challenged me to attend seminary and to allow God full use of my time, talents, and gifts. But this man did not know my story! Unfortunately, Dr. Lee was in my life for only two months, as he and his family were transferred to the east coast for another assignment. His wife, my husband, he, and I, discussed this matter of seminary and spent time in prayer together. My husband, surprisingly, was open to this new idea and did not oppose me at all. So, in September of 1984 I entered Garrett-Evangelical Theological Seminary. My daughter and I moved to Evanston, Illinois, and rented an apartment; my husband remained in our home and visited on his off days. This was one of the most exciting periods of my life. New knowledge, new people, new avenues for expressing ministry!

I had heard of Clinical Pastoral Education, known as CPE, but I could find no Black students who had taken it. The school required a full battery of psychological tests as well as two counseling sessions. God, the mountain will show up! I will not pass these tests, for I am determined to be honest—well, as honest as I can be. I will talk about an abusive father, but I won't say that I was sexually abused. I won't look so bad. I passed! I'm going to take CPE!

I wanted a female supervisor because I felt she would understand better, and I applied to one center where I knew a female would supervise during the summer. I was accepted. Beth Burbank was relatively young and fairly reserved, but she was aware of mental abuse issues, as her mother had a history of psychotic breaks. It was not my issue, but I decided to give it a chance and work toward impacting the mountain.

My goals were to risk being vulnerable; to work on a personal statement of theodicy; to learn how to relax and have fun; and to come to terms with my own mortality. Supervision was not easy for me. I couldn't open up and be honest with Beth. She related that she had never supervised a northern Black woman before, so I wanted to "look good" to this White woman. And I wanted to impress her because I had shared with her that CPE just might be the vehicle for my ministry.

The group experience was so powerful for me. When I finally had a trust level with the group and the process allowed me to risk letting them know about my mountain, I did share—I told of my experience as a child and young adult, with no emotions being expressed. "It happened, I survived." The youngest woman in the group, the one who was the "baby" in our system, told me that she felt my pain and said that I didn't have to be strong. Then she gave me permission to cry. This was a breakthrough! This experience began my grieving process over a lost childhood and innocence; over the rejection by both parents and the lack of love and trust in my life. Finally, I was able to appropriate blame where it belonged—on my father, not onto myself. I was also able to experience anger in such a negative manner, and the church equated anger with "sin," so there was never an open expression of anger being worked through positively in our family. As children, the admission of anger had been cause for a whipping.

One day Beth was sharing "story theology" with us and read *Psalms* 139, which is her favorite passage. As she read verse 13: "For you have formed my inward parts; you have covered me in my mother's womb." The word "formed" seemed to swell within my head. I could actually see myself as a dot sitting on the head of a pin in my mother's womb. I began to watch the forming, shaping, and becoming of "baby" Linda. God seemed to be a mockery to me at that instant as never before. Overwhelmed, I jumped up and ran from the group into the women's toilet. Beth concluded her remarks to the group and found me sitting in a stall, crying. When she inquired what was wrong, I replied, "nothing." When she questioned why I had run out of the group, I replied, "I don't know." Beth then asked, "Linda, are you angry?" I replied, "Of course not!" I could not conceive of anyone who would dare admit to anger at God. Beth managed to talk me out of the stall, and that day, in the toilet, we had one of our best supervisory sessions. She taught me about anger, constructive and destructive. I realized authentic anger that day. I claimed my anger. I chipped at the mountain. The mountain moved.

After only one quarter of CPE, I learned more about myself than I had ever known. I became vulnerable, took risks, and grew because I experienced caring and acceptance, with my faults and limitations, from peers and the supervisor. I entered into therapy after the quarter, for I wanted to learn more and to continue this growth. The time had not fully come that I could explore all of my issues. Beth pressed me to seek therapy.

I wanted a Black, female, feminist therapist but could not find one. I did find a White feminist pastoral counselor, working on a Ph.D. in pastoral psychology at Garrett-Northwestern, and Peggy Garrison and I worked well together. I continued chipping away at the mountain. But I didn't want to touch my mother and her part in my pain. I wanted to lay all of the blame on my father. I wanted to keep the pretense that mother cared and that she really could not have known the horrible trauma I had undergone. Peggy suggested that we role play. "Tell your mother that she failed you. Tell her that she was a poor mother for not protecting you." My mind rebelled. The words would not come. No. My mother was not the issue.

My father died in 1981 and I thought that with his death the mountain would lose some of its hold over me, but I did not find that to be true. I needed my mother. I wasn't ready to KNOW! All of my adult life I had attempted to "buy" my mother's love, as well as that of my brothers and sisters. I refused to confront my mother. But growth demands risk-taking. Removing mountains requires digging into everything around them. My unrealistic expectations of my "perfect" mother had to be faced.

June of 1985 found me living in Lansing, Michigan, and assigned to my first pastorate. Again, Chuck was remaining behind for awhile, so I asked Mother to travel with me and stay for a couple of weeks. In the middle of her second week with me, I asked the question that I needed an answer to and her response was: "I thought it had started again, but I didn't want to know. I needed your father to love me." How sad. How pitiful.

After this confession, all of my illusions were destroyed. I knew that my mother had sacrificed me for what she hoped and wished was love. I refused to see my family for almost a year. I remained in therapy, but found a White, female psychiatrist. I worked on becoming whole; I worked on "cutting the ties" to my family so that I would never need them in the sick, dependent manner I had experienced; I worked on understanding how I was more like my parents than I was different. On April 26, 1986, I had a dream that my mother was trying to join my father.

I knew she was going to die. I had to work on saying appropriate good-byes. I never accomplished this.

On May 18, 1986, my mother had a massive brain stroke; she remained in a coma for twelve days. All the siblings agreed to stop life-support systems and my mother died May 30th. I did not grieve. I was too angry. She was only fifty-nine and had never experienced life. To wait for death is to die by slow torture. To do nothing is to rot. I saw in my mother's death the story of many Black women, wives, mothers, sisters, and daughters. They exist in an empty place, full of a vast interior emptiness.

I knew that if I did not continue to chip away at the mountain, I would be in trouble. So, in May of last year I resigned from the church to take a rest, both mentally and physically. I also tried to immerse myself in "doing" so as to escape the inescapable grief. I realized that as long as my anger remained, the grieving could not begin.

During September of that same year, I began a residency in Clinical Pastoral Education at the Catherine McAuley Health Center of Ann Arbor, Michigan. I was very much in touch with my anger, because it would not allow others to reach me. I had shut down again because I did not want to hurt. I did not fully comprehend that I had to hurt in order to stop the hurt. My goals were to be open to feedback as to the impact of my anger on relationships and to understand what purpose my shutting down and closing myself to feedback served. I had much trust in the group and in the process to see me through what I knew would be stormy times.

I have grown to understand and to accept that the mountain will always be a part of my history—there is no magic "memory eraser." I have come to accept the strength of being a survivor, as well as the negative aspects, which prevent me from knowing what real living is all about. I have accepted as a gift the grace of God that allowed me to come through this situation with the determination not only to help myself, but to reach out to others with mountains in their life they cannot name. Those things in my life that I have worked so hard to hide, tried so desperately to keep secret, have produced some of the greatest "stuff" with which to do ministry. Sharing my story gives hope to others and it also reaffirms the value of who I am.

The greatest gift I received during that year was another woman with the story of incest. One day in group, as I struggled not to break down under the weight of knowing that my primary caregivers were not capable of giving me care, this Catholic nun gently reached over and touched my hand. Who knows at what point of discouragement and despair the simplest act of love may reach a soul and turn it again to the light? This simple act of love taught me that my family of origin might never be there for me, but in the providence of God many others have been sent to reach out and to touch my life with love, concern, compassion, and care.

Many truths came together for me during that intense one-year journey. I realized that my whole life had been lived in greyness. I realized that my mother had only given me birth, for she did not know how to teach me about life; for no one had been there to teach her. I have experienced "the New Birth." I've learned new ways to express my anger so that it is constructive. I have learned how to share and to be vulnerable.

I am committed to learning as much as I can about me and how to be a mountain-mover so that I can be an example for my sisters, for my "mothers," and for my daughters. I have gone through the pain of reconciling with both my parents. I am able to say that I love both of my parents. My anger at the pain they caused me has not dissolved the love. I hate what my father did to me as a child. I hate that my mother was not willing or capable of leaving him when confronted with the truth of my situation. I hate that she had a "poor me" attitude and a victim's stance in life. I hate that he was a sick man and abused me, my sister, and my mother (emotionally).

My mother was a woman with hopes, dreams, and aspirations before she elected to become a wife and mother. My often unfounded expectations of her kept us at a distance for many years. I wanted her to be "perfect" for me, but she was human. She lived the life she chose though often she was sad, disappointed, and hurt. She wanted her own "Prince Charming" and never got him. She wanted a "perfect" daughter. She never got that either. She was a failure as a mother, but this was not her number one priority in life. She chose to be a wife. I am grieving for my mother. I miss her terribly and I love her.

From my father I have gained my love of knowledge and excellence; a love of "good" clothes and grooming habits, and an outgoing personality. Yet I realize that I have a mean, rebellious streak that is just like his and a deep-seated anger that will feed on itself if left unchecked. My father is who and what he was. There is no changing my past. I cannot make him better or different. I have worked hard at reconciling with both my parents, who are now dead.

With continuing therapy, support groups, and re-parenting of my "inner child," I now understand that many of our actions and reactions today are based on early experiences with our parents that we continue to transfer to significant others, mates, children, as well as work, church, and social relationships. Mature awareness gives us the power to change our mental tapes and to re-parent ourselves in a different manner. Every occasion in life is one from which we can learn. Our lives begin with loss, the loss of the security of our mother's womb. To be able to truly "cut the cords" that bound me to both parents was my first step toward living life in its fullness.

TURBULENCE AND TENDERNESS: MOTHERS, DAUGHTERS, AND "OTHERMOTHERS" IN PAULE MARSHALL'S *BROWN GIRL, BROWNSTONES*

Rosalie Riegle Troester

The currents that flow between Black mothers and their daughters are often tumultuous, deepened and intensified by the racism and sexism of White America. Black mothers, particularly those with strong ties to their community, sometimes build high banks around their young daughters, isolating them from the dangers of the larger world until they are old enough and strong enough to function as autonomous women. Often these dikes are religious, but sometimes they are built with education, family, or the restrictions of a close-knit and homogeneous community. Even when relieved by eddies of tenderness, this isolation causes the currents between Black mothers and daughters to run deep and the relationship to be fraught with an emotional intensity often missing from the lives of women with more freedom.

Such intensity may be destructive, especially during adolescence, when a young woman necessarily struggles for independence. The turbulent stream may be kept from overflowing, however, by spillways in the form of other adult women who help guide and form the young girl, thus relieving some of the pressure on the mother-daughter relationship. Sometimes these women, whom I call "othermothers," are grandmothers, aunts, or cousins, united by kinship with the blood mother.[1] But sometimes othermothers live different lives and exemplify values widely divergent from the biological mother. Othermothers provide a safety valve and sounding board and release the teenage girl from the confines of a single role model. They can be gentle and affectionate where the bloodmother must be stern and demanding, thus showing the diversity available to Black womanhood. Often their emotional distance gives them a wise perspective on the mother-daughter relationship. And sometimes they give gifts mothers find hard to give, such as sexual initiation.

Paule Marshall's novel *Brown Girl, Brownstones* immerses us in such a turbulent relationship between a Black mother and her daughter, with the current channeled by the restrictions of an immigrant community and the spillways appearing in the form of three very different othermothers. When we read this novel, which follows a Barbadian family as it searches for economic and social survival in teeming Brooklyn, we swim within the whirlpools of a tense drama and emerge at the end strengthened like the daughter Selina. Our encounter with the Boyce family, and especially with the turbulent yet occasionally tender connections between the daughter Selina and the mother Silla, both strengthens our understanding of the Black mother-daughter bond and gives us tolerance toward the inevitable conflicts within such relationships.[2]

We meet the protagonist Selina sitting on the upper landing of a Brooklyn brownstone, daydreaming in preadolescent awkwardness of the life the former White owners had lived in the elegant house. She wears silver bangles on her arms, symbols that she is an "island girl." Despite the mother Silla's efforts, the Boyce family is still renting their brownstone, while most of their Barbadian neighbors have managed to scrimp and save enough to purchase the coveted houses which signal success and respectability. Silla works tirelessly, baking and selling Barbadian delicacies on the weekends after scrubbing floors for White women all week, but is thwarted in her thrift by her husband Deighton, a charming dreamer whose fear of success colors all his actions. The daughter Selina, of course, loves Deighton, who gives her sunshine, springtime, and laughter, and represents the soft beauty of the islands. He calls her his "lady-folks" and they share secrets both trivial and powerful. In contrast, Silla represents the brownstone, dark and strong and determined, and she gives Selina boundaries and discipline, rarely showing affection.[3] Providing a shadowy foil for Selina's emerging personality is Ina, a prim older sister, not as completely developed as the other three family members. At the opening of the novel, the Barbadian community is hearing the far-off rumbles of World War II, but more immediate conflicts preoccupy Selina, who lives securely within the group, walled in by their customs and protected from the White world by a determined mother.

She is stretching into adolescence, both attracted and repelled by evidence of emerging sexuality, but, more importantly, caught in a mortal conflict between her mother and her father. Against a backdrop of their battles, she grows up during the course of the novel's four books, becoming stronger through her rebellion against her mother and realizing finally that she *is* her mother in some deep and eternal sense.

Three very different and rather unlikely othermothers guide Selina's initiation into adulthood and provide important gifts to her emerging self. Although her father is an important figure, it is the women who mold her personality—her mother most of all, but also the three othermothers who give Selina unconditional love at a time when her mother sees affection as distracting.

In fact, we are introduced to two of these othermothers before we meet "the mother" (p. 16), as Selina calls her bloodmother, implicitly realizing even at the age of ten that the mother is central to her life and will provide her bedrock. From Suggie Skeets, whose "languorous pose, (and) all the liquid roundness of her body . . . hinted that love, its rituals and its passion, was her domain" (p. 13), Selina learns of the pleasures of the flesh. She is "every woman who gives herself without guile and with a full free passion" (p. 18), living for Saturday nights with her perfume, her rum, and her lover. She gives Selina her first taste of warming Barbadian rum and her first glimpse of sex. Like the father Deighton, Suggie is all that is open and laughing in the Black experience but, also like Deighton, she questions her own worth and is hurt by the censure of the Barbadian community.

A second othermother, Miss Thompson, thin and tall and no longer young, operates a beauty parlor and works nights as a cleaning woman. She is protective, gentle, and understanding, giving Selina both love and wisdom born of bitter experience. Miss Thompson comes from the American South and nurses a permanent fetid ulcer on her leg, the telling result of a brutal encounter with a White man who lashed out at her with a rusty shovel because she wouldn't cooperate with his attempted rape. However, Miss Thompson shields this information from Selina until she is old enough to have had encounters with the White world. She plays mama to the love-children of her roommate, finding solace in loving women of all ages and sheltering them from the cruel world she learned about too soon.

At first we find it hard to see what Selina receives from her third othermother, a wizened and senile White servant who lives out her grey days at the top of the Boyce brownstone where she has worked all her life. But Miss Mary has the time for Selina that her bloodmother doesn't, even though, like Suggie, she often doesn't hear the young girl, preferring instead to reminisce about her past life. Miss Mary gives Selina her first connection with the world outside the Barbadian immigrant community. And Selina learns from her that Whites are not all powerful and wealthy. Through the historical perspective that Miss Mary gives, Selina learns that she has other, more global, contexts than the ones she currently experiences.

Suggie Skeets, Miss Thompson, and Miss Mary are important othermothers, providing releasing spillways to the power of *the* mother, Silla. Predictably, Silla harbors animosity towards these women whose lives mirror conditions she dare not bring to consciousness. Miss Mary's endless monologue reminds her of the greyness of a life lived through others; Suggie's sensuality reminds her of her own dormant sexuality; and Miss Thompson's running ulcer recalls the oppression of Black women. In her efforts to achieve economic stability and, not incidentally, remove the othermothers from Selina's life, Silla evicts Suggie and literally scares Miss Mary to death. She needs Selina all to herself.

At the novel's opening, we see immediately the strong current flowing between mother and daughter because Selina always senses her mother coming before she sees her (p. 16). Silla is the quintessential Black mother—strong, protective, purposeful, and determined. If Deighton represents all that is soft and warm and gay in Barbadian life, Silla represents the opposite: the driving push towards economic stability, the denial of many of the island ways in favor of an upward mobility that mimics the White culture, the withholding of affection in order to forge strong character, and the fierce protection from the cruelty of the White world.

The relationship between Silla and Selina is cat-and-mouse, with neither of them able to show any weakness. Selina fears being pounced upon and swallowed up by her mother and Silla fears an adversary stronger than herself. We see these fears in the first confrontation of the novel.

> They were in the kitchen now, immured within its white
> walls, and although they were motionless they seemed
> to be warily circling each other, feinting, probing for an
> opening. (p. 44)

Selina harbors two conflicting fears: first, that the mother's troubles, which the older woman describes in such searing detail, might finally defeat her; second, that the mother's power will keep her own young spirit from flying free. She dares not show either fear because only the mother stands between Selina and chaos. If the mother were to die, "the world would collapse then, for wasn't the mother, despite all, its only prop?" (p. 46) After a tense silence, Selina breaks free of her ambivalence, darts verbally at her mother, and runs from the room.

We leave Silla standing alone in the kitchen, stunned in wonderment. "Look how I has gone and brought something into this world to whip me" (p. 46).

Book One, "A Long Day and a Long Night," introduces the central conflict between Silla and her husband, Deighton. Deighton inherits land in Barbados, and Silla begs him incessantly to sell it so they can buy the brownstone. Book Two, "Pastorale," is a short but important interlude where Selina visits Prospect Park with her girlfriend, Beryl. There they watch lovers on the grass and talk about sex. Selina grieves that she is still girl and not woman, but is comforted by Beryl's tender love.

In Book Three, World War II is declared and Selina begins menstruating. On a fateful Saturday morning, Silla's friends visit her with tales of other Barbadian women buying houses. Suddenly Silla stands tall and seething and announces that she *will* get the land from Deighton. Selina, ever sensitive to her mother, knows, "even as the dread seeped her blood, that this was not just another one of the mother's threats about the land" (p. 75). She fears for her father and for herself as she realizes that Silla will somehow accomplish her goal.

Silla stands in her kitchen, half in sunlight, half in shadow, embodying the age-old human conflict between good and evil (p. 76). She grabs Selina and threatens to kill her if she tells the secret. In a ceremony of initiation, Silla's friend lightly touches Selina's small breasts, reminding her that she is now a woman and can keep secrets as a woman should.

Selina resists the womanly complicity, resists the rolling stream that flows between the mother and her, resists any iden-

tification with adulthood. But in spite of her anger and determination not to be party to the secret, the touch lingers and she
lives with guilt. The dilemma sends her to the othermothers,
but she finds Miss Mary wrapped in her memories and Suggie
in keeping her identity in the face of ostracism from the community. She tries to tell them her secret, tries to deny the bond
she has with her mother, but they don't pay any attention. She
also tries to tell her day-dreaming father, but he, too, denies
what she is saying. Then she travels to the beauty shop to see
Miss Thompson, who gives her wisdom and another initiation.
She interprets the problem with, "Don't nobody listen to nobody
much . . . they's just plain too wrapped up in theyself" (p. 93).
Instead of attacking the conflict directly, she nudges Selina
toward adult life by fixing her hair in curls in place of the childish
braids. Then, contradictorily, she reminds Selina that the problem is between her parents and that, as a daughter, she is not
to meddle.

For the first time, Selina realizes the essential loneliness of
the human condition. Boldly, she determines to go to her mother
at her job in a defense plant, entering the White world for the
first time. In the factory, she listens to the roar of the machinery,
and feels "the familiar grudging affection" (p. 100) for her mother
because only the mother could work calmly amid the noise and
conquer the machines with her indifference. Selina is both respectful and afraid of her mother's strong hands that so rarely
touch her.[4]

In this third major mother-daughter confrontation, Silla is
surprised at Selina's courage and realizes her daughter is like
her own mother. In a desperate attempt to deny the mother-
daughter bond, Selina confesses that she has told everyone of
her mother's plan. The mother has a moment of panic, but when
Selina also confesses that no one listened, the older woman
laughs in triumph. She has again won over the child and she
tells her daughter, "You's like David without a sling!" (p. 106)
The laughter and the realization of failure pierce Selina and
fill her with dread. She is not yet an adult, not yet included
in the community, yet she knows with an adult mind that the
family tragedy will play itself out and that she is powerless to
prevent it.

During one of the several duels between mother and father
over the island property, Selina realizes that part of her always
sides with the mother even though she outwardly supports Deigh-

ton (p. 133). She is beginning to feel the identification with her mother that will eventually make her a woman, but she must survive several initiations before this strengthening.

In the aftermath of the land conflict, Silla has Deighton deported and the turbulence between mother and daughter builds to a climax. She hears Selina call her from the bedroom, intoning "Hitler" over and over again, like a metronome. "Hurt darkening her already numbed eyes" (p. 184), she stumbles into her daughter's room. Selina springs at her and Silla makes no move to resist, accepting the blows her daughter pours on her. Finally, Selina collapses helplessly against her mother and falls asleep.

> Slowly Silla lowered her face and gingerly touched the sore places on her shoulders and arms. She stared down, with a strange awe and respect, at the limp figure huddled against her and the thin arms wound loosely around her neck. Carefully she lifted Selina's legs over the footboard, and with the sheet trailing behind them she carried her out of the room, up through the dim hall to the parlor, and turned on the chandelier. For a long while she sat quietly holding her on the sofa under the brilliant light. Then, almost reverently, she touched the tears that had dried white on her dark skin, traced with her finger the fragile outline of her face and rested her hand soothingly on her brow. She smoothed her snarled hair. Yet, despite the tenderness and wonder and admiration of her touch, there was a frightening possessiveness. Each caress declared that she was touching something which was finally hers alone. (p. 185)

This scene marks the emotional climax of the mother-daughter conflict, with Selina's rebellion finding physical release and Silla finally able to claim her daughter for herself. After this catharsis, eruptions become less frequent. The relationship, however, becomes even more intense because the conflict has sunk deeply into each psyche.

The bond between Silla and Selina is murky with ambivalence. Silla is both tender and cruel, possessive and detached. Selina feels love and respect in the midst of her hatred and both emulates and ridicules her mother's values. The intensity of the bond is both comforting in its closeness and fearful in its strength.

Book Four, the final book of the novel, is called simply "Selina." Here Selina moves out from the mother-bond and enters the world. Her father dies and she grieves for a year in an exaggerated mourning calculated to punish her mother. The mother-daughter relationship reaches a kind of détente. Selina is apathetic with grief but notices in her mother a veiled respect mingling with the possessiveness. Miss Mary and Suggie give her one last gift as it is they who finally convince her to throw off mourning and begin living again.

In her grief, Selina finds Miss Mary's room comforting in its colorlessness. When the old woman finally dies, killed by Silla's wrath and avarice, Selina sees the peace on her face and feels it calling her "to flow out of herself into life, to touch and know it fully and, in turn, to be touched by it" (p. 204). Selina begins to come back to life, strengthened by the peace Miss Mary gives her.

After Miss Mary's funeral, Selina visits Suggie Skeets. For the first time since her father's leaving, she dances and laughs. Suggie begs her, in the name of her life-loving father, to take up her life again. Selina takes her advice and begins college in accord with her mother's wishes. A month later, Silla evicts Suggie under the guise of finding more reputable roomers. But Selina knows otherwise. "It's not you, Miss Suggie. It's just that I'm to have no one, that's all" (p. 211). Silla will brook no competition.

Selina hugs the sense of desertion she feels at Suggie's leaving all through her first year of college. She enters the White world but only as a spectator, distanced and silent, spending hours anonymously walking on Fifth Avenue and observing the chaos of Times Square. These solitary walks prepare her for autonomy.

During her second year in college, two important events shape an emerging identity which increasingly mirrors her mother. She experiences both first love and an initiatory encounter with White racism. Challenged by Miss Thompson to join the Barbadian Association so as to get an understanding of her mother and her community, she rejects their bourgeois values in an adolescent scene. Running out of the room, she meets Clive Barnes. Clive is an experienced and effete West Indian who awakens her sexually and intellectually. He teaches her a larger view of her world with his Greek chorus commentary on the racism of Greenwich Village Whites, on Barbarian ways, on Selina's emerging adulthood, and on mother-child relationships. He shares Selina's ambivalence toward their common heritage and he, too, is securely bonded to his mother, saying with grim knowledge, "[Mothers] form you in that dark place inside them and you're theirs. For giving life they exact life. The cord remains uncut, the blood joined, and all that that implies" (p. 262).

Selina still fights that joining but begins to realize her identity with her mother. When Clive describes Selina as "grabbing life itself by the throat" (p. 247), she realizes with shock that this is her mother's way, the way she thought she rejected so completely. An audacious scheme to win money so she and Clive can run away together finally reveals itself to her as analogous to the ruthless plan her mother executed in order to get Deighton's money. The two women even fall in love with the same kind of man.

When Silla learns of Selina's affair, she is restored to her former power by the strength of her indignation. Selina feels more at home with this familiar mother than with the tender and possessive one. As Silla strikes out at her, Selina's eyes confirm what her mouth conventionally denies, that yes, she is a woman, that she has defied her mother and spilled over the walls of the censuring community. Selina continues to lead a double life, sneaking to Clive's apartment while pretending to be at the library. Silla so desperately wants to deny the affair that she says nothing and pretends to believe her. Silla senses her daughter's independence at this time because, after all, the mother-daughter identification goes both ways. At eighteen Silla convinced her mother to let her emigrate, and when a young girl she, too, knew the joys of sex and laughter, dancing all night in an island pasture (p. 145).

In addition to Selina's sexual and intellectual initiation, she becomes an adult through her first encounter with White racism. Wounded by the cruelty of a White mother, just as Miss Thompson was wounded by a White racist's rusty shovel, she becomes aware of the community of all Blacks in an alien society. She now understands why her mother sometimes raged at her children after she came home from cleaning White apartments and she can only wonder at the woman's survival strength. In a climactic scene where she confronts her Blackness in a window, she realizes that she is both an individual woman and a member of a community whose support she needs. Like all Blacks, she must find a way to know her true identity in spite of a stereotyping White society. She sees the essential loneliness that comes from growth and autonomy.

She must make a final break with the mother even as she realizes their eternal identity. In an afterword to the novel, Mary Helen Washington points out that when Selina really knows

Silla, she sees her not just as the mother but as Black woman in all her complexity (p. 315). As the story ends, we internalize the wholeness of this vision and learn tolerance toward the mother-daughter conflicts that are its necessary predecessors.

Mother and daughter have a final, cleansing confrontation. "Selina felt the old admiration, but none of the old weakening" (p. 304) in the face of her mother's handsome anger. The young woman tells her mother she is going away—alone—and Silla gropes to a chair and "[sits] numb, silent, the life shattered in her eyes . . ." (p. 306) "What is tis you want?" the mother asks. When Selina replies that she doesn't know and confirms that she has been initiated into the harsh White world, Silla begins to understand. She, too, had felt the young urge, had faced her rejection, and had stood eager and alone at the edge of a new world. Selina finally admits the joining with her mother and this admission frees her to leave. In a final gesture of goodbye to childhood, she throws one of her silver Island bangles to the ghosts of her youth, keeping the other as a sign of bonding with her community. Selina/Silla is a woman.

NOTES

1. See Gloria Joseph's "Black Mothers and Daughters: Their Roles and Functions in American Society," in *Common Differences: Conflicts in Black and White Feminist Perspectives*, ed. Gloria Joseph and Jill Lewis (Garden City, NY: Anchor Books, 1981), pp. 75–126, for a sociological discussion of mother-daughter relationships in Black and White cultures. Joseph also emphasizes that Black girls are sometimes socialized by women other than their biological mothers.

2. Paule Marshall, *Brown Girl, Brownstones* (Old Westbury, NY: Feminist Press, 1981.) Subsequent references to pages in the novel are given in the text.

3. To the question, "What about your mother do you respect the least?", the highest category of respondents (21.2%) in Joseph's research answered "Lack of demonstrative show of affection/appreciation" (p. 103).

4. This mingling of fear and respect is another finding in Joseph's sociological questionnaire (p. 98).

P A R T 5

BINDING THE QUILT:
GENERATIONS

They were uppity Black women, our mothers and grandmothers, women who tossed their heads and crossed their legs, read Fanon and dealt with dream cards, wore felt head huggers and high-top shoes. Bold, audacious women of indomitable spirit who believed that all things are possible, they taught their daughters respect for the possibilities in themselves and others. They took the raw fabrics of their lives—rough linings of dark secrets, deep longings, and private memories; tough cotton battings of family and work and church; and the appliquéd pieceworks of their dreams and creative spirit—and bound them together with delicate blind stitches and strong, bias-cut bindings.

We called them Great Gram, Grandma, Nanny, and Momma, these women who bequeathed to us a legacy of hard work, these field hands and teachers, caterers and clothes pressers, nurses and numbers writers. Margaret Walker's grandmothers and Kate Rushin's Granmom told stories—passing on the legacy, teaching their daughters to survive whole. Alice Walker writes lovingly of the Saints and Headragged Generals—crazy women and exquisite butterflies—who kept alive the creative spirit that sometimes burst into song or flowered into gardens.

Often the creative spirit connects mother and daughter, as when Saundra Sharp writes of her mother (also a poet) in "Double Exposure,"

> i am not you anymore
> i am my own collection of
> gifts and errors

Mothers and daughters celebrate womanhood and honor their womenkin with poems and novels, short stories and personal narratives. Poet Naomi Long Madgett chants a litany of love for

her daughter Jill "on the worn rosary of years"; Saundra Murray
Nettles spins a tale of motherhood when her "milk flowed easy
and rich"; and Esperanza Cintrón paints portraits of four generations of women, including her Grandmomma (1928)—spunky
in bangs, felt hat, and coon collar—and her daughter (1988),
outrageous in "pink and green spiked hair." Through their words
and images, grandmamas passed on motherwit; through their
rites and rituals mamas handed down womanspirit: "I learned
the washing ritual—soaking, bleaching, rubbing, boiling, adding bluing, starching." Annette Jones White writes:

> Saturdays were for getting your hair washed, pressed,
> and curled in preparation for church. Sundays meant
> Sunday school and church all day. And so it went day
> after day, week after week, year after year. This was
> our life—my life.

Sitting on their porches or bent over a stove, the culturebearers
passed on the legacy, teaching their girl children about Billie
Holiday, gospel music, Paul Lawrence Dunbar, the *Pittsburgh
Courier*, and hot-water cornbread patted into cakes. Mothers
also warned their daughter-friends about the dark underside of
Black women's lives; Annette Jones White grows up hearing
about rapes, lynchings, and cross burnings. Telling tales and
singing songs of love, spinning dreams of what a girl might
become, passing on the beauty and the pain from generation to
generation until, like Kate Rushin, the daughter exclaims, hands
on hips,

> *Nowadays*
> *I cultivate*
> *Being Uppity*
> *It's something*
> *My Gramom taught me*

> *Miriam DeCosta-Willis*

LINEAGE

Margaret Walker

My grandmothers were strong.
They followed plows and bent to toil.
They moved through fields sowing seed.
They touched earth and grain grew.
They were full of sturdiness and singing.
My grandmothers were strong.

My grandmothers are full of memories
Smelling of soap and onions and wet clay
With veins rolling roughly over quick hands
They have many clean words to say.
My grandmothers were strong.
Why am I not as they?

From *For My People* by Margaret Walker (New Haven: Yale University Press, 1942).

FAMILY TREE

Kate Rushin

I come from
A long line of
Uppity Irate Black Women
Although they were
Church people
And I'm the only one
Who drinks and cusses
When they
Got on the warpath
They had no match
You think I'm bold
Imagine my grandmother Addie
Raising her umpteen children
During the Depression
Imagine the audacity of
This woman who only
Went to the third grade
Joining The-Book-Of-The-Month Club
She gave me a six-volume set of
The World's Best Poetry
When I was seven years old
When I was nine
My grandmother sent
A coupon and one dollar to
Nabisco Shredded Wheat
They sent her a knife
And fork and spoon
She kept them in a yellow
Envelope in the dish closet drawer
She would say they were for me
For when I went away to college
I didn't know what it meant exactly
But I would open the drawer
And look at them
And it made me feel real good

And you ask me how come
I think I'm so cute
Nowadays
I cultivate
Being Uppity
It's something
My Gramom taught me
It's about time
I learned
My lesson

AT MIDDAY

Naomi Long Madgett

A birthday wish for Jill

Woman to woman now, we tell our beads
on the worn rosary of years
together in the same slant of light.
No longer clay and potter,
we are what we have made each other,
your mark indelibly on me
as mine on you.

And so, at midday, I wish you
a taste of cururú and jaca fruit,
aroma of coconut and palm oil,
resonance of agogô bells at Carnival,
your fingers' touch on a berimbau,
and a silver balangandan hung with amulets.

May the *Pretos Velhos* endow you with their wisdom,
Yansan clear your path of storm and rain,
and Yemanjá protect and guide you
as you sail forever toward Brazilian shores.

GLOSSARY

Cururú: greens cooked with fish, pepper, and palm oil
Agogô: double metal bell played at Carnival and candomblé rites
Berimbau: string instrument consisting of a bow, gourd, and small stick
Balangandan: gold or silver brooch worn by Black women in Bahia
Pretos Velhos: African ancestral spirits
Yansan: Yoruba goddess of wind and storm
Yemanjá: goddess of the sea

DOUBLE EXPOSURE

Saundra Sharp

in the mirror
she holds on
again

> if u can't leave
> u can't stay here
> get off my face!

if i leave this room
people will
see i am
not my own face

> if u can't leave
> u can't stay here
> get off my face!

she stays,
much too comfortable

> i left
> to flee your
> hand-me-down fears
> our answers
> no longer matched

she stays, as if i am
still on duty
in Her image

> i am not you anymore
> i am my own collection of
> gifts and errors

> so woman spirit
> if u can't leave
> u can't stay here

and finally, she moves off
(as in retiring to Her room
                    after a trying day)

                    don't you
                    remember
                    the sunshiny days?

i smooth in the camouflage
    smudge the brown red rouge
        assemble it all
            hoping
                if u can't leave
hoping to hold on
                if u can't leave
to my own face
            u can't stay here
for a few days
            get off my face!
please?

FOUR WOMEN
(a cycle of poems because of nina simone, ray waller, & judith siegel pearson)

Esperanza Cintrón

GRANDMOMMA 1928

Posed against a scarred backdrop
    of Lucky Lindy's plane
Brand new coat, coon collar
    pulled up high
Touching the snug felt head hugger
Dark fingers press gleaming bangs
    to a pair of sweaty brows

Car'mel man darting in and out
    of his camera box
Feeling rich, looking good
    hand on hip
Tightning knots on real silk stockings
Showing some knee and lean brown legs
    'cause he kind a cute

Thoughts of Greystone on Monday night
    of dance and The Duke
Big, fine, spending, yellow man
    on my arm
Blues swaying down in Paradise
Repenting in church on Sunday
    for temperance beer last Monday

Know I was born, just the right time
    of slavery gone
Smelling up-north promises
    kiss my free
Six dollar a day earning man

Sweat, dig, haul, colored jobs, for true
  but men bathe and money's good

Ice box, trolley, FORD, ain't no south
  of cotton Poplars
Don't have to clean they baseboards
  on my knees
There's two men to ev'ry woman
No need nursing no pale children
  'sides don't mind washing what's mine

Everybody come up this way know
  of the dark Valley
Folks squeezed in and piled atop
  pool tables
Looking toward ironing my man's clothes
North End moving and babies come
  'cause Dr. Sweet showed we got rights

Pat pasty powder on my face
  of Neisner's five and dime
Wish they made some for colored
  dull the shine
Lights blaring, glaring in my face
He say smile. Feeling good, collar high
hand on hip, smile sly, . . . there—POP!

MOMMA 1956

She talking on the phone
Hot comb heating on the stove
Sister gets out the Brownie
She laugh and cover her face

        close-up, click

Lips painted a wild red
Part in an inviting smile
Fresh tinted jet black hair
Glistens as she tosses her head

Mouth wide, teary eyed laughing
At the lewd jokes of admiring men
Men dressed in loose cut suits
Small brimmed hats and shining shoes

Change jingling in their pockets
As they wait patiently, for her
Etta James's cool cuts through the heat
Nat grins out from the little round screen

Cain't be worried 'bout no bomb shelters
Air Raid Drills ain't gone save nobody
Folks sitting in where they not wanted
Boycotting, folks going to court, life's too short

She fans her hand at the TV
Crosses her leg, sucks on her cigarette
Switches to an interview with Dorothy Dandridge
Smiling, she sits back sipping her beer

click . . . click . . . click

DAUGHTER 1972

ungrown when 12th street went
smelled the fire, felt the flame
saw juice from Stein's
pickle barrel run down sidewalks

black boys wearing blue jeans
bent over with booty
scrambled amidst scattered glass
as shot-guns screeched from scout cars

clickclickclickfrontpage

young girls in short skirts
herded into wagons
saw wide-eyed wearied elders
point fingers screaming wait

when there are folds of fists
martyrs to follow, and cause
spirit of the people, baby
stopped waiting for the revolution

grew up fanning the flames
discontent eating eager brains
saw gaping holes
dying to be filled with truths
about neo-colonialist fascist pigs

me with my towering afro rallying with
bell-bottomed flower-carrying hippies
swearing they understood
what it be like to be black in america
when they don't even know who Gil-Scott is

panthers prowled demanding real dreams
being beautiful black and realizing we're a
species of hybrids
reading FANON and reprints of WRIGHT'S rage
listening to Stokley rapping 'bout unity

brothers and sisters anticipating power
finding out its cool to vote and buy black
stress killing young men and
political power pulls Coleman in
a new black bourgeosie is born

                                        click

THE BABY 1988

She
        has
             pink and green
        spiked
hair

                                        click

Ground zero
      threatens
         her
and Nostradamus reigns

From one ear
      hangs
   a tarnished crucifix
           the other bears
   a zicron stud

Loose-fitting
   men's clothes
        drape her body
      and high top shoes
   of grandma's day

                click—click

Rhythmic poets
   vie for audio space
      with spastic electric guitarists
        and Prince peers from her walls

High tech   video   laser
   Must have RAM
          ATARI   VCR   Laserdiscs   and
   Call forwarding to FERMI II

Next to Prince
   an exhibit announcement for
      Diego Rivera
and she knows who
      Mandela is

Lounging across her bed
      we talk
   of her future
      she smiles
       and says
         Cain't be worried 'bout no bomb shelters

TO MY DAUGHTERS

Saundra Murray Nettles

My milk flowed easy and rich
Bringing with it
Wholegrain breads and fresh fruit
Six-month checkups and no cavities
Saddle oxfords with plaid dresses
Sunday school and museums,
    though these were less for the
    joy than the substance.

Oh, you got a taste of mom's honey
It leaked
But in little drops
When we took tap dancing together
With my thirty-six years of rhythm and
    your seven of grace
When we stole away from company picnics
    to walk in the woods, where you
    watched bumblebees and flies
    and asked why is there pollen?
    it makes our eyes so red and runny.

But most of the honey is still trapped
    inside me.
You ask for it sometimes
And when it doesn't come
You turn aside and
    learn to love life
    with someone else.

I want to give you
Much more of my sweet sticky stuff
So
We'll stop and play
    even when our work is pressing
Go to plantations

just to walk in gardens
and admire beautiful old things.
We can swim
even though our hair gets messy
and my belly is no longer flat like yours.
And we'll cook up interesting things
even though we don't have
all the right ingredients.

But with mom's milk and her honey too
You have enough to see you through.

DYAD/TRIAD

Annette Jones White

My grandmother was fifteen years old when she married my grandfather—little more than a child. While he worked, she continued to play with her friends as usual, until her mother called her inside one day and told her she was a married woman whose playing days were over. Eleven months later, at home and in fear and ignorance of the reality of *birthin' babies*, she and a midwife brought my mother into the world.

Eighteen years later, my mother married my father. A year after that, I was born in the same house where my mother had been born. My arrival was attended by the only black female doctor in southwest Georgia.

My parents and grandparents lived in the same house for thirty years. I was reared by the four of them in theory, and by my grandmother and mother in actuality—my grandmother's influence, at first, more actual than my mother's.

My grandmother was very strong of character and was convinced she had most, if not all, of the answers. Quite often, she did have them, to the exasperation of my mother. My grandmother's personality, for a time, overshadowed my mother's and I thought my grandmother was the mother of us all.

She made all of the decisions concerning herself and my grandfather and quite a few concerning my mother and me. She had no control over my father and was quite agitated when he refused to follow her wishes.

When I was in elementary school, my grandmother decided what I would wear every morning. She often combed my hair and tied my ribbons or adjusted my caps. I did not want her to do this but my mother allowed it. I liked the way I looked under my mother's supervision. My mother would set my beret jauntily up front and to the side of my head, while my grandmother would pull it down to my ears. She said if I didn't keep my head warm, then I would have consumption before I was fifteen years old. That was one of the few times that she was wrong.

If I asked my mother for an apple or a piece of cake, my grandmother quickly answered as to the advisability of my having it. I would look at my mother, hoping she would veto my grandmother's opinion and stand up for me and for herself. She never did. Until the day my grandmother died, in 1981, my mother acquiesced to her wishes—ever the obedient child.

Although my mother allowed my grandmother to be heavy-handed in my life, she was never so. She let me make choices and decisions whenever we were alone. I cherished those times even though I loved my grandmother very much. We all loved her in spite of herself.

An only child, my mother grew up in an era where children were seen and not often heard. Consequently, she spent a great deal of time alone in her room. As a result of this, she became an avid reader for life. I grew up seeing her reading whenever she had a free moment. I developed the habit and often sat near her reading my book while she read her book. By the time I was twelve years old, I had read many of her books, including *Les Miserables*, *The Hound of the Baskervilles*, *Young Bess*, *And So Victoria*, *Dark Waters*, and several Agathie Christie novels. In retrospect, I realized what an incredible booklist she possessed, given the time and her circumstances. She was a high school graduate at age sixteen, having completed eleven years of study. She wanted to go on to nursing school, but the age limit for admittance was eighteen. By the time she was old enough to go, she had met and married my father. Her reading seemed to satisfy a yearning she had but could not fulfill in other ways. She also passed on her love for the printed word to the four other children she later bore. I, in turn, have passed it on to my daughters.

My mother always said that a person could have so many experiences just by reading books. A great many of her experiences were lived vicariously through her books.

I often watched her read the local newspaper or the *Pittsburgh Courier*. The *Courier* was my introduction to the horrors of lynchings and racism. The pink colored paper was filled with pictures of atrocities visited upon "Negroes"—as we were called then. I particularly recall a picture of a Black woman hanging from a tree. A fire was burning beneath her, and, in her agony, she had given birth and the baby had dropped into the fire. I had seen pictures of lynchings in the paper before, but they were always pictures of men or young boys—horrible still, but males. Not mother, not me. As I looked at my mother I thought, "That could have been us." That picture brought the horror closer to home.

Nowadays, children are not allowed to see pictures of a similar nature. However, my mother and I talked about those pictures. She wanted to make sure I knew the danger so I would exercise caution when I ventured outside our door.

In those days, Black people had few rights and lived constantly on tiptoe and in a react mode. But there was a closeness, a togetherness in the community, that appears to be missing today. Perhaps, Blacks *had* to stick together then for mere survival.

I grew up hearing how my grandmother had been chased by the Ku Klux Klan when she was thirteen years old. I grew up hearing about the Scottsboro Boys, the Monroe Georgia Massacre, Mrs. Ingram and her sons, and lynchings in general. I saw the Klan ride through my neighborhood once. They wore white robes and hoods and sat on the trunks and hoods of slow moving black cars. As they yelled threats, I looked out of the window and was terrified at the sight. I couldn't see their eyes, just black holes where eyes should have been, and it frightened me. Another thing that frightened me was that policemen were escorting them.

My mother comforted me. She told me how she sent money to the N.A.A.C.P. each month. She said it was an organization that helped "us" if we had trouble. She called it N-double-A-C-P. When she told me that, I felt better, and I was thrilled knowing my mother was making this possible by paying her dues.

Racial tensions created an atmosphere of fear, yet there was courage; they created a sense of powerlessness, yet there was determination. My grandmother survived and reared her daughter to survive. My mother reared me to survive in her own fashion. She gave me heroes and heroines to be proud of. She told me about George W. Carver, Joe Louis, Booker T. Washington, Paul Lawrence Dunbar (for whom my father was named), Phillis Wheatley, Madame Walker, and others. She taught me how to turn away wrath with a soft answer but without letting anybody make me think I was inferior to them.

She also tried to keep me informed of the dangers I might face so that I could avoid situations that would put me in danger. She tried to keep me out of situations that could lead to humiliation and "incidents." For example, on one of the few times she took me downtown, she avoided a confrontation. It was generally known that Blacks were supposed to step off the sidewalk if they were meeting a group of Whites. To not do so invited several things—a tongue lashing, a vicious elbow to the chest or side, or, possibly, arrest. As we walked, we approached a group of Whites. My mother quickly walked to a store window and we window shopped until the Whites passed by. I knew why and she knew I knew why but we never discussed it. That was her way of avoiding an incident.

Another time, when I was about ten, a White man yelled from a car at my mother as we walked along the street.

"Hey, you girl, I need a nigger wench to do some ironing."

My mother ignored him but it made me angry and resentful. Girl? This was my mother. She stood ten feet tall in my book. Her word was my law. She could kill a chicken, pluck it, and reach inside and pull out unimaginable things. Then, she could cook it so you would forget where it came from. The same hands that did that also washed on a rubboard and scrubbed floors with Octagon soap, yet still remained soft enough to rub away my stomachaches in the wee hours of the morning. Girl? This woman did laundry for doctors and handwashed, stiff-starched and flat-ironed white coats and pants by the dozens. This woman knew how long an egg should boil—could make a meal from almost nothing. Girl? This woman presented herself, her children, and her husband (no easy task) at church every second and fourth Sunday. I was furious!

The more I saw her avoid confrontations, the more resentment I felt. My resentment had no form so it just bubbled around inside, no doubt festering like Langston Hughes's "Dream Deferred" until it finally burst years later and thrust me into the Civil Rights Movement of the sixties. But before that happened, I just felt angry. My mother's careful rearing of me made me see how wrong, unfair, and humiliating it was to have to live in fear that your children might come to harm for just being themselves.

By introducing me to books and the *Pittsburgh Courier*, my mother opened up a whole new world to me, part good, part bad. The horrors of racism and lynchings were bad but the closeness they generated in the Black community was good. Through books, I found out that there were machines that washed clothes in minutes. I had thought that everybody washed all day on Monday the way my mother did, using a rubboard and boiling the clothes in a big black pot. By reading, I learned about vacuum cleaners, boiled lobsters, inside plumbing, and so many other things. I would never be the same again. I began to think things like "when I have a daughter, she won't have to do the things I've done." I swore that when I grew up, I would never do certain things again as long as I lived. To this day, I do not wash on Mondays. I do not hang clothes outside on a line. I do not parboil meats.

When I grew older, I heard talk at school about sex. I wanted to ask mother about it, but I didn't know what to ask. All I had been told was to be nice and don't be fast, and that some girls messed up and had babies. That confused me because my grandmother told me the stork had brought me. One day Aunt Ida told me babies were found under cabbage leaves. When I told my grandmother this, she said, "Ida doesn't have any children; she doesn't know what she's talking about." Later, I found out that if I had asked my mother direct questions about sex, then she would have answered. We have never been able to share our sexuality as women, except as it relates to our mother-daughter relationship.

However, I noticed, as a child, that my mother got ready for my father to come home from work. She would put on a clean dress and comb her hair. She never wore makeup. I would see them kiss each other when he came home. It made me feel very secure and warm.

I was aware of many nuances by observing my mother. Maybe each mother passes on to her daughter, unconsciously, certain ways or wiles which have resulted from living in a racist and sexist society. Often, my mother would make statements about Whites or some of their actions. The way she said it or the way she held her mouth gave me a clue as to the attitude I was to adopt concerning them or their particular action.

I could always tell when she wanted my father to do something. I could not have told how I knew because I was too young to understand what I somehow *knew*. Perhaps, it was the way she acted—her mannerisms, her eyes. Instinctively, I learned that certain things were not said around my father. He was never told certain things that my mother and grandmother had discussed before he came home from work, things like the waste of ingredients in a cake that fell and was thrown away, or the amount of money left over from the grocery money.

One day, in my presence, a man made advances to my mother, who promptly put him in his place. I did not mention this to my father and I was known for running off at the mouth. Yet, another time, when a woman smiled and winked at my father,

I promptly reported it to my mother when I was out of earshot of my father.

During my elementary and secondary school years, I was very active in the goings-on at the schools. My mother attended every activity I was a part of. She seemed to live through me and, later, through the other children. She always told me how proud she was of me and of whatever I was doing. Her approval was very important to me and I did my best in school so I could win awards and blue ribbons to present proudly to her. She still has those awards. She never bragged about my accomplishments, rather she accepted them with a deep sense of pride.

There were certain things that created and strengthened bonds between my mother and me and the rest of the family. First, there were our close ties to the church. Wordlessly and by deeds, my mother let it be known that a wife, a mother, saw to it that her family went to church and went well turned out. She was proud that she could get my father to go to church and that he looked so nice in his snow white shirts with the starched and nicely ironed collars and cuffs. I saw that women were often the reason men went to church. For, in truth, my father did not really want to go all of the times he went.

Second, at our house, there was a relationship between major chores and the day of the week. On Mondays we washed. I learned the washing ritual—soaking, bleaching, rubbing, boiling, adding bluing, starching. I learned all the things that I would never use as an adult. It always amazed me that my mother never knew when the clothes had boiled long enough, but my grandmother knew. Later, I realized that no matter how long they boiled, my grandmother would never admit that my mother had judged correctly. It was my grandmother's way of holding on to her authority, of being in charge. For my mother knew as much about almost everything as my grandmother. There were no more mysteries. My grandmother realized she was losing her reputation of being all-knowing and she grasped at small things to preserve her status and her dignity.

The next thing in our week of chores was my mother's laundering of doctors' coats and pants. My father did not want her to work outside our home, so she took in laundry. She washed it on Tuesdays.

On Wednesdays, my mother ironed our clothes that had been washed on Monday. On Thursdays, she ironed the doctors' clothes. The routine chores of bedmaking, dishwashing, and mending were also done, but each day was known for a special chore.

Friday was the day she shopped for groceries. This day represented more than just the acquisition of food. This was a day my mother reigned supreme. She was mother earth. She was the dispenser of life-saving food, of treats. She controlled my very soul as I danced excitedly around the mountain of food she had pulled exultantly from the sacks. She had real power on Fridays. She let my father know how cleverly she had bargained. She even surprised him and my grandmother with some special treat. Power, and she gloried in it.

Saturdays were for getting your hair washed, pressed, and curled in preparation for church. Sundays meant Sunday school and church all day. And so it went day after day, week after week, year after year. This was our life—my life. It was the way things were, the way they were supposed to be. My mother's life cried out to me: "This is what being a woman is. This is what a wife and mother does. Woman is wife and mother. This is what I am, this is what you will become, what I am teaching you to become."

She knew I would be more, however, because she wanted me to go to college. I think her hopes were for me to be wife, mother, schoolteacher or nurse.

As I grew older, I learned what she taught me, but deep in my heart, I accepted some things and rejected others. For instance, I liked makeup and high heels and short hair. What must she have thought, after having tried to "raise me right," when at seventeen, I stood before her, teetering on high heels, lips red, bangs self-cut, with the radio blasting "Honey Love" by Clyde McPhatter? Probably the same thing I felt when my daughter stood before me with three earrings in each ear, a fuchsia muscle shirt on, a pair of pants on that were a cross between riding breeches, harem pants, and blue jeans, bright blue eye-liner, fuchsia lips and nails, and the stereo blasting "Like A Virgin" by Madonna. But I only felt that way for a few minutes; remembering how I had felt at seventeen, I related it to how my daughter must have been feeling and decided that the feelings were of equal value. Whenever I find myself beginning to be intolerant or insensitive with my daughters, I think back to a similar incident I put my mother through and I smile and understand their need to be themselves. As a result of my upbringing, I am open with my daughters and we can talk about anything. I have given them more freedom to be themselves than I had, and so far they have handled it well.

I have tried to pass on the things I accepted from my mother and have omitted the things I rejected. One day, my daughters will no doubt do the same thing.

I owe my mother a great deal. She gave so unselfishly of herself and made many sacrifices for me. I hope she is proud of the person I have become.

IN SEARCH OF OUR MOTHERS' GARDENS

Alice Walker

> I described her own nature and
> temperament. Told how they needed a
> larger life for their expression....I
> pointed out that in lieu of proper channels,
> her emotions had overflowed into paths
> that dissipated them. I talked, beautifully
> I thought, about an art that would be born,
> an art that would open the way for women
> the likes of her. I asked her to hope, and
> build up an inner life against the coming
> of that day....I sang, with a strange
> quiver in my voice, a promise song.
>
> JEAN TOOMER, "Avey," *Cane*

The poet speaking to a prostitute who falls asleep while he's talking—

When the poet Jean Toomer walked through the South in the early twenties, he discovered a curious thing: Black women whose spirituality was so intense, so deep, so *unconscious*, that they were themselves unaware of the richness they held. They stumbled blindly through their lives: creatures so abused and mutilated in body, so dimmed and confused by pain, that they considered themselves unworthy even of hope. In the selfless abstractions their bodies became to the men who used them, they became more than "sexual objects," more even than mere women: they became "Saints." Instead of being perceived as whole persons, their bodies became shrines: what was thought to be their minds became temples suitable for worship. These crazy Saints stared out at the world, wildly, like lunatics—or quietly, like suicides; and the "God" that was in their gaze was as mute as a great stone.

Who were these Saints? These crazy, loony, pitiful women?

Some of them, without a doubt, were our mothers and grandmothers.

In the still heat of the post-Reconstruction South, this is how they seemed to Jean Toomer: exquisite butterflies trapped in an evil honey, toiling away their lives in an era, a century, that did not acknowledge them, except as "the *mule* of the world." They dreamed dreams that no one knew—not even themselves, in any coherent fashion—and saw visions no one could understand. They wandered or sat about the countryside crooning lullabies to ghosts, and drawing the mother of Christ in charcoal on courthouse walls.

They forced their minds to desert their bodies and their striving spirits sought to rise, like frail whirlwinds from the hard red clay. And when those frail whirlwinds fell, in scattered particles, upon the ground, no one mourned. Instead, men lit candles to celebrate the emptiness that remained, as people do who enter a beautiful but vacant space to resurrect a God.

Our mothers and grandmothers, some of them: moving to music not yet written. And they waited.

They waited for a day when the unknown thing that was in them would be made known; but guessed, somehow in their darkness, that on the day of their revelation they would be long dead. Therefore to Toomer they walked, and even ran, in slow motion. For they were going nowhere immediate, and the future was not yet within their grasp. And men took our mothers and grandmothers, "but got no pleasure from it." So complex was their passion and their calm.

To Toomer, they lay vacant and fallow as autumn fields, with harvest time never in sight: and he saw them enter loveless marriages, without joy; and become prostitutes, without resistance; and become mothers of children, without fulfillment.

For these grandmothers and mothers of ours were not Saints, but Artists; driven to a numb and bleeding madness by the springs of creativity in them for which there was no release. They were Creators, who lived lives of spiritual waste, because they were so rich in spirituality—which is the basis of Art—that the strain of enduring their unused and unwanted talent drove them insane. Throwing away this spirituality was their pathetic attempt to lighten the soul to a weight their work-worn, sexually abused bodies could bear.

What did it mean for a Black woman to be an artist in our grandmothers' time? In our great-grandmothers' day? It is a question with an answer cruel enough to stop the blood.

Did you have a genius of a great-great-grandmother who died under some ignorant and depraved White overseer's lash? Or was she required to bake biscuits for a lazy backwater tramp, when she cried out in her soul to paint watercolors of sunsets, or the rain falling on the green and peaceful pasturelands? Or was her body broken and forced to bear children (who were more often than not sold away from her)—eight, ten, fifteen, twenty children—when her one joy was the thought of modeling heroic figures of rebellion, in stone or clay?

How was the creativity of the Black woman kept alive, year after year and century after century, when for most of the years Black people have been in America, it was a punishable crime for a Black person to read or write? And the freedom to paint, to sculpt, to expand the mind with action did not exist. Consider, if you can bear to imagine it, what might have been the result if singing, too, had been forbidden by law. Listen to the voices of Bessie Smith, Billie Holiday, Nina Simone, Roberta Flack, and Aretha Franklin, among others, and imagine those voices muzzled for life. Then you may begin to comprehend the lives of our "crazy," "Sainted" mothers and grandmothers. The agony of the lives of women who might have been Poets, Novelists, Essayists, and Short-Story Writers (over a period of centuries), who died with their real gifts stifled within them.

And, if this were the end of the story, we would have cause to cry out in my paraphrase of Okot p'Bitek's great poem:

> O, my clanswomen
> Let us all cry together!
> Come,
> Let us mourn the death of our mother,
> The death of a Queen
> The ash that was produced
> By a great fire!
> O, this homestead is utterly dead
> Close the gates
> With lacari thorns,
> For our mother
> The creator of the Stool is lost!
> And all the young women
> Have perished in the wilderness!

But this is not the end of the story, for all the young women— our mothers and grandmothers, *ourselves*—have not perished in the wilderness. And if we ask ourselves why, and search for and find the answer, we will know beyond all efforts to erase it from our minds, just exactly who, and of what, we Black American women are.

One example, perhaps the most pathetic, most misunderstood one, can provide a backdrop for our mothers' work: Phillis Wheatley, a slave in the 1700s.

Virginia Woolf, in her book *A Room of One's Own,* wrote that in order for a woman to write fiction she must have two things, certainly: a room of her own (with key and lock) and enough money to support herself.

What then are we to make of Phillis Wheatley, a slave, who owned not even herself? This sickly, frail Black girl who required a servant of her own at times—her health was so precarious— and who, had she been White, would have been easily considered the intellectual superior of all the women and most of the men in the society of her day.

Virginia Woolf wrote further, speaking of course not of our Phillis, that "any woman born with a great gift in the sixteenth century [insert "eighteenth century," insert "Black woman," insert "born or made a slave"] would certainly have gone crazed, shot herself, or ended her days in some lonely cottage outside the village, half witch, half wizard [insert "Saint"], feared and mocked at. For it needs little skill and psychology to be sure that a highly gifted girl who had tried to use her gift for poetry would have been so thwarted and hindered by contrary instincts [add "chains, guns, the lash, the ownership of one's body by someone else, submission to an alien religion"], that she must have lost her health and sanity to a certainty."

The key words, as they relate to Phillis, are "contrary instincts." For when we read the poetry of Phillis Wheatley—as when we read the novels of Nella Larsen or the oddly false-sounding autobiography of that freest of all black women writers, Zora Hurston—evidence of "contrary instincts" is everywhere. Her loyalties were completely divided, as was, without question, her mind.

But how could this be otherwise? Captured at seven, a slave of wealthy, doting Whites who instilled in her the "savagery" of the Africa they "rescued" her from . . . one wonders if she was even able to remember her homeland as she had known it, or as it really was.

Yet, because she did try to use her gift for poetry in a world that made her a slave, she was "so thwarted and hindered by . . . contrary instincts, that she . . . lost her health. . . ."

In the last years of her brief life, burdened not only with the need to express her gift but also with a penniless, friendless "freedom" and several small children for whom she was forced to do strenuous work to feed, she lost her health, certainly. Suffering from malnutrition and neglect and who knows what mental agonies, Phillis Wheatley died.

So torn by "contrary instincts" was black, kidnapped, enslaved Phillis that her description of "the Goddess"—as she poetically called the Liberty she did not have—is ironically, cruelly humorous. And, in fact, has held Phillis up to ridicule for more than a century. It is usually read prior to hanging Phillis's memory as that of a fool. She wrote:

> *The Goddess comes, she moves divinely fair,*
> *Olive and laurel binds her golden hair.*
> *Wherever shines this native of the skies,*
> *Unnumber'd charms and recent graces rise. [My italics]*

It is obvious that Phillis, the slave, combed the "Goddess's" hair every morning; prior, perhaps, to bringing in the milk, or fixing her mistress's lunch. She took her imagery from the one thing she saw elevated above all others.

With the benefit of hindsight we ask, "How could she?"

But at last, Phillis, we understand. No more snickering when your stiff, struggling, ambivalent lines are forced on us. We know now that you were not an idiot or a traitor; only a sickly little Black girl, snatched from your home and country and made a slave; a woman who still struggled to sing the song that was your gift, although in a land of barbarians who praised you for your bewildered tongue. It is not so much what you sang, as that you kept alive, in so many of our ancestors, *the notion of song*.

Black women are called, in the folklore that so aptly identifies one's status in society, "the *mule* of the world," because we have been handed the burdens that everyone else—*everyone else*—refused to carry. We have also been called "Matriarchs," "Superwomen," and "Mean and Evil Bitches." Not to mention "Castraters" and "Sapphire's Mama." When we have pleaded for understanding, our character has been distorted; when we have asked for simple caring, we have been handed empty inspirational appellations, then stuck in the farthest corner. When we have asked for love, we have been given children. In

short, even our plainer gifts, our labors of fidelity and love, have
been knocked down our throats. To be an artist and a Black
woman, even today, lowers our status in many respects, rather
than raises it: and yet, artists we will be.

Therefore we must fearlessly pull out of ourselves and look at
and identify with our lives the living creativity some of our great-
grandmothers were not allowed to know. I stress *some* of them
because it is well known that the majority of our great-grandmothers knew, even without "knowing" it, the reality of their
spirituality, even if they didn't recognize it beyond what happened in the singing at church—and they never had any inten-
tion of giving it up.

How they did it—those millions of black women who were not
Phillis Wheatley, or Lucy Terry or Frances Harper or Zora
Hurston or Nella Larsen or Bessie Smith; or Elizabeth Catlett,
or Katherine Dunham, either—brings me to the title of this
essay, "In Search of Our Mothers' Gardens," which is a personal
account that is yet shared, in its theme and its meaning, by all
of us. I found, while thinking about the far-reaching world of
the creative black woman, that often the truest answer to a
question that really matters can be found very close.

In the late 1920s my mother ran away from home to marry my
father. Marriage, if not running away, was expected of seven-
teen-year-old girls. By the time she was twenty, she had two
children and was pregnant with a third. Five children later, I
was born. And this is how I came to know my mother: she
seemed a large, soft, loving-eyed woman who was rarely impatient in our home. Her quick, violent temper was on view
only a few times a year, when she battled with the white landlord
who had the misfortune to suggest to her that her children did
not need to go to school.

She made all the clothes we wore, even my brothers' overalls.
She made all the towels and sheets we used. She spent the
summers canning vegetables and fruits. She spent the winter
evenings making quilts enough to cover all our beds.

During the "working" day, she labored beside—not behind—
my father in the fields. Her day began before sunup, and did
not end until late at night. There was never a moment for her
to sit down, undisturbed, to unravel her own private thoughts;
never a time free from interruption—by work or the noisy in-

quiries of her many children. And yet, it is to my mother—and all our mothers who were not famous—that I went in search of the secret of what has fed that muzzled and often mutilated, but vibrant, creative spirit that the black woman has inherited, and that pops out in wild and unlikely places to this day.

But when, you will ask, did my overworked mother have time to know or care about feeding the creative spirit?

The answer is so simple that many of us have spent years discovering it. We have constantly looked high, when we should have looked high—and low.

For example: in the Smithsonian Institution in Washington, D.C., there hangs a quilt unlike any other in the world. In fanciful, inspired, and yet simple and identifiable figures, it portrays the story of the Crucifixion. It is considered rare, beyond price. Though it follows no known pattern of quilt-making, and though it is made of bits and pieces of worthless rags, it is obviously the work of a person of powerful imagination and deep spiritual feeling. Below this quilt I saw a note that says it was made by "an anonymous Black woman in Alabama, a hundred years ago."

If we could locate this "anonymous" black woman from Alabama, she would turn out to be one of our grandmothers—an artist who left her mark in the only materials she could afford, and in the only medium her position in society allowed her to use.

As Virginia Woolf wrote further, in *A Room of One's Own:*

> Yet genius of a sort must have existed among women as it must have existed among the working class. [Change this to "slaves" and "the wives and daughters of share-croppers."] Now and again an Emily Brontë or a Robert Burns [change this to "a Zora Hurston or a Richard Wright"] blazes out and proves its presence. But certainly it never got itself on to paper. When, however, one reads of a witch being ducked, of a woman possessed by devils [or "Sainthood"], of a wise woman selling herbs [our root workers], or even a very remarkable man who had a mother, then I think we are on the track of a lost novelist, a suppressed poet, of some mute and inglorious Jane Austen. . . . Indeed, I would venture to guess that Anon, who wrote so many poems without signing them, was often a woman. . . .

And so our mothers and grandmothers have, more often than not anonymously, handed on the creative spark, the seed of the flower they themselves never hoped to see: or like a sealed letter they could not plainly read.

And so it is, certainly, with my own mother. Unlike "Ma" Rainey's songs, which retained their creator's name even while blasting forth from Bessie Smith's mouth, no song or poem will bear my mother's name. Yet so many of the stories that I write, that we all write, are my mother's stories. Only recently did I fully realize this: that through years of listening to my mother's stories of her life, I have absorbed not only the stories themselves, but something of the manner in which she spoke, something of the urgency that involves the knowledge that her stories—like her life—must be recorded. It is probably for this reason that so much of what I have written is about characters whose counterparts in real life are so much older than I am.

But the telling of these stories, which came from my mother's lips as naturally as breathing, was not the only way my mother showed herself as an artist. For stories, too, were subject to being distracted, to dying without conclusion. Dinners must be started, and cotton must be gathered before the big rains. The artist that was and is my mother showed itself to me only after many years. This is what I finally noticed:

Like Mem, a character in *The Third Life of Grange Copeland*, my mother adorned with flowers whatever shabby house we were forced to live in. And not just your typical straggly country stand of zinnias, either. She planted ambitious gardens—and still does—with over fifty different varieties of plants that bloom profusely from early March until late November. Before she left home for the fields, she watered her flowers, chopped up the grass, and laid out new beds. When she returned from the fields she might divide clumps of bulbs, dig a cold pit, uproot and replant roses, or prune branches from her taller bushes or trees—until night came and it was too dark to see.

Whatever she planted grew as if by magic, and her fame as a grower of flowers spread over three counties. Because of her creativity with her flowers, even my memories of poverty are seen through a screen of blooms—sunflowers, petunias, roses, dahlias, forsythia, spirea, delphiniums, verbena . . . and on and on.

And I remember people coming to my mother's yard to be given cuttings from her flowers; I hear again the praise showered on her because whatever rocky soil she landed on, she turned into a garden. A garden so brilliant with colors, so original in its design, so magnificent with life and creativity, that to this day people drive by our house in Georgia—perfect strangers and imperfect strangers—and ask to stand or walk among my mother's art.

I notice that it is only when my mother is working in her flowers that she is radiant, almost to the point of being invisible—except as Creator: hand and eye. She is involved in work her soul must have. Ordering the universe in the image of her personal conception of Beauty.

Her face, as she prepares the Art that is her gift, is a legacy of respect she leaves to me, for all that illuminates and cherishes life. She has handed down respect for the possibilities—and the will to grasp them.

For her, so hindered and intruded upon in so many ways, being an artist has still been a daily part of her life. This ability to hold on, even in very simple ways, is work Black women have done for a very long time.

This poem is not enough, but it is something, for the woman who literally covered the holes in our walls with sunflowers:

> They were women then
> My mama's generation
> Husky of voice—Stout of
> Step
> With fists as well as
> Hands
> How they battered down
> Doors
> And ironed
> Starched white
> Shirts
> How they led
> Armies
> Headragged Generals
> Across mined
> Fields
> Booby-trapped
> Kitchens
> To discover books
> Desks
> A place for us
> How they knew what we
> Must know
> Without knowing a page
> Of it
> Themselves.

Guided by my heritage of a love of beauty and a respect for strength—in search of my mother's garden, I found my own.

And perhaps in Africa over two hundred years ago, there was just such a mother; perhaps she painted vivid and daring decorations in oranges and yellows and greens on the walls of her hut; perhaps she sang—in a voice like Roberta Flack's—*sweetly* over the compounds of her village; perhaps she wove the most stunning mats or told the most ingenious stories of all the village storytellers. Perhaps she was herself a poet—though only her daughter's name is signed to the poems that we know.

Perhaps Phillis Wheatley's mother was also an artist.

Perhaps in more than Phillis Wheatley's biological life is her mother's signature made clear.

1974

P A R T 6

LOOSENING THE THREADS:
SEPARATIONS

Throughout the preceding sections of this anthology, we have explored the fabric and contours of the ties that bind Black mothers and daughters in the various and sundry dimensions of our relationships. Poetry, personal narratives, fiction, and essays have been the vehicles by which we have examined how roles and relationships are formed and shaped; the richness of the threads, colors, and designs that create the quilt of our experiences laid whole; the ways in which we carve out territories for ourselves and others; the pulls and tears that wear us out and down; the patterns and trademarks that help to sustain us, to keep us feeling warm, vibrant, resilient.

"Loosening the Threads" looks at yet another dimension. As the final section, it sheds light on how daughters face and work through the despair which comes when ties are loosened and made separate by the experiencing of death and dying. In the throes of death's separations, often we feel too much of our *one-ness*. We feel the spaces around us, and we despair in our search for connectedness. With patience and persistence, however, sometimes we see patterns that reveal the connections that fasten our lives to the lives of our mothers, bindings that are resilient and remain worthy even through death. Sometimes we are able to transcend our despair and use these moments of fragility to renew our sense of balance and power and strength.

The selections in this section offer lenses through which we can filter these moments. They allow us to notice a range of ways in which we are made separate, and a range of responses through which we acknowledge loss and despair and find peace, balance, reconnection.

Marilyn Nelson Waniek reminds us that often as young children we experience symbolic moments of "death" when we are separated temporarily in unexpected circumstances from our mothers. These moments strike fear in our hearts and souls as our imaginations take hold of us. We are brought to the brink of despair and magically saved, a magic which we crave sometimes when real separations occur.

From other perspectives, SDiane Bogus and Pinkie Gordon Lane illustrate how ties wear out through the strains of living Black, poor, and female; whereas Judy Scales-Trent describes the symbolic and psychological separation that a daughter must make in order to forge her own identity.

Lois Lyles and Gloria Wade-Gayles paint the pain and emptiness which comes from the aggressive loosening of illness and disease. Occasionally, we transcend this despair in mystical ways and come to understand that death and dying offer challenges, opportunities, and also "lessons."

In the loosening, mothers and daughters pay homage to each other. Sometimes daughters come to understand as Lorde does that "death is not a disease," and like Lane they are able to carry mothers "like a loose sweater that sucks out the chill on a snowy winter night."

The collective visions expressed in this section show us how we face fragility and strength. We can see the multidimensionality of our singular and our collective experiences. As readers, we can be affirmed, we can transcend, and we can be renewed as we go with them metaphorically, vicariously, resonantly through separation. They show us ourselves and our legacies, the threads that our mothers leave behind.

Jacqueline Jones Royster

THE LOST DAUGHTER

Marilyn Nelson Waniek

One morning just before Christmas
when I was four or five years old
I followed Mama's muskrat coat
and her burgundy cloche
from counter to counter in The May Co.
as she tested powders and colognes,
smoothed silk scarves and woolen vests,
and disappeared down the aisle
into the life she lived before I was born.

The mirrors rendered nothing more
at my eye level than a small brown blur;
I understood why the salesclerks didn't see
a little girl in a chesterfield coat,
plaid bows on her five skimpy braids,
or stop me as I wept my way
toward the outside doors
and was spun through their transparency
out into the snow.

On the sidewalk Santa rang a shiny bell
and shifted from his right boot to his left
as the fingers in my mittens froze
and fell off, one by one.
My skin, then my bones turned to stone
that parted the hurrying crowd,
until at last I drifted, thinned as the smoke
from an occasional pipe or cigarette,
through the thick white words people spoke.

Sometimes a taxi squealed its brakes
or beeped to pierce the solid, steady roar
of voices, wheels, and motors.

The same blue as the sky by now,
I rose like a float in the parade
I'd seen not long before:
a mouse tall as a department store
that nodded hugely as it moved
above our wonder down the avenue.

When Mama spat out my name
in fury and relief, I felt my face
fly back into focus. I formed again
instantaneously under her glaring eyes.
In the plate glass window I recognized
the shape Mama shook and embraced—
the runny nose, the eyes' frightened gleam,
the beret askew on hair gone wild—
and knew myself made whole again, her child.

"MAWU"

Audre Lorde

to Linda

In this white room full of strangers
you are the first face of love   remembered
but I belong to myself in the rude places
in the glare of your angriest looks
your blood   running through my dreams
like red angry water
and whatever I kill
turns in the death grasp
into your last   most beautiful
silence.

Released
from the prism of dreaming
we make peace with the women
we shall never become
I measured your betrayals
in a hundred different faces
to claim you as my own
grown cool   and delicate   and grave
beyond revision

So long as your death is a leaving
it will never be my last.

Departure sounds bell through the corridor
I rise and take your hand
remembering   beyond denials
I have survived
the gifts   still puzzling me
as in the voice of my departing mother
antique and querulous
flashes of old toughness   shine through like stars
teaching me how to die   insisting
death is not a disease.

PROSE POEM: PORTRAIT

Pinkie Gordon Lane

for Inez Addie West Gordon

My mother died while walking along a dusty road on a Sunday morning in New Jersey. The road came up to meet her sinking body in one quick embrace. She spread out like an umbrella and dropped into oblivion before she hit the ground. In that one swift moment all light went out at the age of forty-nine. Her legacy: the blackened knees of the scrubwoman who ransomed her soul so that I might live, who bled like a tomato whenever she fought to survive, who laughed fully when amused—her laughter rising in one huge crescendo, and whose wings soared in dark despair. She asked for little except "to be," and never preached values to me because of her own example. With only an eighth-grade education, she found her escapes in dime-store detective novels (describing lurid crimes) and Saturday night double features at the local movie theater. One afternoon after her death, I came across a pack of letters, five in all, neatly tied with a ribbon, tucked in the corner of a dresser drawer beneath a pile of clothes. They had been written to my father before marriage.

> Dear William, when I think of you and long for you, my
> heart faints with despair.

The irony of that life still haunts me—she a battered wife in later years, who never found the way to release the hope, the dream, even while she tumbled around in the tight little drum of a house in north Philadelphia, guarding its walls fiercely as if they belonged to the Smithsonian.

They lowered her coffin into the ground in 1945, when I was just beginning to think of her as "sister." I carry her with me now like a loose sweater that sucks out the chill on a snowy winter night.

Originally published in *Black American Literature Forum*, vol. 23, no. 3 (Fall 1989); reprinted with the permission of the author.

ON THAT DARK AND
MOON-LESS NIGHT

Judy Scales-Trent

On that dark and moon-less night

my mother opened the door
at the back of the house

quietly
quietly
so as not to waken
the others.

I stood by the door
looking out
into the snow-covered fields and mountains.

She had given me warm clothing and boots.
She had filled my knapsack with food for the journey.
The family dog would come as companion and guide.

My mother opened the door for me
that cold and snow-lit night

and set me free.

CONNECTED TO MAMA'S SPIRIT

Gloria Wade-Gayles

As soon as I opened my eyes, I looked at my Black history calendar with its amateurish drawings of Black leaders and three-sentence summaries of lives that deserved volumes. APRIL, printed in bold black letters, seemed to speak to me. I was running out of time. In five months a new school year would begin, and my semester's leave would come to an end. If I didn't begin to make headway on the book, I would return to work with nothing to show for my time off except stacks of note cards, folders of xeroxed essays somebody else had produced, and conversations with Alice Walker in the margins of four novels.

There was no time for breakfast or the morning paper. I threw on a robe, made a cup of instant Taster's Choice and sat down at the computer to work. "Please wait," the machine ordered. I waited. A second later I had a blank screen. To the far top left was the lighted cursor. At the far bottom right was the line, "Doc 1 Pg 1 Ln 7," which revealed how unproductive I had been for months.

I placed my hands in typing position—my right index finger on "j," my left on "f," and both thumbs on the space bar. I wanted a compelling and poignant opening sentence on Alice Walker's artistic visions. The keys began moving. On the blank screen, lighted in amber, I saw the words, "It is time to go home." I turned off the computer, dressed hurriedly and went searching for the best rates on a rental car.

If I were to share such an experience with Mama, she would explain it as one of those psychic feelings we get but can't explain.

"People get them. All the time," she would say. "You can feel someone thinking about you, pulling you toward them." She believed there is a dimension where the spirits of the living and the dead come together.

"Some people are more psychic than others," she had told me many years ago, and many times. "They're born that way." And

she added proudly, "We're psychic, you know. Your grandmother was real psychic and she passed it on to all of us."

I would admit that her readings of "signs" (which I did not
see) often came true, but I held to my interpretation: mere
coincidence.

"Call it what you want," Mama would say. I know what it is."

We would debate for hours about politics, sex, women and
men, children, the church, and White people. I was never her
match. She would draw on her brilliance and her passion, her
experience and her ability to shape analogies with precise and
colorful words. The bantering was entertainment for us, games
that gave us a chance to spread our mental feathers for each
other.

But when it came to that "other dimension," Mama played no
games. There was no bantering. She would end a conversation
on its way to a debate with a four-word sentence that slapped
me hard in the face: "Just keep on living."

If I gave her an irreverent shrug, her caveat would put my
college degrees in proper perspective: "I don't care how much
education you get, if you lock out the spirit, you're empty. Being
connected is a blessing, but it can be taken from you."

When I returned to the apartment with the rented car, I called
home to announce my plans. I would be leaving for Memphis
early in the morning and returning to Atlanta in two days. With
Mama! She had been living with my aunt for six months; it was
past time for her to live with her daughters.

Each time my sister Faye and I arranged for Mama to live
with us—or at least visit for an extended period of time—my
aunt wouldn't release her. Couldn't. "You're still in school,"
she would tell us. Or "It's too cold. Wait until the weather
changes." Or "Bertha's not ready to leave home yet." Or "She's
not feeling up to a motor trip right through here." This time had
to be different.

"I'll be there tomorrow," I said in an upbeat voice.

"Tomorrow?" my aunt asked.

"Tomorrow," I answered. "It's time for Faye and me to take
care of Mama. And—we're concerned about you, Aunt Mae."

"Concerned about me?" She responded as Faye and I had
predicted she would. Selfless in her love, she was the last person
to make herself first.

"I'm not gonna let you put this on me," she said. "I'm fine
and Bertha and I are having a ball. No children. No pets. No

men during the day. Just the two of us doing what we want to do when we want to do it. It's like heaven here."

"Tomorrow, Aunt Mae."

Mama came to the phone. "Why are you so bent on coming to get me tomorrow? You're not giving me time to get ready."

"I'll get you ready."

"Well, suppose I'm not ready to go with you."

"Remember how you used to give Faye and me your final word with a final word?"

"I remember."

"Well, I'm giving you the final word. I will be there tomorrow afternoon by four, and we will leave for Atlanta in two days."

"Well," she said," pretending that she was giving in to something she was not ready to accept, "Drive safely. Don't speed."

"Don't worry. I'll be careful."

"And if you get sleepy, just pull over to the side of the road . . ."

"I know, Mama. Pull over and sleep in the car the way we used to do when White folks wouldn't let us into motels."

"And if the cops stop you, don't get smart because—well, you got this racial thing so bad that . . ."

"Don't worry, Mama. I'll obey all the rules. See you and Aunt Mae tomorrow around four or five in the afternoon."

The city was asleep when I pulled away from the complex at five the next morning, earlier than I had planned. Except for the lights of a few passing cars and motels' neon signs with missing letters, I drove in darkness. And yet, the highway in front of me seemed to be illuminated by a strange light. My mind began to play tricks on me. I felt as if my car were being pulled by this light. I chuckled to myself, "This is one of those strange phenomena Mama would attribute to the other dimension. I guess I could close my eyes and reach Memphis, drive right up to Mama's front door."

"Naw," I said. "There's nothing to all of that talk about the other dimension. Pre-dawn darkness is just eerie, that's all. Just eerie."

The world began to yawn and stretch by the time I reached the Alabama state line. Cows walked slowly in pastures to my right and my left, dropping huge pies. Farmers, all of them White, were boarding tractors for early morning work in the fields. Lights came on in distant houses as if they were answering each other. I was headed West toward Birmingham. The sun was rising in the East behind me, strips of rose on the hood of my car. I pressed down on the accelerator.

I had six or seven hours alone to think and feel—to get connected to the other dimension. I wondered where it was, what it was, if it *was* real. One side of me knew that I had "it," the psychic thing. Another wanted to reject "it," out of fear. Anything that gets into your life without your permission and leaves without your permission, never explaining why it came in the first place, is frightening. You're out of control, at the mercy of something you can't see or hear, just feel.

I knew I had "it" in 1965 when something pulled me from my bed at four in the morning. The dense darkness in my graduate student's apartment didn't prevent me from finding my way to the phone and dialing, without error, Mama's number: 1-901-458-6223. As I dialed, I knew she wasn't home. My stepfather's sleepy voice answered the phone.

"What's wrong with Mama?" I asked with surprising calm.

"Who told you?"

The calm left me. "Who told me what?" I all but screamed into the phone. "Where's Mama? What's wrong with Mama?"

He took too long to answer, and I became hysterical. "Where is my mama? What's happened to her?"

They had tried to keep it from my sister and me, he began explaining, because that was what Mama wanted them to do. "You know how she don't like to worry you and your sister, being that you're so far from home," he said.

It was an eternity before he told me that Mama was scheduled at six that morning for a brain scan. For several weeks she had had double vision; the doctors feared a stroke.

"But who told you?" he asked after I had calmed down.

I had no answer.

I hung up the phone and called Mama at the hospital. I knew she was awake and waiting for the phone to ring. When she heard my voice, she took a deep breath, remained silent for a second, and with a smile shaping her words said, "I told them you'd know. Somehow you'd know."

I was thinking about that experience when I reached the Mississippi state line. "Mississippi, the Magnolia State," the large sign read. "The spirit must have flown right over Mississippi," I told myself. "Just ignored our people. Left them disconnected to everything except pain."

Mama was born in Clarksdale, Mississippi, the oldest child of an A.M.E. minister and a strong-willed mother who had more experiences with pain than Mississippi had "mean pecker-woods," my grandmother's word for White people. Her step-father, a sharecropper, was an abusive man who beat his children and his wife at will.

"But I can say one good thing for him," Mama would add when she talked about Grandmother's childhood in Mississippi. "He didn't turn any of his girls over to White men. When that peckerwood who owned the land requested your grand-mother. . . . Dirty dog. And she was only twelve. That was it. Her stepfather moved the whole family in the middle of the night."

I hated Mississippi, grew up hating it. In Mississippi my grandmother was widowed at a young age and with four children. Church people who had loved her as the elder's wife avoided her, fearful that she might ask for their assistance. In Mississippi my grandmother struggled "to make ends meet" with the small widow's pension the church provided until she had enough of preachers' sexual propositions and preachers' loose hands.

"Damn hypocrites!" Mama would say.

She moved to Memphis with her children and "somehow mak-ing a way out of no way," she told my sister and me, "we had a roof over our heads, food in our stomachs, and clothes on our back. All of my children finished high school. We made it and I never once worked in a White woman's kitchen. And my daughters didn't either."

I wanted to get out of Mississippi, as my Grandmother had years ago, and on to Memphis, but the Tennessee border was hundreds of miles away. I became anxious and exhausted. Highway 78 was a mean road. It turned and crooked through small towns that offered the same things: fireworks, Indian artifacts, statues of colored jockeys, chenille bedspreads, and two-pump gas sta-tions where red-necked White men spat chewing tobacco. I was held below the speed limit by tractors I dared not pass and mean-looking White drivers I did not trust to let me in if I got out there. I began to sing songs from the Movement, appropriate on this highway. "Keep your eyes on the prize. Move on."

That was Mama's philosophy. Set a goal for yourself, keep your eye on it, and "you'll get there." In the prime of health, I was now stronger than Mama, but not as wise or as brave. She had a way of seeing around sharp corners, over high fences, beneath thick layers of confusion and uncertainty to the very center of truth and practicality. She had a "single eye," she would tell my sister and me. "A single eye." That "eye" was focused on my sister and me, on our wholeness, our ability to stand tall in the light of our own suns.

She talked philosophically about "means to an end," but not the Machiavellian notion that the end justifies the means. For her, "means" meant struggle and sacrifice for an end we had chosen for ourselves. Nothing could derail her. She stayed on track. She stayed on track. Extraneous nonsense that had nothing to do with her "single eye" she just didn't see, wouldn't see.

I remember running home from high school with the good news that a local sorority had chosen me to be a debutante. That was an honor for me. I wasn't light-skinned (as we used to say). I didn't have long hair or short "good" hair, and I lived in a housing project. I had been chosen in spite of my background. The only debutante from the housing project.

"What's it for?" Mama asked, trying to embrace my joy. I recall that she was cooking hot-water cornbread for our full-family Friday dinner. She was pouring boiling water into a mixture of corn, lard, and salt. When the consistency was right, she began rounding the wet meal with her strong hands, never looking up at me.

"My debut," I answered, giving the French pronunciation. Laughing I said, "Not my dee-but."

Mama laughed, too.

"What's it for?" she asked again. I knew now we were going to have court.

"Huh?"

"What will it do for you?"

"Mama!" I was exasperated. This was going to be one of those tests for practicality and values, Mama's favorite word. "It's an honor. I mean, they chose *me* to be a debutante."

"Well, that's because they're smart. No one is more beautiful and graceful than my girls." She had placed four cornbread patties on a sheet of wax paper. They were perfect circles. She turned up the flame under the cast-iron skillet. "What will you need?"

I swallowed hard. Mama already knew what I would need, but she was forcing me to say it, to *hear* myself say it.

"It won't cost that much," I said.

"What will you need?" she asked again, making more corn-bread patties.

I read the list, fast. "A long white formal dress, a tiara, elbow-length white gloves . . ."

She stopped me with a you-gotta-be-kidding chuckle that came from deep inside. "Now what do you need with elbow-length white gloves? Even Cinderella didn't wear elbow-length gloves." I was surprised she didn't jump on the tiara.

"This isn't about Cinderella, Mama."

"Oh but it is," she said. I knew she had chosen Cinderella for a reason. No one was better at analogies than Mama. "It's all fantasy. White dresses, a crown, a ball, and a Prince Charming to boot."

"Mama, you're not being fair to me. This is a *debutante* ball. The biggest event in the city. It symbolizes my debut to society."

"It symbolizes my debut to society," she repeated, mimicking me. "Society?" Mama looked up at me for the first time. "So-ciety? Colored people in Memphis don't have a *society*, baby. Don't you know that? We have communities and churches and families, but not a *society*. They're just copying White folks."

"Well, maybe they are," I said, knowing that she was right. "But what's wrong with that?"

"For people who want it, need it, and can afford it—nothing. We don't need it, can't afford it, and you know I don't want it."

"But we can use it, Mama?"

"How? How can we use a debutante ball that will cost us money. How?"

"It will look good on my resume and give me connections when I apply to college."

"Connections. Don't ever depend on connections, baby," she said sweetly. "That's like depending on somebody else. Connect to yourself. Study, make good grades and. . . ."

I cut her off. "But, Mama, those people are very careful about the girls they choose to be debutantes. I mean, every girl at school wants to be a debutante and those people chose *me*."

"*Those* people?" I had shown my hand. It wasn't about feeling pretty in a long white dress after all. It was about wanting to be with a certain class of people. It was all over for me.

Mama placed the meal patties in the skillet carefully because the oil was piping hot. They made sizzling and popping sounds. "*Those* people?" Mama repeated. I don't care who *those* people are—doctors' wives, dentists' wives, preachers' wives. You know how I feel about people."

I didn't answer.

She separated the meal patties with a black-handled spatula and stepped back from the stove. She looked at me and her eyes told me what was coming. As if she were standing on the top of the world with a bullhorn, she all but shouted her favorite saying, "EVERYBODY IS SOMEBODY AND AIN'T NOBODY NOTHIN'."

I was on my way to popularity, and she was blocking my way. Mixing meal, lard, and hot water in a kitchen which was like all the other kitchens in the project, she was saying no to my chance to be with the right people.

"A colored debutante ball! Hmph. As the old folks used to say, 'Some people don't have a pot to piss in or a window to throw it out of' and we're going around spending money on debutante balls."

Whenever she started sprinkling her wisdom with bits of profanity, I knew I had lost.

"You won't let me have this dream, Mama." I screamed at her, more hurt than angry. "You're taking it away from me."

"It wasn't your dream, baby," her voice softened. "It was a dream somebody else gave you. It doesn't even fit you."

She reached to embrace me, but I ran from her, shouting, "It does fit me. It does. It does."

The hurt lasted for only a few days because I knew Mama was right. She wasn't being mean; she was being practical. She was being herself, a proud woman who was opposed to showy things, phoniness and the slightest hint of elitism. "Phony things can mess up your values," she would tell us. "If you start trying to be like other people because of who they are, or who you think they are," she explained, "you'll end up not being yourself."

That was the only major conflict Mama and I ever had. Even during the turbulent and tumultuous adolescent years when mothers and daughters are supposed to become antagonists in a bitter war that can cast a shadow over adulthood, Mama, Faye, and I were friends. We did silly and wonderful things like walking in the rain for the heck of it and walking home from the neighborhood theater bumping hips against hips, three bodies moving as one.

Mama was a practical joker and an entertainer. I loved her imitation of the man who sold hot tamales in the cold of winter.

He would come down the driveway in the project, singing his song and pushing a two-wheel cart filled with hot coals.

"Hey, hot tamale man. Hey. I got your redddd hotttt tamales. Two fo adime."

I have vivid memories of her bargaining with the Italian market man over the price of thin bunches of greens, too-hard okra, and potatoes that had too many eyes. He would come on Saturday morning, singing no songs, driving a wagon pulled by a horse that salivated profusely.

I also have vivid memories of a brief period in her life when she was having a difficult time with her personal life. She was there for my sister and me, and yet she seemed to be away from us, depriving us of her humor and her wit, her laughter and the dance that made her so delightfully wonderful. I did not like her during this period because she was impatient and vacant. Before I could make peace with having her there and yet not there, she returned to us, never to leave again.

She was an easy mother. She did not wake us up early on Saturday mornings, as some of the other mothers did their daughters, to complete a long list of household chores. We seemed always to have time for ourselves which, I now understand, was her gift to us. She sacrificed to give us that which she did not have when she was growing up—leisure, emotional space, and education.

She did not set unreasonable curfews for us or preach pious sermons about our generation's definition of fun. And when we returned from dates, she did not run her eyes over our bodies— suspiciously, menacingly. She was a sensuous woman who talked openly and vividly about passion and sex, subjects most parents avoided. Sex could be thrilling, we learned from Mama, but "not in the back of a car and not before marriage." She believed in romance and the excitement of young love, but "loving someone and being a fool are two different things."

One neighbor, hinting at Mama's easy parenting style, or jealous of Mama's success at rearing what folks called "good girls," told Mama, "I knew a girl who got pregnant while her Mama was upstairs in bed asleep."

"Is that so?" Mama responded. "Do you think where her mother was sleeping had anything to do with her getting pregnant?"

Mama said that too many of the mothers in the project saw their daughters as potential victims of everything people thought happened to Black girls, especially those growing up in housing projects. She saw us as achievers. Their orientation was shaped by where they lived—in a housing project, a stone's throw from Beale Street. Mama's orientation was shaped by what she saw in her "single eye": two college-educated women in charge of their lives.

Up ahead, the sign read, "Memphis—30 Miles." I pressed down on the accelerator and began singing one of Mama's favorite songs. A Billie Holiday tune which was the blues rendition of Mama's insistence on self-reliance. I pressed down harder on the accelerator and sang, "Mama may have. Papa may have. But God bless the chile that's got his own. That's got his own."

At 1:30 in the afternoon, I pulled into my aunt's driveway. Before I could get out of the car, I heard the screams from inside the house. "She's here, Bertha. She's here." They had been sitting at the kitchen table waiting for me.

"Thank you, Jesus. Thank you, Jesus." Mama kept repeating.

Aunt Mae covered me with kisses. "Girl, you are something else," she said. "Driving all the way here by yourself. Making it here on time."

Mama held me the way a child holds a doll she has wanted for years and finally gets. "You made it," she said. "All by yourself you made it."

Being cute helped me fight back the tears. "A piece of cake, Mama," I said. "No tickets. No cops. No snoozes. Zip. Zip. Zap. And heeerrr I am. Tahdah!" I bowed theatrically.

She turned me around. "Let me see those hips." She was satisfied with my weight. "Now when you lose some pounds, remember not to lose those hips. A black woman without hips is a pitiful sight. We gotta keep our hips."

She went to the phone and dialed my sister. "She made it," Mama said. "Yeah. She looks good. Still got that militant hair cut," she said, "but she looks good." She handed me the phone.

Faye and I had worked everything out before I left Atlanta. It made sense for me to make the trip to Memphis because I was on leave from Spelman for a full semester and Faye was working full-time, and over-time, in a large inner-city Chicago high school. Mama would stay with me this summer and through Chicago's harsh winters and with Faye next summer. As much as my aunt loved Mama and cared for her, we wanted Mama with us. Mothers, we believed, belonged with daughters.

I went to the phone prepared to answer Faye's questions: Had Mama lost weight? Was she steady on her feet? How did she look?" I answered her truthfully, "Mama was beautiful."

Only later that night, after Mama had gone to bed, did I tell the larger truth. Mama was thinner than she was when I had seen her four weeks earlier, and not as steady on her feet. She was not well, but she didn't appear to be seriously ill. She was witty, full of fun, feisty/smart. HERSELF, only older.

The next morning Mama and I went to her house to prepare for her trip to Atlanta. My aunt and I moved about as if this were one of those mornings that followed Mama's overnight away from home. It seemed so routine. But there was nothing routine about what was happening. Mama was leaving for an extended visit in Atlanta and in Chicago. Reluctantly, Aunt Mae was letting go, and yet holding on.

People in the South Memphis housing project in which we grew up thought they were going places. They had hopes, dreams, books in their units, clothes in their closets, and even a bit of vanity in their walk. The housing project was only a stopping-off place for all of us, we believed. But in Mama's North Memphis community, people seemed to survive by standing still.

If you missed the weather-beaten street sign, SHASTA AVE-NUE, you knew when to turn onto Mama's street by the sight of Black men congregating at the corner. Were it not for city streets and city lights, her small community could have been any place in the rural South where Black people sat on porches or hung out in fields with no promise of tomorrow.

"Nothing has changed," Mama said when we reached her street. "We're still so pitiful. So pitiful. Got so many problems."

Mama had moved to Shasta when she married Joe, a hard-working skilled laborer who came from the deep rurals of Tennessee. This area was his stomping ground, and it became Mama's community. After his death seven years ago, she remained and called it home.

When we drove up in front of the house, Mama's next-door neighbor, who had the key to Mama's house, was sitting on the porch. She ran from the porch to meet us at the car. Mama seemed steadier on her feet as she returned Helen's hugs.

"Bertha! Girl, you know I'm glad to see *you*. Girl, you know you look good being as how you been sick. I think you just been hiding out from us."

"Laying up in bed, honey," Mama responded, "trying to get well."

"Well you did it, girl," her neighbor said, looking Mama over. "You looking healthy. Real healthy. You know ev'rybody been missing you." She followed us into the house, sat down in her favorite chair, and started bringing Mama up on what had been happening while she was away.

Word spread quickly that Mama was back and, one by one, the neighbors made what seemed like a pilgrimage to the house. They marveled at how good Mama looked and, as I watched her with them, talking as animatedly as they were, she looked stronger, healthier, and happier. I called my aunt.

"Aunt Mae, you should see her. You wouldn't think she's known a day in bed," I said. "Maybe all she needed was to get out, to return home, to be here with her neighbors."

There was a cohesiveness about poor Black communities before integration that today's middle-class Black communities do not have, or do not need. Everybody had something to contribute to the whole. One woman, my grandmother for example, could make a dress or a suit without a pattern; another could cook everything good from scratch. One could fix things better than men; another could grow a dying Woolworth's twig into a plant healthy enough for cuttings. One, my mother for example, could fix hair without a day of training; another could prepare a potion for mosquito bites or the common cold.

It was that way with the women in Mama's neighborhood. Each gave to the whole out of her special talents and experiences. Mama's gifts were uniquely hers. She wrote letters for her neighbors, filled out job applications, notarized papers, and preached self-reliance. The women would take Mama their bruised egos, or bruised faces, and she became a midwife birthing them new, only to birth them again, and again. They had long since given up receiving pablum from Mama. She served red hot pepper advice.

"You don't have to be a slave to nobody," she would tell them. "First time a man hit you or act like he's gonna hit you, pack your bags. You can take care of yourself."

Tears got nowhere with her in such conversations. She was compassionate, but she had no patience with weakness and self-pity. "You can cry and feel sorry for yourself," she would tell the women, "or you can dry your eyes and get on with your life. If you take mess, you're asking for it, and you'll get it. Don't be no fool-woman. You can change your life. It's about will. If you will something to happen and work at it, it can happen."

I could repeat her sermon verbatim because it is the same one my sister and I heard repeatedly when we were growing up. It always ended with Mama saying, "You don't turn your life over to circumstances or other people."

"Bertha sho will tell you what she think," her next-door neighbor often told my sister and me. "If you don't wanna hear it, don't ask her." That Mama had given her the key to her house gave her status in the community, especially since Mama's house was the only one on the street with shelves of books and souvenirs her children and her grandchildren had sent her from places as far away as Germany.

"But Bertha don't put no stock in stuff like that," she would say. "Bertha don't act like she better than the rest of the folks around here. All of us women get together, sit on the porch, and Bertha, she just like us. She ev'rbody's friend. Everybody love her cause she like that."

When Mama settled in on Shasta and bonded with the community of women, I was, to be quite honest, a bit ashamed. But the community grew on me because it was a part of Mama's life. It was home for her. It would take some maturing and years in the Civil Rights Movement for me to understand and respect Mama's belief in the connectedness of all human beings. She truly believed that "Everybody was somebody and ain't nobody shit." She was not given to the syrupy/sweet hugging and kissing I have witnessed among women who are supposed to be bonded. In fact, she was not demonstratively affectionate with people outside the family, and she didn't like clubs or organizations that put people into groups. But she believed in bonding, believed in love. "Love is the only thing we have that never runs out," she often said. "You can't empty a cup of love. The more other people drink from it, the fuller it is."

Two days later, Mama and I left before dawn for Atlanta. Much to my surprise, she did not look back at her house or at the avenue as we turned from Shasta onto Hollywood, making our way to Highway 78. This was to be her trip. We took with us Mama's tape recorder and a bag of tapes my aunt and I had purchased the day before: selected favorites by B.B. King, Muddy Waters, Billie Holiday, Sarah Vaughan; sermons; and the latest in religious commercialism. We were going to sing our way to Atlanta.

"Caldonia. Bang. Caldonia. Bang. What make your big head so hard." Mama sang along, moving her hands as if she were playing piano. She especially liked the blues and the talking-sensual sounds of B.B. King's guitar. She couldn't carry a tune, but she knew all the lyrics. I laughed at her atonal rendition of "Muddy Water Blues." "I'd rather drink muddy water," she sang, "and sleep in a hollow log."

We played Billie Holiday several times. Using reverse and fast forward, I found Mama's favorite song, and she sang along with Billie: "Mama may have. Papa may have. But God bless the chile that's got his own. That's got his own."

"If things had been different," Mama said, "Billie Holiday would not have had a tragic life."

"Different how?" I asked.

"Just different for Black women. We've had a rough life, still having it. Women love so hard, give so much, give up so much."

"Black men, too," I added.

"Now you know I know that," she explained. "Black men have always had a hard life, still do. But I spend my emotions on Black women because I'm a woman and because women have the children. Made by God to have the children. That makes our lives different from Black men's."

We listened to Billie singing a less well-known song in the background. "Besides," Mama picked up the conversation, "Black women take so much from everybody. In my lifetime, Baby, I have seen some terrible things happen to Black women."

"Out on Shasta?" I asked.

"Everywhere I've been," she answered solemnly. "We give so much and all we want is love. Put on "Women do get weary." I changed tapes, fast-forwarded and rewound until I found the song. Mama sang along: ". . . wearing the same ragged dress. But when she's weary, try a little tenderness."

We reached Tupelo and started counting the signs announcing, "The Birthplace of Elvis Presley." Mama liked Elvis, and I didn't.

"I don't care anything about his music," she said, defending herself. "I just like the fact that he was a poor white boy who never forgot his roots."

"A poor white boy who made it big copying us," I responded.

"Yeah, you're right," she said. "He and a whole lot of them.

But I just respect Elvis. He made a fortune and shared it with his family. "Remembering who you are takes character."

She always talked about roots, about values that were anchored in loving yourself, but also in loving your people. Your roots. "Little people make big people," she would say, "and big people become small people when they forget where they came from."

The highway and the weather cooperated with us. The temperature was in the mid-seventies, and the traffic was light to moderate. After we left Tupelo, the highway became a moving carpet. We rode it together. The signs announcing the number of miles to Atlanta became more frequent, larger it seemed, reaching at times into the car and propping up on the dashboard for our eyes only.

"Hot dog!" Mama said when we reached Carrollton, right outside Atlanta. "Hot dog! We're almost there."

Her emotional mood turned from blues to Amazing Grace. I liked that about Mama. She was connected to different rhythms of life as much as she was connected to different people. She could be secular and earthy when she wanted to be, a high stepper I'd take to anyone's dance. And she could be spiritual and religious, still with her soul and filled with the holy ghost. She embraced and affirmed both parts of herself.

"I'm gone from home now," she said. "I don't think I'll ever get back." She began singing a popular White gospel: "One step at a time, sweet Jesus. That's all I'm asking of you."

She was full. Very full.

"Not many daughters would do what you and Faye are doing," she said.

I reached over and touched the back of her neck, rubbing it gently. "That's only because they don't have mothers like you. I mean that, Mama. I mean that for Faye and for me." The song continued to play.

I pressed down on the accelerator. "Mama," I said, turning down the tape. "We love you."

The phone rang as soon as we entered the apartment. I took a chance and answered by beginning a conversation with Aunt Mae. "A piece of cake," I said. "A piece of cake. Tahdah. We're here. Sang all the way to Atlanta."

"How's Bertha?" she asked. She was letting go and holding on.

Mama went to the phone. "Ola, I didn't get tired one time.

Didn't take a nap. Didn't feel sick. I'm fine. When are you coming to visit?"

We hung up the phone, and it rang again. This time Faye was calling. "How did Mama fare on the trip?" she asked. I handed Mama the phone.

"Hey, baby," she said. "Your mama is doing fine. Just fine. Didn't get tired one time. Didn't take a nap. Didn't feel sick. You would have been proud of me."

Faye must have begun to cry. She had been worried about the length of the trip, and she was hurting because she wasn't with us. "Why are you crying?" Mama said. "You have to stop worrying about me. I'm fine. The only thing that's wrong is I'm missing you. Real bad."

Mama was happy in Atlanta, and each day she seemed to get stronger. I pampered her as she had pampered Faye and me when we were young girls, and even after we became adults. During the day I did what she wanted me to do—sit at the computer and write. She would stand over me sometimes and listen to the click-clapping of the computer keys.

"How's it coming?" she would ask with pride.

"It's coming," I would answer.

"I'm glad. I'm glad you know how to use the computer." It was a gift from her. "I'm glad you're writing. I just wish Faye would write. She's really gifted. If she ever sits down to write, watch out."

Mama loved to hear the sound of the printer. That was proof of my productivity. Sometimes, just to please her, I would call up old essays or course syllabi and print them. I didn't feel guilty about deceiving her because she would say, not knowing what was being printed, "Now that's what I call being busy." And she always referred to Faye's talents. The old saying that a mother loves one child more than she loves another did not apply to Mama. My mother had two daughters, two daughter-friends, in her "single eye."

Nights with Mama were wonderful. Intimate. Spiritual. Peaceful. I would lie in the bed next to her, sometimes in the crook of her right arm, watching television or listening to the pleasant sound of her memories. Other times I would sit in a chair with my feet propped up on the bed, as she ordered. She would share stories with me for "the book," and as she talked she rubbed my feet continuously.

There is something about the night that makes space for subjects we do not discuss during the day. It was at night that Mama
talked about "the other dimension," about our psychic family,
about feelings that came from somewhere neither of us had been,
and yet had been.

"You still don't believe you're psychic, do you?" she asked
one night.

"Here we go again," I said, wanting to change the subject.

"Well, if you don't want to be psychic, that's your business,"
Mama said. "But I know I'm psychic. I know I am connected
to that other dimension. I feel things."

"Do you hear voices?" I was being irreverent, mainly out of
fear.

"My own," she said, "talking to me." She was rubbing my
feet, laying her spiritual hands on me, and I could feel her
strength finding its way to my arms, hands, legs, heart, soul.

"Keep on living, baby," she said. "You'll have experience
after experience that will convince you that the other dimension
is real. We are connected to it."

"Let's just enjoy ourselves in this dimension," I told her.

"We are, and that includes the other dimension. Right now
things are happening in the other dimension that we will experience right here in this room. And people who live there can
see us."

"Mama, I am NOT ready for this conversation."

She continued. "Remember that Mama never saw Prince until
after he had died?" She was referring to her brother, who died
while Grandmother was in the hospital.

"All those times she was laid up," she continued, "Mama
never said, 'Prince came to see me today. Didn't you see him?
He just left.' He didn't visit her until after his death. How do
you explain that?"

"I can't," I answered, "but then I don't try to explain it,
Mama."

"And remember that her mama came to your grandmother in
a dream to tell her something about a large hole and heavy rains.
Remember, she had that dream *after* Prince died."

I remembered that the doctors had advised the family to keep
Prince's death from Grandmother. We didn't want to, but we
had no choice. Doctor's orders. I remembered that it rained so
hard on the day of his burial that the grave was filled with water
by the time we arrived at the cemetery.

"You can't ignore things like that," Mama said. "They're real. There is another dimension to life, and there are spiritual and psychic things here because we are connected to that dimension. Don't fight the connection, baby. Don't fight the connection."

Strange experiences I had had raced through my mind, shouting the truth I did not want to accept. Not now. I was afraid that accepting the truth would release Mama to that "other dimension." I wanted us to live fully and forever in our idyllic world of quiet days and intimate nights. In this dimension.

I took my feet off the side of her bed, stood over her, kissed her, and said, "I love you madly."

"I know," she responded, stroking my hand. "You and Faye are my blessings." I kissed her again.

"You love me so much," she said as I turned to leave the room. "And Faye loves me so much. And Ola Mae loves me so much. And Loren and Jonathan and Monica and . . ."

"What's up with this love's roll call?" I asked, wanting to change a mood I was not ready for. "Of course we love you. All of us do."

"I know," she said in a young girl's voice so uncharacteristic of her.

"So?" I questioned. What's new, Mama? We've always been a family of love."

"I know," the young girl's voice answered. "And it makes me happy. My life has been full because all of you love me, because we've loved one another. That's what life is all about: family and love."

I pretended to play a violin.

"I've never been rich," she continued, ignoring my antics. "Never really wanted to be rich with money and things. But I have been a wealthy woman. Truly blessed. All a mother can ever want in life is to see her daughters become women who like themselves and others. Who can take charge of their own lives. I thank the Lord for my blessings."

"You're the blessing, Mama." I kissed her again and walked out of the room. I pulled myself into bed, feeling a sense of heaviness. Moments later, Mama called to me from her room.

"Remember the time you knew I was in the hospital?"

"I remember, Mama. Now go to sleep."

"Remember the doctors told me that I would just have to live with the double vision? There was nothing they could do for me?"

I couldn't fight the truth any longer. Mama's double vision went away in a phone call. A woman whom Mama met at the hospital, a psychic woman, began calling Mama daily. In each conversation she would tell Mama that the double vision was leaving. Mama knew my silence meant I was recalling the experience.

"Even the doctors couldn't explain it," she said from the other room. "Call it God, call it Jesus, call it whatever you want, I know there's something else to my life than what we see and hear. Goodnight, baby."

"Goodnight, Mama."

Minutes later, she called again from the other room. "Gloria, are you asleep yet?"

"Far from it, Mama."

"You know I am not going home again."

I worked hard that night to communicate with the force, the power, the spirit in the other dimension. "If you could take away Mama's double vision," I said. "If you could send me a sign that she was in the hospital. If you could let Prince visit Grandmother. You can do anything. I know you can. If you're listening to me, and I know you are, please, please don't take Mama away from us. Not yet. Not yet."

When Aunt Mae came to visit, Mama was ecstatic. It was almost like old times in Memphis. She and my aunt got up at the crack of dawn for their coffee and spent the day savoring each minute as if it were vintage wine kept in a cellar only they could enter. They were intoxicated with a love that knew no boundaries. In Atlanta, they shared the same bed; in life, the same heart.

Faye came from Chicago burdened with worries about Mama's health. We were very different, my sister and I. I was the mischievous child; Faye was the lady. I was the child who, in early grades, could care less about school. Faye was, from the very beginning, exceedingly bright and well-mannered. I was playfully feisty with Mama. Faye was indulgent and gentle. I was one half of Mama's life; Faye was the other. Mama lived for the whole.

Faye bought Mama a VCR, and we spent a fortune on movies Mama wanted to see. Her favorites were "The Color Purple" and "Cry Freedom." *The Color Purple* was the last book Mama read before her eyesight began to fail her. Growing up in Mississippi and in Memphis in the early twentieth century, she had met many Celies, she said. She marveled in Celie's wholeness, Sofia's strength, and Mister's redemption. She loathed the oppressors of our people in South.

Faye pampered Mama with good home-cooked meals. A special treat since I could never cook to please Mama. I made casseroles and bland things she called "White folks' food." She enjoyed greens and peas and roasts that Faye touched magically with a culinary ability she got from Mama.

Faye took every breath that Mama took, watching her closely, unable to conceal from me her concern and worry. In a strange way, I worried at times more about Faye than about Mama. If anything should happen to Mama, Faye, I feared, would simply fall apart. She was connected to Mama in a special way. "Mama is my strength," Faye would say. "I can't imagine life without her."

Faye wanted Mama to live forever. Mama wanted Faye to write the book that was burning inside. She was quite right in her evaluation of her two daughters. Faye was truly gifted. I was not as gifted, but I was driven. I would fight my way through the thickets, running at breakneck speed. Faye would get through, Mama believed, but she would do so with grace and style, taking her time. What mattered to Mama was the getting through.

Faye's departure from Atlanta was stiff, awkward, and painful. "I don't want to leave my mama," she told me the night before she left. I understood, but she had to check her tears. "You know how Mama is about signs," I told her.

Both of them deserved a medal for pretense. Faye was dry-eyed. So was Mama. They talked about Faye's return in October for Mama's birthday. Everyone was coming for the celebration. Mama was sitting in the rocking chair we had purchased for her. Faye hugged her, just long enough but not too long. "I love you, Mama," she said.

"I know," Mama answered. "I know."

As soon as the door closed, Faye released her pain in unchecked tears. She told me about the conversation she and Mama had had the day before. They were drinking coffee early that morning while I slept late. Mama looked at Faye with a radiant smile and said, "Whatever happens to me, don't let them cut me open." Before Faye boarded the plane, she turned to me and said, "When it's time for Mama to come to Chicago, let her go. I can't wait to have my Mama with me."

Mama and I returned to our quiet days and intimate nights, but it just wasn't the same. I wanted the Black history calendar over my desk to read OCTOBER because everyone would be coming for her seventy-fifth birthday. She was born on the tenth of October, a Libra like my daughter. Strange thing about Mama. She believed in a spiritual world, but didn't think much about signs. A generational difference, I suppose.

The first four months of Mama's visit were productive for me. Words and ideas came faster than I could write them. In late July, they began to run from me.
    Mama said, "I'll catch them."

Sometime during July, I returned home from grocery shopping to find Mama more excited than she had been since Faye and Aunt Mae had returned home. She had taken a message from an agent regarding a manuscript I had sent her. Mama thought it was *the* book. When I returned from shopping, she was so excited she could hardly speak.
    "You didn't tell me you had finished the book!"
    "I haven't," I told her.
    "The agent called. Honey, the agent called and said she got it and she would be in contact with you in a few weeks."
    I realized that Mama was talking about the manuscript of poetry I had mailed. I never told her about it because I didn't want her to get her hopes up.
    "Oh, that's not the book, Mama," I explained. "That's my poetry."
    "Whatever," she answered, no less excited. "It's something you wrote and it's gonna be published."
    "Let's just cross our fingers," I told her.
    "You got the good news," she said. "The agent called didn't she and . . ."
    "That's not *good* news, Mama," I corrected her. "That's a professional response."
    "You'll hear from her. Just believe me," Mama said. "I can feel it. You will hear from her. I won't be around when you do, but you will hear from her."
    "In the meantime, lady love of mine," I became theatrical.

That was usually my way with her when I was uncomfortable. "Let's not wait for the phone to ring."

A month later, I was back at work, and very distraught because the woman I had hired to stay with Mama for three days a week took another job. As if she were a fortuneteller, or a woman who could really *feel* things before they happened, Mama had told me in Memphis that my plans would not work out.

"And when I go back to work," I remember telling her, "Miss Miller will stay with you. . . ."

She had interrupted me with a knowing smile. "No, she won't. Nobody will be there."

Mama was stoic and valiant, even convincing when she told me that she could do for herself. "I'm not an invalid, you know," she told me. "I can cook, wash, straighten up a bit. You don't need to pamper me."

I had no choice. I returned to work and left Mama at home alone. Luckily, my department chairperson had given me the schedule I requested. I had only one class on Tuesdays and Thursdays, and it did not begin until 1:00. I left home at 12:30 on those days; I was back by 3:00.

Mondays, Wednesdays and Fridays, however, were my more difficult days. I had three classes, but thank God I had a break between 1:00 and 3:00. I always went home to check on Mama. Each time she was watching television, napping, or cooking. I was relieved.

On Friday, September 17th, I did not go home during my break. Instead, I drove to a vacant lot behind abandoned apartments that were once dormitories for an adjacent college. I sat in the car staring ahead, looking into an abyss of loneliness. The skies were heavy with the darkness of a tornado which hit Atlanta somewhere to the West. There was no air and, though I was close to I-20, there were no sounds of passing cars. There was no world. I knew where I was and yet I could not remember how I got there.

I was late reaching my 3:00 class. Where I had been, I could not remember. When I walked into the classroom, my feet were iron weights pounding the floor, and yet I felt that I was floating into the room.

The class, Images of Women in Literature, was beginning a

unit on "woman as mother." I asked the students to try to *see* their mothers as persons. To get them started, I talked about Mama. The images of her came faster than I could share them with the students, speaking without my voice and moistening the eyes of everyone. I remember ending the class by saying, "If you could meet my mother, you would love her."

When I returned home, Mama was unusually energetic. She had cooked a big pot of chicken stew and a pan of cornbread. I learned later from my aunt that Mama had called her long distance and talked for over an hour.

That night we cuddled together in the bed watching MASH. Mama's laughter was hearty and her wit had never been sharper.

"How's your writing coming?" she asked me. Before I could answer, she said, "You're gonna hear from that agent."

We talked about Faye, "who must write," Mama said, and Aunt Mae and the grandchildren—everyone in the family. Nothing maudlin. We seemed to be returning to the joy of her first days with me.

"You've had a long day," she said.

"But, just think, Mama. It's Friday." I jumped from the bed and did a silly dance. "It's Friday, and tomorrow is Saturday. I will be here all day."

"That will be good," she said, sitting up on the side of the bed. "Hand me my purse."

She opened it and took out several cards wrapped with a rubber band. "These are my insurance cards." She reached in for a five by seven blue notebook wire-ringed at the top. "All of my medicines are written down here."

I was speechless.

"Don't let them perform surgery on me for anything. Don't let them put me on life-support systems. Don't. . . ."

"Mama, why are you doing this?"

"Hush," she said, "and listen to me. I know what I am doing." She continued, repeating her first "don'ts." "Don't let them perform surgery on me for anything. Don't let them put me on life-support systems. And don't let them do an autopsy."

"Mama, I . . ."

"Do what I tell you, Gloria," she said with firmness and serenity. "Put all of this in your purse. And don't worry about me. Wherever I am, I will be connected to you and Faye. I'll be fine. Now give me a kiss and turn off the light."

I did not sleep well that night. I kept thinking about Mama's belief in psychic feelings and the "other dimension." Her heavy breathing in the next room reassured me. She was fine. As long as I could hear her, we were in *this* dimension.

That's where we were when I awoke on Saturday morning. Mama was unusually beautiful. Glowing really. Her skin was firm and her eyes were tiny jewels, glittering. It was a beautiful sunny day. The world outside was a perfect skyblue decorated with fluffy white clouds close enough to touch.

Mama's energy and beauty, combined with the sunshine, inspired me to plan a day away from home. Dinner out. A movie. She agreed to everything. She would take a nap for two hours, and I would grade student essays. It was going to be a perfect day.

I was behind with my paper grading, especially the themes I had assigned the freshmen two weeks ago. When I began grading the papers, I smiled to myself, "I must have been teaching Mama in all of my classes." The papers were portraits of mothers. I had finished the last essay in the set and was writing, "You should show this to your mother. It is a testimony of your love for her," when I heard what sounded like the gasp one makes when surprised. I hesitated for only a second before running to Mama.

Mama never returned to Memphis. We buried her in Atlanta. For weeks after her death, I went to the cemetery every day, sometimes twice a day. Always I went during the break between classes. Without my hands or my eyes, my car left Spelman's campus, drove down Westview and took the turns from the gate to the far end of the cemetery. I knew I was losing my mind slowly, and I really didn't care. When you lose your mother, you lose a part of yourself. Nothing would ever be the same again in my life.

My aunt, whose loss was as great as mine and Faye's, talked to us about "the other dimension," using Mama's cadence. "You have to believe that she's still with us," Aunt Mae said. "Only her body is gone. We'll always have her spirit."

For a second I thought of how empty platitudes are when you're hurting so badly you can't even cry out. But my aunt was not speaking platitudes. She was stroking us with her faith, which was Mama's faith, stroking us and forcing us to heal.

"The way to begin to heal," she would tell us, "is to be connected to her spirit. She's still with us." My aunt was split in two, hemorrhaging in her soul, but she was stoic for us. Again and again, she told us, "Your mother left the way she wanted to leave—at peace, smiling and ready." And my aunt added, "If you don't believe what she believed and what I believe, just keep on living. You'll see the signs."

A month after her death, I found the courage to sleep in Mama's bed. I wanted to feel her spirit, even prayed, insane woman that I had become, for an apparition or a voice. I saw nothing. I heard nothing. I felt nothing except pain.

I had not been able to work on the book since Mama's death. Perhaps, I told myself, lying in her bed will bring some words to me. I went next door to my room and returned to Mama's bed with a legal pad and several sharpened pencils. Nothing came to me except the beginning of a letter: "Dear Mama, I miss you so much."

The phone rang. The voice on the other end said, "I never make business calls from my home, but I'm making this one. I just finished your manuscript and . . ." There was a pause. "Something had been directing me to it for days. I read it before reading others I received before yours." There was another pause. "It's . . . I just can't tell you what a moving experience it was. I love your poetry."

The words I had wanted to hear, had wanted Mama to hear, did not move me. Instead of responding jubilantly, I said, "I lost my mother a month ago and . . ."

The agent interrupted me. "Now I understand everything," she said. "I know what was happening to me. Gloria." She called my name. "Gloria. Gloria. I am your mother's medium."

TO MY MOTHER'S VISION

SDiane Bogus

My earliest reader was my mother; a lover of poetry herself, she often quoted Longfellow from memory as she went about the harsh chores of our cold-water flat. I'd come dashing home from school in those latter days following the publication of the "Bogus boys," and plop my new "hearts and flowers" creation before her. With the eloquence of Sojourner Truth, she'd intake a breath, and read aloud the sentimental, slightly unrhythmical "mistress-piece" (apologies to traditionalists). On one of those days, she declared, "You're going to be a writer when you grow up. I think I'll get you a typewriter when you become sixteen."

What age was I then? Eleven? Twelve? Thirteen? I don't know; it doesn't matter because I've never forgotten the moment. What she had done was to define me, to offer the future to me, to approve of my talent, to encourage it. That day, I stood before her as she sat in bed, she was ill. My heart pounded anticipatorily as if age sixteen was a moment or two away. I stood there dreaming of legions of readers, legions who would, like my mother, read my work, not with envy, but love, pride, and awe. Her declaration of my future had slain envy of my brothers and other writers, and I was free to become a writer compared to none. Oh, how I dreamed!

Waiting for sixteen, I churned out poems and stories with the facility of a first-grade finger-painter. I marveled at my ability, and to get better at it, I would read books during my school's "library hour" in order to get an idea of how I'd want my books to be when I grew up. I read *The White Stag, Caddie Woodlawn, Alexander Hamilton, The Young Lion*, and many others. Outside of school, I visited the public library like a nun goes to prayer, habitually, religiously, and seriously.

By now, my mother was in the hospital in Chicago, and I was living with an aunt on the other side of town. Children under sixteen weren't allowed to visit people in the hospital; so, I mailed my staple-bound notebooks to my mother. She wrote back, infrequently, commending my vocabulary, my ideas, and reminding me of the promised typewriter come my sixteenth year. I was fourteen then, but my anticipation remained great. My dreams were grand. My writing advanced (for a ninth grader). My mother died. She died young, died of cancer, died of overwork, worry and Blackness in an underpaid poor person's factory job.

No single setback to my career has ever been as devastating as that first one. With my mother dead so were my dreams. She had been the repository for them. She would have been the one to make them real and official by buying me a typewriter. But she was dead and so was the writer in me. I did not write again for two years.

Meanwhile I was shipped from Chicago to Birmingham, Alabama because my father did not think he could raise me without my mother. I was enrolled in high school, and I promptly fell in love with one of my schoolmates, the girl next door. It was a hide and seek affair. We hid to kiss and fondle, and sought a means to do it again and again. She reminded me of my mother, and some time around 1962 I wrote a poem that exorcised my grief and resurrected my talent:

TO MY MOTHER

Though Death took you from me
While yet in younger years
I feel, Dear Mother, in time of need,
Your memory calms my fears.
I wondered on the day, they laid you away,
My eyes full to tears and sorrow
Oh, Mother, I loved you so
What's in store for tomorrow?

LAST CHRISTMAS
GIFT FROM A MOTHER

Lois F. Lyles

Tis the season to be jolly, I think, seeing the string of gold tinsel someone has used to bind her hair into a question mark atop her skull. No smile decorates my lips. Seeing her face averted on the pillow and her gelatinous eyelids drooping, I step back from the bed. No time for small talk now. She needs rest, after what she's been through.

"Lois, sit down," Dad commands. As he sits, his arms are locked across his chest and his legs are crossed. The toe of his shoe swings nonstop like the arm of a metronome.

"No, thanks." I look beyond the foot of the bed at the empty seat between Dad and my son Ahmed. "I'm not tired."

"You're making *me* tired!" Dad's mouth knots.

"No thanks."

Crossing my arms over my chest, I stroll to the window. The broad window ledge is lined with get-well cards and big, luxuriant potted plants. On a velvety red leaf of the poinsettia I wired her from New Jersey, a fragment of the last sunlight has settled. I grimace as I touch the card I sent with the plant. The gay card contains the message, "Get well soon."

"Dad, Ahmed and I are going outside." He nods. His eyes close.

My twelve-year-old and I step into the clean, bright hospital corridor, lined with doors bravely sporting large cut-outs of stars, bells, and Christmas trees, against backgrounds of artificial snow stuck to shiny red, green, blue, or silver paper. Not far to the left is a large, artificial Christmas tree weighted with "snow" thick as cotton batting and a multitude of satiny, white balls. A few yards to the right, at the end of the hall, is a picture window. Ahmed and I gaze at the fiery setting sun; and, as he weaves me tales of denizens of other galaxies, of superheroes with blazing swords and impeccable constitutions, I silently entreat for her, a woman only sixty-three years old, the Christmas gift of hope.

Looking at the brilliant sun, I remember a different, infinitely colder orb. The night he told me, the round white neon light on the kitchen ceiling leered like an evil moon. He'd called, long-distance, to tell me she was having an operation; that's all I'd known, until my first night in D.C., home for the holidays.

"I know you find it hard to accept, but—"

"What did you say?" I hissed. His words of a minute before were still lingering, hooked into me, sucking my blood.

And Dad repeated, "Lois, your mother has terminal cancer."

I stare at the sun. The frozen gray apartment buildings scin-tillate with its ruby glory. But, in what seems like seconds, the sun is gone, leaving a mere ash of daffodil and rose in the tenebrous vault of the sky.

"Gol-lee!" Ahmed's jaw drops. "Where did the sun go?"

"So fast!" I whisper, in sorrow and wonder.

NIGHTGOWN

The pink and white flowered gown I wear to bed is three years old, and threadbare. It had been witness to my first experience of loving a good man. Both the gown and the good man are still with me.

Now my gown is again a witness. It carries a black smudge (the watery mascara from the blotting of my midnight tears) just above the ruffle at the hem. I cannot cry in the daytime. I must, like my relatives, look at my mother in the hospital bed and pretend nothing is wrong. Besides, I must try to be cheerful, to keep her spirits up.

Sometimes she, either from pain or from fear of the axe of doom hovering over her neck, explodes in a tempest of nervous tears. Then my father, scowling, exclaims, "Aw, Minnie, don't cry!"

Twice when she and I have been by ourselves in the room, we have cried together. She doesn't mind my tears, I know, and hers don't bother me. When nobody is looking at us, we can cry, and then it is all right.

It's not all right when I am at the house; if I cry there, father or son is sure to reproach me for the weakness of sorrow. So, at night, I go into my room and shut the door. I pull my old, warm gown, first the gown of love, and now of grief, over my head. The soft white flannel balls into my palm as soon as the room is dark and my feet have slid between the cool bedsheets. In a few minutes, the flannel is damp. Can I get a witness? I've got my gown.

NEEDLEWOMAN

She is not quite so knocked out so much now. She was operated on a week before Christmas. Now, the second week of her hospital stay, she is gradually healing after the mastectomy, so the nurses have eased up on the painkillers. We crank up the hospital bed and she sits up and talks with the family. As she chats, her hands are busy with a square of linen stretched under an embroidery hoop. Her needle plies in and out, and white French knots bloom into flowerlets on the wheat-colored cloth. I remember how she taught me to make French knots. I am a needlewoman like my mother.

She asks me to make her another eyeshade to replace the one she uses to help her sleep when the nurses are in and out of her semi-private room all night, flashing lights on and off. She plans to give her black satin and lace eyeshade to a friendly nurse who admired it.

When I was a young girl, Mama taught me to sew by hand and by machine. To save money, during the years I and my sister Mary were growing up, she had made our clothes and many of her own.

I am glad she taught me her craft. Now I can sew for her. And I have been able to help myself with the art of the needle. When I moved into my current apartment, I saved money by making some of my own furnishings. Not having a sewing machine, I made, by hand, five sets of curtains, four of them from remnants of cloth I'd saved, just as she used to save pieces of cloth from the bolts that had, on her cutting board, yielded up the rudiments of whole garments.

ENTERING THE WHIRLPOOL

Happy New Year. She is home for the first time since her operation. As the front door swings inward to admit her, the first thing visible in the living room is a bright army of boxes, large and small, massed on a white sheet draped around the base of a Christmas tree. The cheery wrapping on the boxes is largely her work; most of the gifts are the ones she bought and wrapped for us, weeks before she entered the hospital.

Christmas was over a week ago, and the gift boxes, resplendent in their red, their green, lie ignored on the floor.

Just inside the front door she sees the bunch of rolled-up newspapers, still in their plastic sheaths, on the piano top. There are ten papers, one for each day she was hospitalized.

"I'm going to call and cancel the *Post*. I have *no* interest in that at all," she says; then, wearily, trods upstairs.

And now we hear the hum of the whirlpool. We are to live submerged under waves of heat, light, and sound. Dad sets the heat at eighty-five so that she will not come down with something. The light in the master bedroom where she sleeps will stay on, turned either to bright or dim, at all hours. The color television in her room will never cease to babble. And the telephone will begin to ring, shattering the quiet every two or three minutes. It is beginning, the time of warmth that chokes, of light that cannot relieve our darkness, of sound that deafens, of time that is quicksand, leading nowhere but down.

New Year's is the last occasion I will know what day it is for a long time. Or what happens, when. Thought, word, emotion, event—all of these will eddy round and round in the muddy water of my brain. There is no time in a whirlpool.

We are all in the whirlpool—she, most of all. She is to ex-perience time as a circle, not as a progression; she will surely pass the stages of her age and youth. There is no time in a whirlpool.

NEW YEAR'S AFTERNOON

As she reclines, I kneel at her bedside. She is telling me her final wishes: "Don't ever let any man get next to your money. Don't put anybody before the welfare of your child. Ahmed loves you. He must always come first."

She moves on to a less important concern: what to do with her possessions. "As for my clothes, donate them to charity. I don't know of anybody who'd want them except me." I glance at the rack of fifteen-year-old polyester skirt-and-blouse sets and pantsuits in the closet behind me, and nod. The beauty of her existence has always lain in her generosity, not in the costly adornment of her body. She has always been thrifty, hoarding money for her children and grandchildren. She has monitored every tablespoon of soap powder and dishwashing liquid, every hank of thread, every portion of paper and plastic, to prevent waste. Only sporadically has she seen the dentist, the doctor. She has watched her money more than her looks; valued her pennies more than her life.

On the bed next to her are the two smiling, stuffed toys Cousin David gave her in the hospital. Mama never had many toys while she was growing up. She has her toys now. She takes the pink-and-blue clown and the panda with the neck-tag reading, "I need bear hugs!" to her breast and gives them a brief, intense caress. Then she sets the toys down on the bed, and sighing, looks at me.

"I hope you will always try to stand up for yourself, Lois. I am sure the way your great-aunt treated me contributed to my low self-esteem." She tells me about New Orleans: the start of her long, hard road.

New Orleans: my great-aunt Minnie, adopting my mother, age three, after both parents, the blacksmith father and the school-teacher mother, died young. And the older Minnie verbally torturing the younger, sheltered and fed (it was what relatives, in those times, felt obliged to do), though my great-aunt could barely support herself. (In the Depression hard-scrabble, my great-aunt was a manicurist, staring all day at White folks' hands.) Under a barrage of curses from her only parent, little Minnie retreated into herself. She learned never to trust anyone with either her successes or her problems. Secrecy was her only weapon.

New Orleans: schooling from the Sisters of the Blessed Sacrament, the shimmering heat and rain, the tropical stink, the endless wealth of magnolia and palm, the kaleidoscope splendor of carnival season, the fishy taste of Lent. New Orleans: the blue-vein caste to which my mother belonged, the Creole patois. The on-your-knees housework, the quilting, embroidering, and crocheting (fine arts for a Black girl), no money for much of anything; Aunt Flo, the eldest, worked and paid Mama's college fees at Xavier, no money even for Kotex, wash your bloody rags instead.

New Orleans: the Crescent whistling her name when she was twenty-one. Like so many of her kin who'd heard the freedom whistle of a northbound train, and had ended up in Philly, New

York City, Cleveland, Detroit, she showed her back to the crack-
ers and Jim Crow. D.C. became home.

Mama interrupts her reminiscing to sit up and gently rub a
large bruise on my right forearm. "Lois, what is this?" she asks,
tenderly as she might had I been five years old instead of thirty-
five. I shrug and reply, "I don't know how I got that." She smiles
sadly, then comments, "Sometimes I hurt myself, too, and don't
know how I did it."

"Mama," I blurt out, "How long did you know there was a
lump in your breast?"

She shakes her head, and reclines again. Her hands cross
upon her stomach. "Lois, I am ashamed to tell you." Tears are
welling up in her eyes.

"Why—why didn't you tell somebody sooner? See a *doctor?*"
I watch her lips tremble, and her face twist with shame. "Was
it because you were afraid?"

Behind the unstylish reading glasses, her eyes are wet. She
nods vigorously, then whispers, "Ye-es."

WAITING ON THE SICK

Mama is down, I am up. Up, and up, and up. She wants vaseline
for her char-dry lips, her Saint Francis church bulletin, her
rosary. The vase on the dresser must be moved out of the way
of the black-faced digital clock. Two twenty-five, New Year's
afternoon. She stares at the red numerals, each like an imp or
an infernal flame, as the five becomes a six; the six, a seven.

"Water the plants, Lois."

Nervously, I dribble water into the flowerpots. I work fast.
She has approximately one request every three minutes.

"Thank you, darling. I feel so worthless and useless. Why
can't I do anything?"

"Mama, you are not worthless. You are a beautiful person.
You still look beautiful to me," I say, and mean it. She was my
childhood idol. Her soulful-eyed, smooth-haired beauty was my
first acquaintance with romance.

"No, I'm not," she whimpers; then says, "Thank you, darling."

"Mama, whatever happens, I'm with you, and I'm for you."

She cries. Her misery makes me recall how my fear of death
had once made me, to my mortal shame, abandon a sick woman
I loved. I am the namesake of Mama's sister Florence, who died

of cancer four summers ago. Florence is my middle name. Mama must be thinking of Aunt Flo, too, for she says, "I took care of Sister when she went up to her bedroom three days before she died and never came downstairs again. I remember she was amazed that I would wash her down there, you know, her private parts. She didn't want me to have to do that." After pausing, my mother adds, "I thought, Lois, it would help you after this is over, to be with me now when I need you, and do things for me."

I am astonished at her, the good mother. She has called me to her sickbed, not so much to help her as to help *me*. I, in childhood, was never hungry, never homeless, never seriously ill; and was never exposed to the sight of physical suffering. My parents had made sure of all that. But an easy ride of a life is only a half-truth. Now Mama's gift is to let me know her pain. She is letting me see if I am strong enough to grapple, by proxy, with Death.

HER NAMES

The phone cries unceasing alarm. Three nurses, a nurse's aide, an oncologist, a dermatologist, the family physician, a lawyer, a social worker, the medical insurance people. Nephews, nieces, sisters, daughter Mary, friends. "Anything I can do? So sorry. Call me if you need anything. So sad." So sorry to hear about Miz Lyles, about Minnie, about Auntie Minnie, about Nanny, about Mary (this last, the name my mother chose to call herself after she, upon retirement, developed her own business; she had always hated "Minnie").

She has some other names. To my son, whom she reared, she is alternately "Ma" and "Grandma." To "the Frye bunch," my sister's four, she is "Big Grandmommy," in contrast to Mrs. Alberta Frye, "Little Grandmommy."

Ahmed, Odeyo, Sekou, Fela and Lia, children of Mrs. Lyles's children, light a candle of hope for Big Grandmommy. Remember her now, for she always, on holidays, remembered you; and on birthdays, celebrated your lives with neat sums, an extra dollar to each child with each new birthday, the money keeping pace with the slowly accumulating fund of years.

Mama is hunched over in the wheelchair as I, moaning under my breath and clutching her shoulders, sit behind her on the bed. The emergency medical technicians, all in blue shirts and trousers, seem to take up too much space in this bedroom, that, for the first time, is receiving the scrutiny of strangers.

"What's her name?" the big, blond technician asks.

"Mrs. Lyles."

"First name?"

"Minnie."

He bends toward her and trumpets, "Minnie, can you hear me?" His Southern accents grates on my ears.

"Her name is *Mrs*. Lyles." I stare at the man.

"I'm sorry!" He twirls the end of his thick yellow moustache between thumb and index finger. "She is a very sick woman. What's more important, that I check her condition, or that I call her by her proper name?" The young man's brow knits, and he shakes his head.

I think, "He's young, White, she never would have let him call her by her first name. *They* always did that to us, down South."

NO MORE CORNBREAD

The red flashing lights of the ambulance tunnel through the blackness. The siren is a merciless hammer on the anvil of the night. We are going fast, fast up Branch Avenue to Alabama, right on Alabama Avenue, all the way to Sears, then left at the Sears parking lot, on, on fast, to Greater Southeast Hospital. I've known these streets since I was a teenager. But if I know the landscape, why does this seem like a journey through hell?

Mama is alert now, and when I say, "I love you, Ma," she says, clearly, "I love you too, Lois."

The blond medic questions me: What is her age? Her medical history? What kinds of pills is she taking? "She is a cancer patient," I say. It is the first time I have said "cancer" in connection with her. The word makes her disease real to me in a way it had never been before.

Muffled and sweating in my quilted winter coat, I sit in the crowded emergency waiting room. I think, sorrowfully and angrily, "She can't even eat cornbread anymore. I tried to please her by making something she liked, but look what happened! Nothing I do for her again will do any good." In my mind, I see her as she had looked not long before. She had suddenly slumped back on the bed, unable to chew; the yellow dough had balled up in her mouth. Her eyes had rolled up in her head, and the muscles of her left hand and arm had gone slack.

Dazed, I wonder, "Is this real?" Yet my name is real, and the loudspeaker barks it out.

I am in an emergency ward for the first time in my life. Unreal, the white-curtained cubicles, the quiet precision of the white-clothed nurses, the azure-smocked, azure-trousered doctors. A nurse shepherds me to a cubicle where, within the perimeter of shade cast by long drapes, my mother lies on the cold white bed.

"Lois, why am I here? What did I do?" she pleads, eyes ballooning with fear. Her tone promises that if her family and doctors will let her go, she will never make this much trouble again. I am crumbling as I look at her, prone, struggling so to hold on to normalcy, decency, dignity.

"Lois, I wasn't doing anything wrong. I was just eating a piece of cornbread," she protests, like a child maliciously accused of misconduct. "I was all right," she insists, over and over.

Later, a doctor confers with me and with my father, who drove, following the ambulance, to the hospital. "She's had a transischemic attack—a temporary stroke. There's nothing more we can do for her here. The type of episode she experienced tonight is not unusual for a person with her illness. She said she wanted to go home. For a woman in Mrs. Lyles's condition, following her wishes would be the best thing to do." His compassionate tone communicates clearly to me, left in ignorance of my mother's prognosis by our family physician, all I need to know. She's dying.

The next morning, when my mother awakens in her own bed, she says, "I never want to see another piece of cornbread in my life."

DOG

My mother is a dog. She snarls, rather than talks. She seemed all right at first, but a relapse came after the temporary stroke. That her speech is half-gone frightens and hurts me above all else. I have always loved the richness, cadence, clarity of the human voice.

My mother is a dog. It is easier to think of her that way. Since the stroke, I have not kissed her hands or face. Did I promise that I'd always be her support, no matter what happened? Well, I lied. I am afraid of her now. *Liar, liar,* I taunt myself. You only loved a woman beautiful or whole.

This is early morning on a bad day. All the days now are bad. Since the stroke. When was that? What's today? I remember dinner last night, that's all.

Now I have to watch her when she eats the way you watch a baby. Her hair dangles in the plate and crumbs of meat and vegetables stick to the white strands. *Now I have to chop and mash her food, just like a baby's. Only she's not a baby*. With her left hand, she claws for the bread on her lap tray. "Why can't I use my left hand? Why is everybody well but me?" she moans. The bread, clawed to fragments, spatters all over her pajamas.

"Mom, don't try to use your left hand. It's weak. Use your right."

Still, her left hand scratches over the slick surface of the plastic tray, seeking the recalcitrant remnants of bread.

"Mom!" I move her left hand to her thigh, hold it there. *Be still*.

Night is worse than mealtimes. I am up every few hours to help her take her pills. She is getting too weak to swallow them. To medicate her, I get my hand behind her back, and heave her into a sitting position. Then I support her shoulders against my chest so that she will not fall. She is boulder-heavy. How can one little body just under five and a half feet long, weighing under a hundred pounds, be so maliciously, grossly heavy? *Dead weight*.

She is calling me. I wake up in the dark, hearing her. How long has it been since I gave her the midnight pills? "Lo-was. Lo-was." I run across the hall. In the light of the pink, char-treuse, and indigo figures flickering on the TV screen, Mama is lying on the floor, her legs splayed out over the bathroom lintel, her head just underneath the bed.

"Mama! Mama!" I bend over her, tugging at her to get her all the way out into the bedroom and sitting up.

"I wanna use the toilet," she growls, slowly, sullenly, like a drunk. I try to help her up, but she is all dull, insensate weight.

"Daddy! Daddy!"

Together he and I lift her back onto the bed, but she tries to roll out. "Gotta use the bathroom," she insists.

"No, Ma!" I run to the linen closet, get towels, shove them under her. Dad and I tell her it is better to mess the bed than fall and get hurt. But she is obstinate. Her leg keeps pummeling the side of the bed.

"Minnie, if you've got to go, just cut loose." Dad is frowning, exasperated.

"No. I'm not gonna go in the bed. Can't do that."

"Mama!" Dad and I lean over her and press back her squirming hips and thighs.

"Put these chairs up against the bed," Dad says. He is pulling up one of the chairs we have brought in here for visitors. Soon Mama is imprisoned by three high-backed chairs. *This is what you do to keep a baby from rolling out of bed,* I think. She still begs us to let her get up.

"Tomorrow I'll have to get a bedpan," Dad says. He pads downstairs.

In a little while, the bitter odor of urine is on the air. I pull the wet towels from under her and remove the wet pajama bottoms. Her sex is a forlorn, desiccated rose in a desert of loose, sandy flesh. Her privates simultaneously repel, shame, and fascinate me. I cannot remember ever having seen my mother's nakedness. *This is the body from which I came.*

Gingerly, I wash her genitals and thighs, and change her clothing. What about the soaked bedding? Moving her to the other side of the bed is a task for a weightlifter. How do you move a helpless woman?

"Ma, you gotta move to the other side of the bed," I say. I stand cupping my jaw in my right hand, looking down at her, but not meeting her eyes. Since the temporary stroke, I have avoided looking her full in the face.

A dovelike touch greets my hand. I bend over her.

"Ma, what is it?"

Her right arm curves gracefully as a swan's neck around the back of my head, and her hand settles politely on my neck.

"Oh! You remembered!" I look in her eyes now, as she tries to raise her shoulders. *She* had remembered; I had not.

The first time the nurse had come, I'd asked, *How do I help her sit up?* And the nurse had explained, *Mrs. Lyles, put your arm around your daughter's neck. Lois, slip your left hand behind her back, and hook your right around her waist. Then, ease her up gradually.*

I smile at Mama. *My mother is not a dog.*

Mama died forty days after Christmas. I celebrate the daily beauty of her life with these words, chosen by Dad for the written program of her funeral: *Her crown was her heart.*

AFTERWORD

Paula Giddings

One seldom hears a child cry in Africa. No matter the economic status of the mother, she seems to rear her children with such a precise balance of indulgence and discipline that they have no need, or desire, to pierce the air with public complaint. It is as if with the birth of a child, the African mother steps into a universe especially created for her and her child alone. The child, in turn, is indulged with such rapt maternal attention that it is all-consuming and satisfying. On the other hand, too much discipline is demanded of an African child for it to be "spoiled" in the Western sense of the word.

I think it is this balance of indulgence and discipline, and the maternal absorption which it allows, that invests African motherhood with its almost mythic qualities—the qualities that moved W.E.B. DuBois to observe that "The great Black race in passing up the steps of human culture gave the world, not only the iron age, the cultivation of the soil, and the domestication of animals, but also, in peculiar emphasis, the Mother idea."

Reading the essays and poems in this volume made me think about how this Mother-idea has fared in North America. How it was hoisted onto foreign ships and replanted in New World soil. I think about how it had to be tended in a garden so rejecting of color; how, under such conditions, Black mothers maintained such a delicate balance. What happened to their special universe when, both during slavery and after, it could suddenly be so violated by outsiders? I think about the impassioned adjustments that had to be made.

Discipline was still expected of slave children but indulgence wasn't always possible. In her narrative, Sojourner Truth, abolitionist and feminist, noted how "The Lord knows how many times I let my children go hungry, rather than take secretly the bread I liked not to ask for." In other instances, though traditional lines of communication were broken, indulgence seemed to be measured in quantities just sufficient to sustain self-respect. This certainly seemed true of Aunt Sally, who in her

slave narrative observed how stern her mother was, "rarely talking with her children, but training them to the best of her ability
in all industry and honesty. Every moment she could gain from
labor," the narrator wrote, "was spent in spinning and knitting
and sewing to keep them decently clothed."

The balance could careen most radically when the consuming
focus of maternal attention was directed toward daughters. The
non-African earth was not only disrespectful but ravenous toward
Black women. For the mother and female child, the universe
became one where the daughter's "almost certain doom [was] to
minister to the unbridled lust of the slaveowner," as stated in
the narrative of Bethany Veney. So now, in addition to the already general emotional struggle, there was also the particular
"painful, patient and silent toil of mothers to gain title to the
bodies of their daughters," as the writer and intellectual Anna
Julia Cooper noted.

I think about how a desperate discipline took its toll. The
narrative of Linda Brent talks about how the vigilance of a
daughter reaching puberty had a "tendency to drive her from
maternal councils." Even Black mothers who themselves could
not escape exploitation, vowed that their daughters would. A
Northerner, commenting on mothers who were concubines in
Mississippi, noted that "they had too much pride and self-respect
to rear their daughters for such a purpose. "If driven to des-
peration," he continued, the mother "destroyed herself to prevent it, or killed them." The Mother-idea has always had a
certain intensity. Too much, sometimes, for some women to bear.
I think it was the caring too much, rather than not enough, that
made other slave mothers sometimes give birth only to abandon;
to stop trying to cultivate fragile petals, letting survival-prone
wildflowers grow in their stead.

Of course, the struggles associated with the ancient Mother-
idea did not end with slavery. At the turn of the century, the
activist Fannie Barrier Williams would note that "It is a significant and shameful fact, that I am constantly in receipt of
letters from the still unprotected women in the South, begging
to find employment for their daughters . . . to save them from
going into the homes of the South as servants as there is nothing
to save them from dishonor and degradation." Certainly this was
an additional motive of Black mothers who migrated, or sent
their daughters North in search of safe haven and decent
employment.

What has happened to the Mother-idea in the latter part of the twentieth century? As this volume shows us, myriad legacies unfold. There are those of us who reside in a universe of perfected equilibrium. Others are caught in an uncontrollable lurch whose unwieldy motion began generations ago. Still others are the wildflowers who survived; or the lonely whose abandonment began in centuries past. There are those of us who have been sent to safer havens to escape the storm that still rages, though more quietly now. The painful, patient, and silent toil of the late twentieth century is restoring the balance for all.

SUGGESTED READINGS

Janet Sims-Wood

GENERAL BOOKS, RESEARCH REPORTS, AND CHAPTERS IN BOOKS

Abramson, Jane B. *Mothermania: A Psychological Study of Mother-Daughter Conflict*. Lexington, MA: Lexington Books, 1986.

Arcana, Judith. *Our Mothers' Daughters*. Berkeley, CA: Shameless Hussy Press, 1979.

Bernard, Jessie. *Women, Wives, Mothers: Values and Options*. Chicago: Aldine, 1975.

Burton, Linda M., and V. L. Bengston. "Black Grandmothers: Issues of Timing and Meaning in Roles," in *Grandparenthood: Research and Policy Perspectives*. Beverly Hills, CA: Sage Publications, 1985.

Butts, June Dobbs. "Adolescent Sexuality and Teenage Pregnancy from a Black Perspective," in *Teenage Pregnancy from a Family Context*, Theodora Ooms, ed. Philadelphia: Temple University Press, 1981.

Chess, Stella, and Jane Whitbread. *Daughters: From Infancy to Independence*. New York: Doubleday, 1978.

Chilman, Catherine. *Adolescent Sexuality in a Changing American Society: Social and Psychological Perspectives for Human Service Professionals*. New York: John Wiley and Sons, 1983.

Chodorow, Nancy. *The Reproduction of Mothering: Psychoanalysis and the Sociology of Gender*. Berkley, CA: University of California Press, 1978.

Davidson, Cathy, and E. Broner, eds. *The Lost Tradition: Mothers and Daughters in Literature*. New York: Frederick Ungar, 1980.

Dowling, Colette. *Perfect Women: Daughters Who Love Their Mothers, But Don't Love Themselves*. New York: Pocket Books, 1989.

Fastman, Raisa. *A Portrait of American Mothers & Daughters*. Pasadena, CA: NewSage Press, 1987.

Firman, Julie, and Dorothy Firman. *Daughters & Mothers: The Journey Toward Independence & Reunion*. New York: Crossroad, 1989.

Fisher, Lucy R. *Linked Lives: Adult Daughters & Their Mothers*. New York: Harper & Row, 1986.

Flax, Jane. "Mother-Daughter Relationships: Psychodynamics, Politics, and Philosophy," in *The Future of Difference*. Hester Eisenstein and Alice Jardine, eds. Boston: G. K. Hall, 1980.

French, Marilyn. *Her Mother's Daughter*. New York: Ballantine Books, 1988.

Friday, Nancy. *My Mother/My Self: The Daughter's Search for Identity*. New York: Delacorte, 1977.

Friedensohn, Doris, and Barbara Rubin. *Generations of Women, In Search of Female Forebears*. Jersey City, NJ: Jersey City State College Press, 1984.

Guttmacher, Alan. *Teenage Pregnancy: The Problem that Hasn't Gone Away*. New York: Alan Guttmacher Institute, 1981.

Hammer, Signe. *Daughters and Mothers, Mothers and Daughters*. New York: Quadrangle/New York Times, 1975.

Hirsch, Marianne. *The Mother-Daughter Plot: Narrative, Psychoanalysis, Feminism*. Bloomington: Indiana University Press, 1989.

Joseph, Gloria, and Jill Lewis. *Common Differences: Conflicts in Black and White Feminist Perspectives*. Garden City, NY: Anchor Books, 1981.

Kent, Estelle O'Connor. "I Always Wanted My Mother to Be Proud of Me, But I Never Really Turned Out to Be Nothin'," in *Drylongso: A Self-Portrait of Black America*, John Langston Gwaltney, ed. New York: Random House, 1980.

Koppelman, Susan, ed. *Between Mothers & Daughters: Stories Across a Generation*. New York: Feminist Press, 1984.

Ladner, Joyce. *Tomorrow's Tomorrow: The Black Woman*. New York: Doubleday, 1971.

Moses, Yula. "Christ Warned Us by His Life and Death, So Who Am I that I Should Not Warn My Daughter by My Life?" in *Drylongso: A Self-Portrait of Black America*, John Langston Gwaltney, ed. New York: Random House, 1980.

Neumann, Erich. *The Great Mother: An Analysis of the Archetype*. Princeton, NJ: Princeton University Press, 1972.

Payne, Karen, ed. *Between Ourselves: Letters of Mothers and Daughters, 1750–1982*. Boston: Houghton Mifflin, 1983.

Pearce, Diana, and Hariette McAdoo. *Women and Children: Alone and in Poverty*. Washington, D.C.: National Advisory Council on Economic Opportunity, 1981.

Powell, Gloria. "Growing Up Black and Female," in *Becoming Female: Perspectives on Development*. C. Kopp, ed. New York: Plenum, 1979.

Rafkin, Louise, ed. *Different Daughters: A Book by Mothers of Lesbians*. Pittsburgh, PA: Cleis Press, 1987.

Reid, Pamela T. "Socialization of Black Female Children, in *Women: A Developmental Perspective*. Phyllis W. Berman and Estelle R. Ramey, eds. Bethesda, MD: National Institutes of Health, 1982.

Rich, Adrienne. *Of Woman Born: Motherhood as Institution and Experience*. New York: Norton, 1976.

Rodgers-Rose, LaFrances, ed. *The Black Woman*. Beverly Hills, CA: Sage Publications, 1980.

Saunders, Ellen. "My Daughter Listens to Me Sometimes, but I Listened to My Mother All the Time," in *Drylongso: A Self-Portrait of Black America*, John Langston Gwaltney, ed. New York: Random House, 1980.

Stack, Carol. *All Our Kin: Strategies for Survival in a Black Community*. New York: Harper & Row, 1974.

Staples, Robert, ed. *The Black Family, Essays and Studies*. Belmont, CA: Wadsworth, 1971.

Strom, Kay, and Lisa Strom. *Mothers & Daughters Together: We Can Work It Out*. Grand Rapids, MI: Baker Books, 1988.

Trebilcot, Joyce, ed. *Mothering: Essays in Feminist Theory*. Totawa, NJ: Rowman and Allanheld, 1983.

Wade-Gayles, Gloria. *No Crystal Stair: Visions of Race and Sex in Black Women's Fiction*. New York: Pilgrim Press, 1984.

Walker, Alice. "One Child of One's Own: A Meaningful Digression Within the Work(s), in *In Search of Our Mothers' Gardens*. New York: Harcourt Brace Jovanovich, 1983.

Washington, Mary Helen. "I Sign My Mother's Name: Alice Walker, Dorothy West, Paule Marshall," in *Mothering the Mind: Twelve Studies of Writers and Their Silent Partners*, Ruth Perry and Martine Watson Brownley, eds. New York: Holmes and Meier, 1984.

ARTICLES AND NARRATIVES

Alexander, Adele Logan. "Adella and Ruth: A Granddaughter's Story." *SAGE: A Scholarly Journal on Black Women* 2 (Fall 1984): 32–33.

Aug, Robert, and Thomas Bright. "Study of Wed and Unwed Motherhood in Adolescent and Young Adults." *Journal of the American Academy of Child Psychiatry* 9 (1970): 577–594.1.

Avery, Billye Y. "Breaking the Silence about Menstruation: Thoughts from A Mother/Health Activist." *SAGE: A Scholarly Journal on Black Women* 1 (Fall 1984): 30.

Bell-Scott, Patricia. "A Critical Overview of Sex Roles Research of Black Families." *Women Studies Abstracts* 5 (Spring 1976): 1–9.

Bell-Scott, Patricia, and Beverly Guy-Sheftall. "For Mothers and Daughters." *SAGE: A Scholarly Journal on Black Women* 1 (Fall 1984):2.

Bray, Rosemary L. "Between Mothers and Daughters." *Essence* 15 (May 1984): 98–100, 153.

Brown, Josephine, et al. "Interactions of Black Inner City Mothers with their Newborn Infants." *Child Development* 46 (1975): 677–86.

Bundles, A'lelia P. "A Letter to My Great-Great-Grandmother, Madame C. J. Walker." *SAGE: A Scholarly Journal on Black Women* 4 (Fall 1987): 57–58.

Bundles, A'lelia P. "Madame C. J. Walker to Her Daughter A'lelia Walker—The Last Letter." *SAGE: A Scholarly Journal on Black Women* 1 (Fall 1984): 34–35.

Butts, June Dobbs. "Goodbye, Mama! Be Home When I Get Back!" *SAGE: A Scholarly Journal on Black Women* 4 (Fall 1987): 45–48.

Cason, Candice S. "Telling My Mother's Story: Notes from a Daughter." *SAGE: A Scholarly Journal on Black Women* 1 (Fall 1984): 31.

Caswell, Geraldine C. "Mothering." *Essence* 8 (May 77): 63, 136, 138.

Cooper, Annie L. "Notes for My Daughter on Premenstrual Syndrome." *SAGE: A Scholarly Journal on Black Women* 2 (Fall 1985): 43–45.

Crastnopol, M. "Disturbances in the Mother-Daughter Relationships of Women Offenders." *Counseling and Values* 26 (1982): 172–79.

Davies, Carole Boyce. "Wrapping One's Self in Mother's Akatado-Cloths: Mother-Daughter Relationships in the Works of African Women Writers." *SAGE: A Scholarly Journal on Black Women* 4 (Fall 1987): 11–19.

Fox, Greer, and Judith Inazu. "The Influence of the Mother's Marital History on the Mother-Daughter Relationship in Black and White Households." *Journal of Marriage and the Family* 44 (February 1982): 143–54.

Fox, Greer. "Mother-Daughter Communication about Sex." *Family Relations* 29 (July 1980): 347–52.

Fox, Greer. "Patterns and Outcomes of Mother-Daughter Communication about Sexuality." *Journal of Social Issues* 36 (Winter 1980): 7–29.

Fu, Victoria R., et al. "Maternal Dependency and Childrearing Attitudes among Mothers of Adolescents. *Adolescence* 19 (Winter 1984): 795–804.

Gispert, M., and R. Falk. "Sexual Experimentation and Pregnancy in Young Black Adolescents." *American Journal of Obstetrics* (1976): 56–79.

Greene, Beverly. "Sturdy Bridges: The Role of African-American Mothers in the Socialization of African-American Children." *Women and Therapy* 10 (1990): 205–25.

Grimes, Nikki. "Life After Death: Coping with Loss." *Essence* 15 (May 1984): 106–8, 169–70.

Gutelis, M. "Childbearing Attitudes of Teenage Negro Girls." *American Journal of Public Health* 60 (1970): 93–104.

Guy-Sheftall, Beverly. "Mothers and Daughters: A Black Perspective." *Spelman Messenger* 98 (1982): 4–5.

Guy-Sheftall, Beverly, and Patricia Bell-Scott. "Turbulence And Tenderness." *SAGE: A Scholarly Journal on Black Women* 4 (Fall 1982): 2.

Hammonds, Karl. "Mothers, Daughters and the First Period." *Body Garage* 2 (March-April 1984): 12, 14.

Harrison, Algea O. "Dilemma of Growing Up Black and Female." *Journal of Social and Behavioral Sciences* 20 (Spring 1974): 28–40.

Hirsch, Marianne. "Mothers and Daughters." *Signs* 7 (Autumn 1981): 200–222.

"Introducing: Most-Watched Couple on Campus." *Ebony* 37 (March 1982): 45–46, 48.

Jamison-Hall, Angelene. "Remembering Me and Yana: A Story." *SAGE: A Scholarly Journal on Black Women* 4 (Fall 1987): 82–88.

Ladner, Joyce A., and Ruby Gourdine Morton. "Integenerational Teenage Motherhood: Some Preliminary Findings." *SAGE: A Scholarly Journal on Black Women* 1 (Fall 1984): 17–21.

Laws, Janice, and Joyce Strickland. "Black Mothers and Daughters: A Clarification of the Relationship as an Impetus for Black Power." *Black Books Bulletin* 6 (1980): 26–29, 33.

Lee, Helen E. "Rearranging Hands." *SAGE: A Scholarly Journal on Black Women* 4 (Fall 1987): 89–90.

Leonard, Gloria Ratliff. "My Daughter Drove Me Crazy, So I Sent Her to Her Dad." *Essence* 14 (February 1984): 131–32.

Macke, Anne, and William Morgan. "Maternal Employment, Race and Work Orientation of High School Girls." *Social Forces* 57 (September 1978): 187–204.

McPhail, Fabienne. "Mothers and Daughters Talking Together: An Interview with Filmmaker Cheryl Chisholm." *SAGE: A Scholarly Journal on Black Women* 4 (Fall 1987): 53–56.

Marshall, Paule. "From Daughters." *Callaloo* 13 (Winter 1990): 1–8.

Mullen, Harryette. "A Summer in School with Mother." *SAGE: A Scholarly Journal on Black Women* 2 (Spring 1985): 60–61.

Nelson, Jill. "A Mom's Rap." *Essence* 18 (April 1988): 126.

Ohayon, Ruth. "Rousseau's Julie; Or, the Maternal Odyssey." *CLA Journal* 30 (September 1986): 69–82.

Oliver, Stephanie Stokes. "Mother-To-Mother." *Essence* 16 (May 1985): 186, 188.

Omolade, Barbara. "It's a Family Affair: Black Single Mothers, the Real Deal." *The Village Voice*, July 10, 1986.

Pearson, Jessica. "Mothers and Daughters: Measuring Occupational Inheritance." *Sociology and Social Research* 67 (January 1983): 204–17.

Peters, Marie, and Grace Massey. "Socialization of Black Children: A Critical Review of the Literature on Parent-Child Relationships in Black Families." *Resources in Education* (March 1976).

Pettis, Joyce. "Difficult Survival: Mothers and Daughters in *The Bluest Eye.*" *SAGE: A Scholarly Journal on Black Women* 4 (Fall 1987): 26–29.

Philliber, Susan, and Elizabeth Graham. "The Impact of Age of Mother on Mother-Child Interaction Patterns." *Journal of Marriage and the Family* 43 (February 1981): 109–16.

Pickard, Mary A. "I Remember Mama When . . ." *Essence* 8 (May 1977): 62–63, 138, 140.

Randolph, Laura B. "Mothers and Daughters: The Special Connection." *Ebony* 43 (February 1988): 158–62.

Rowland, Sonya, and Karen Wampler Smith. "Black and White Mother's Preferences for Parenting Programs." *Family Relations* 32 (July 1983): 323–30.

Sojourner, Sabrina. "Loving Us Both." *SAGE: A Scholarly Journal on Black Women* 4 (Fall 1987): 59–60.

Subryan, Carmen. "Circles: Mother and Daughter Relationships in Toni Morrison's *Song of Solomon.*" *SAGE: A Scholarly Journal on Black Women* 5 (Summer 1988): 34–36.

Sulaiman, Madeline. "An Open Letter to Mommie." *about . . . time* 11 (May 1983): 22–23.

Wade-Gayles, Gloria. "The Truths of Our Mothers' Lives: Mother-Daughter Relationships in Black Women's Fiction." *SAGE: A Scholarly Journal on Black Women* 2 (Fall 1984): 8–12.

"Walker, Alice. "In Search of Our Mothers' Gardens." *Ms.* (May 1974): 64–70, 105.

Washington, Mary Helen. "Alice Walker: Her Mother's Gifts." *Ms* (June 1982): 38.

Williams, Ida B., Thelma O. Williams, and Ora Williams. "Between a Mother and Two Daughters: The Williams Family Letters." *SAGE: A Scholarly Journal on Black Women* 4 (Fall 1987): 61–66.

Willis-Ryan, Deborah, and *SAGE* staff. "Photographic Essay—Mothers And Daughters." *SAGE: A Scholarly Journal on Black Women* 1 (Fall 1984): 4–7.

Wilson, Melvin N. "Mothers' and Grandmothers' Perceptions of Parental Behavior in Three-Generational Black Families." *Child Development* 55 (August 1984): 1333–39.

DOCTORAL DISSERTATIONS

Brown, Martha Hursey. "Images of Black Women: Family Roles in Harlem Renaissance Literature." Dissertation Abstracts International 37A (1976), 2836–37.

Cox, Gayle J. "Black Daughters' Perceptions of Their Elderly Mothers' Needs." Dissertation Abstracts International 49A (1989), 3869.

Cunningham, Terry. "An Exploratory View: Attitudes of Black Teenage Females Toward Familial Relationships." Atlanta: Atlanta University School of Social Work, 1980.

Friedman, Jennifer. "Mothers and Daughters: Negotiations for Control over Their Lives." Dissertation Abstracts International 49A (1989), 3324.

Gilkey, Joyce Katherine. "From Their Daughters' Eyes: Parent/Daughter Relationships and College Adjustment in Young Women." Dissertation Abstracts International 50A (1989), 267.

Kilpatrick, Hortense Emma. "A Study of Early Adolescent Pregnancy: Self-Perceptions of Mothers and Their First-time Pregnant Adolescent Daughters." Dissertation Abstracts International 50A (1990), 2650.

Kohn, Amy F. "A Study of Mother-Daughter Relationships among Pregnant Teenagers." Dissertation Abstracts International 49A (1989), 3507.

Tatje, Terrence. "Mother-Daughter Dyadic Dominance in Black American Kinship." Dissertation Abstracts International 35A (1974), 3202.

MASTER'S THESES

Reilly, Andelaide. "The Relationship of 55 Negro Adolescent Unmarried Mothers Toward Their Own Mothers." Master's Thesis, Catholic University of America, 1962.

West, Frankie. "A Mother-Daughter Study of Thirty Families as Bases for a Vocation Guidance Program." Master's Thesis, Hampton Institute, 1964.

SPECIAL JOURNAL ISSUES

"Daughters and Mothers." *Ms* 3 (June 1975).

"Mother Love." *Essence* 15 (May 1984).

"Mothers and Daughters in Literature." *Women's Study Quarterly:* 6 (1979).

"Mothers and Daughters." *Frontiers: A Journal of Women's Studies* 3 (Summer 1978).

"Mothers and Daughters I." *SAGE: A Scholarly Journal on Black Women* 1 (Fall 1984).

"Mothers and Daughters II." *SAGE: A Scholarly Journal on Black Women* 4 (Fall 1987).

"The Mother-Daughter Thing." *Essence* 22 (May 1991).

"Teaching About Mothering." *Women's Studies Quarterly* 11 (Winter 1983).

"Third World Lesbian Mothers." *Azalea: A Magazine by Third World Lesbians* 3 (1979–1980).

"Toward a Feminist Theory of Motherhood. *Feminist Studies* 4 (June 1978).

FILMS

"Black Mother, Black Daughter." 29 minutes. A celebration of black womanhood through oral histories, song, and interviews.
National Film Board of Canada
1251 Avenue of The Americas
New York, NY 10020

"On Becoming a Woman: Mothers and Daughters Talking Together." 104 minutes. Mothers and daughters talk about sexuality, motherhood, birth control, and the joys and sorrows of life.
Women Make Movies, Inc.
225 Lafayette Street, Suite 211
New York, NY 10012

CONTRIBUTORS

Maya Angelou, author of the best-selling *I Know Why the Caged Bird Sings,* several autobiographical works, and collections of poetry, is Z. Smith Reynolds Professor at Wake Forest University.

Patricia Bell-Scott, professor of child and family development and of women's studies at the University of Georgia, is founding editor of *SAGE: A Scholarly Journal on Black Women* and co-editor of *All the Women Are White, All the Blacks Are Men, But Some of Us Are Brave: Black Women's Studies.*

SDiane Bogus lives in Turlock, California. To preserve her soul, she meditates, chants, prays, makes love, writes, listens to music, and performs. Her works include *I'm Off to See the Goddamn Wizard, Alright!, Woman in the Moon, Sapphire's Sampler,* and *Dyke Hands.*

Elsa Barkley Brown teaches in the department of history at the University of Michigan. She is associate editor of Carlson Publishing's *Black Women in United States History* series. Her articles on African American women's history have appeared in *SAGE: A Scholarly Journal on Black Women* and *Signs: Journal of Women in Culture and Society.*

Esperanza Cintrón was born in Detroit and is of Puerto Rican descent. Recognition of her work includes a Michigan Council for the Arts Individual Artist Grant and the Judith Siegel Pearson Poetry Award. She is a founding member of Sisters of Color (SOC), a women's writers' collective. Her first novella, *Shades,* is nearing completion.

Pearl Cleage is an Atlanta-based writer who serves as artistic director of Just Us Theater Company and editor of *Catalyst Magazine.* She is mother of one daughter, Deignan, and author of a new book, *Mad at Miles.*

Johnnetta B. Cole, anthropologist and editor of *All American Women: Lines that Divide, Ties that Bind* and *Anthropology for the Nineties,* is president of Spelman College.

Willi Coleman holds a doctorate in comparative culture from the University of California, Irvine. She is interested in nineteenth-century

African-American women as social activists. Her poetry has appeared in a variety of Black and women's publications.

Patricia Hill Collins is an associate professor of Afro-American studies and sociology at the University of Cincinnati. She has published numerous articles on African-American women and sociological thought and is author of *Black Feminist Thought: Knowledge, Consciousness, and the Politics of Empowerment.*

Miriam DeCosta-Willis, Commonwealth Professor of Spanish at George Mason University, has edited or co-edited *Blacks in Hispanic Literature, Homespun Images: An Anthology of Black Memphis Writers and Artists,* and the forthcoming *Erotique Noire/Black Erotica.* Her articles on Afro-Hispanic and Afro-American literature and history have appeared in such journals as *Callaloo, Latin American Literary Review,* the *West Tennessee Historical Society Papers,* and the *Revista/Review Latinoamericana.* She is also associate and book review editor of *SAGE: A Scholarly Journal on Black Women.*

Toi Derricotte is author of *Empress of the Death House, Natural Birth,* and *Captivity.* She has been awarded fellowships from the National Endowment for the Arts, the Maryland State Arts Council, and the New Jersey State Council on the Arts. Her poems have been published in *Callaloo, Black Scholar, American Poetry Review, Ploughshares, Black American Literature Forum, Conditions, Iowa Review, Massachusetts Review,* and many other journals.

Lucille P. Fultz, assistant professor of English at Rice University, is associate editor of *SAGE: A Scholarly Journal on Black Women.* She recently completed a dissertation on Toni Morrison's *Beloved.*

Paula Giddings, author of *When and Where I Enter: The Impact of Black Women on Race and Sex in America* and *In Search of Sisterhood: Delta Sigma Theta and the Challenge of the Black Sorority Movement,* holds the Laurie Chair in Women's Studies at Douglas College/Rutgers University.

Ann T. Greene is a short story writer and librettist. Her fiction has appeared in *Callaloo.* In collaboration with composer Leroy Jenkins and choreographer/director Bill T. Jones, she created a dance opera, *The Mother of Three Sons,* which premiered at the 1990 Munich Biennale.

Beverly Guy-Sheftall, founding director of the Spelman College Women's Research and Resource Center and associate professor of English, is founding co-editor of *SAGE: A Scholarly Journal on Black Women;* co-editor of *Sturdy Black Bridges: Visions of Black Women in Literature;* and author of *Spelman: A Centennial Celebration* and *Daughters of Sorrow: Attitudes Toward Black Women, 1880–1920.*

Linda H. Hollies, a graduate of Garrett-Evangelical Theological Seminary, is senior pastor of the Richards Street United Methodist Church in Joliet, Illinois. Because of her history and clinical pastoral education, she has developed an intensive and extensive workshop design, "WOMANSPACE," which she conducts for sisters across the country. Married to Charles H. Hollies, they are the parents of Greg, Grelon, and Grian Eunyke.

Karla F. C. Holloway, professor of English at North Carolina State University, is author of books on Zora Neale Hurston, *The Character of the Word,* and Toni Morrison, *New Dimensions of Spirituality,* with S. Demetrakopoulos. She is completing *Moorings and Metaphors: A Critical Theory of Black Women's Literature,* which she began during her year as a Rockefeller Humanist-in-Residence at the Duke/ University of North Carolina Center for Research on Women.

Bell Hooks, writer, feminist theorist, and cultural critic, is associate professor at Oberlin College. She speaks widely on the issues of race, class, and gender and has authored *Ain't I a Woman: Black Women and Feminism, Feminist Theory from Margin to Center, Talking Black: Thinking Feminist, Thinking Black,* and *Yearning: Race, Gender and Cultural Politics.*

Gloria T. Hull is chair of women's studies and professor of English at the University of California, Santa Cruz. She is co-editor of *All the Women Are White, All the Blacks Are Men, But Some of Us Are Brave: Black Women's Studies,* and author of *Give Us This Day: The Diary of Alice Dunbar-Nelson* and *Sex, Color, and Poetry: Three Black Women Writers of the Harlem Renaissance.*

Valerie Jean is a poet, undeniably Black and woman. She writes as much as she can while raising her daughter.

June Jordan has published nineteen books, most recently *Naming Our Destiny, New and Selected Poems.* She is professor of African-

American studies and women's studies at the University of California, Berkeley.

Gloria I. Joseph is a revolutionary spirited Black Feminist of West Indian parents, who views the world from an Afrocentric perspective with a Socialist base. She lives in St. Croix, Virgin Islands. She is a political activist, educator, and writer, and she raises honey bees.

Malia Kai, daughter of Nubia Kai, is a fine arts major at Howard University. Her work has been exhibited in the Detroit area.

Nubia Kai is a poet, playwright, and novelist whose works have been published in *Black World, Black Scholar, Solid Ground, Obsidian, Black American Literature Forum, City Arts Quarterly,* and *Essence.* Her collection of poems, *Solos,* was published by Lotus Press. A recipient of three Michigan Council of the Arts Awards for poetry, drama, and fiction, she has also received a National Endowment for the Arts Award for poetry.

Dolores Kendrick teaches at The Phillips Exeter Academy. She is the recipient of fellowships and awards from the National Endowment of the Arts, the Yaddo Writers' Colony, and the Fulbright program. She has also authored three books, *Through the Ceiling, Now Is the Thing to Praise,* and *The Women of Plums,* for which she received the Anisfield-Wolf Award.

Pinkie Gordon Lane was appointed Poet Laureate of Louisiana by Governor Buddy Roemer. She is professor emeritus of Southern University, Baton Rouge, and the author of three volumes of published poetry. Many of her poems have appeared in literary magazines.

Lois Florence Lyles received her Ph.D. from Harvard University. She teaches English Renaissance literature and contemporary American literature at San Francisco State University.

Audre Lorde is a Black Feminist Lesbian Warrior Poet Mother who now lives in the Virgin Islands, where she is still rebuilding after hurricane Hugo, writing a novel, and making trouble.

Irma McClaurin was born in Chicago, Illinois on April 2, 1952. She has an M.F.A. in English from the University of Massachusetts at Amherst, where she is presently working on a Ph.D. in anthropology.

Pearl's Song is her third book of poetry. Part of a biography-in-progress appears in *Black Writers Redefine the Struggle: A Tribute to James Baldwin.*

Naomi Long Madgett is author of seven collections of poetry, most recently *Octavia and Other Poems,* which won the College Language Association Creative Achievement Award. She is professor emeritus at Eastern Michigan University and editor at Lotus Press in Detroit. Her daughter, Jill Witherspoon Boyer, is author of two poetry collections and has a fourteen-year-old daughter of her own.

Saundra Murray Nettles is principal research scientist at the Johns Hopkins University Center for Social Organization of Schools. She also writes poetry and short stories.

Louise Robinson-Boardley is a New Englander by birth and a Virginian by lineage. She believes in naturalness, the beauty and power of language, and the eloquence of the human spirit as it struggles to become.

Belvie Rooks lives on and writes from California's Pacific north coast. Her previously published works have appeared in *Essence, Bookpublisher, San Francisco Review of Books, San Francisco Chronicle,* and *Women's Voices.* She is currently working on a series of reflective, nonfiction pieces entitled "Where the River Meets the Sea."

Jacqueline Jones Royster, director of the Spelman College Comprehensive Writing Program and associate professor of English, is founding senior associate editor of *SAGE: A Scholarly Journal on Black Women* and is completing a book on *Literacy and Social Change.*

Kate Rushin was raised in Camden and Lawnside, New Jersey and graduated from Oberlin College. She is winner of the 1988 Grolier Poetry Prize and a member of the Cambridge, Massachusetts-based New Words Bookstore Collective. Her work has appeared in *Callaloo, Home Girls: A Black Feminist Anthology,* and *An Ear to the Ground: An Anthology of Contemporary American Poetry.*

Sonia Sanchez holds the Laura Carnell Chair in English at Temple University and is author of thirteen books, including *Homecoming, We a BaddDDD People, Love Poems, I've Been a Women: New and Selected Poems, A Sound Investment and Other Stories, Homegirls and Hand-*

grenades and *Under a Soprano Sky.* A recipient of awards from the National Endowment for the Arts and Pennsylvania Coalition of 100 Black Women, she also won an American Book Award in 1985, the Governor's Award for Excellence in the Humanities in 1988, and the Peace and Freedom Award from the Women International League for Peace and Freedom in 1988.

Judy Scales-Trent is professor of law at the State University of New York at Buffalo School of Law. She gave herself the name "Scales-Trent" to show respect and love for all of her family; "Scales" is her mother's family name, and "Trent" is her father's family name.

Saundra Sharp is a writer/actress/filmmaker who has authored four volumes of poetry and a stage play. She has also produced three award-winning film shorts.

Janet Sims-Wood, founding associate editor of *SAGE: A Scholarly Journal on Black Women,* is assistant chief librarian at the Reference/ Reader Services Department of the Moorland-Spingarn Research Center of Howard University. Compiler of several bibliographies, including such landmark works as *The Progress of Afro-American Women, The Psychology and Mental Health of Afro-American Women,* and *The Ku Klux Klan,* she has also authored numerous articles and chapters on African-American women's history.

Rosalie Riegle Troester is associate professor of English at Saginaw Valley State University, University Center, Michigan. She holds the doctor of arts in English from the University of Michigan and specializes in women's literature and the teaching of writing. She is editor of *Historic Women of Michigan: A Sesquicentennial Celebration.*

Gloria Wade-Gayles is author of *No Crystal Stair: Race and Sex in Black Women's Novels, 1946–1976,* a study of race and gender in Black women's novels, and *Anointed to Fly,* a collection of poetry. Her scholarly essays and poetry have appeared in a number of books and journals. She is currently completing an autobiographical novel, which will highlight the resilient strength of women in her family and women in the southern community in which she was reared. She is professor of English and women's studies at Spelman College.

Alice Walker, prize-winning author, has written numerous essays, several volumes of poetry, two collections of short stories, and four novels, including *The Color Purple* and *The Temple of My Familiar.*

Margaret Walker, professor emeritus of English at Jackson State University, is author of nine books, including *Jubilee, For My People,* and *Richard Wright: Daemonic Genius.*

Michele Wallace, author of *Black Macho and the Myth of the Superwoman* and daughter of artist Faith Ringgold, was born and raised in Harlem. She has written fiction and cultural criticism for a variety of popular journals. She teaches women's studies and Afro-American literature at The State University of New York at Buffalo.

Marilyn Nelson Waniek has written *For the Body, Mama's Promises,* and *The Homeplace,* all published by Louisiana State University Press, and two collections of verse for children. Her honors include two Pushcart Prizes; fellowships and grants from the Danforth Foundation, the National Endowment for the Arts, the Connecticut Commission for the Arts, and the Cultural Ministry of Denmark; and the 1990 Connecticut Arts Award. Married and the mother of a ten-year-old son and a four-year-old daughter, she is professor of English at the University of Connecticut and a teacher in the Vermont College Master of Fine Arts in Writing Program.

Renita Weems teaches at the Vanderbilt School of Divinity and has published in *SAGE: A Scholarly Journal on Black Women* and *Essence.*

Annette Jones White, director of the Spelman College Nursery-Kindergarten School, is a graduate of Spelman and Virginia State University. Her essays and poetry have appeared in *Black World, Southern Exposure, World of Poetry, American Anthology of Poetry,* and *SAGE: A Scholarly Journal on Black Women.*